FIGHTING SCARED

To Tegan

Who Dares Wins!

FIGHTING SCARED

Para, Mercenary, SAS, Sniper, Bodyguard

Robin Horsfall

CASSELL

Cassell Military Paperbacks

an imprint of Orion Books Ltd,
Orion House, 5 Upper St Martin's Lane,
London WC2H 9GA
An Hachette Livre UK company

5 7 9 10 8 6

First published 2002

British Library Cataloguing-in-Publication Data
A catalogue record for this book is available from the British Library

ISBN 978-0-3043-6462-6

Printed and bound in Great Britain by
Cox & Wyman Ltd, Reading, Berkshire

The Orion Publishing group's policy is to use papers that are
natural, renewable and recyclable products and made from wood
grown in sustainable forests. The logging and manufacturing
processes are expected to conform to the environmental regulations
of the country of origin.

www.orionbooks.co.uk

To Hazel Anne and Geoffrey Granville Horsfall

God bless you both

Contents

Acknowledgements

IT TOOK ME six years to write *Fighting Scared*. During that time the final chapters of the book actually took place. There were only a few individuals who influenced me and it is important that I convey my thanks to them.

Thanks to: Geoff Thompson of Coventry for helping me to start writing, and Ineke Allez who persuaded me that I had to write the story alone, without assistance; to Diana Lovell-Pank and Elizabeth Sinclair House who read, encouraged and advised on the text; and to Ian Paten for providing the literary polish that turned a story into a book.

Finally I have to thank my wife Heather, who helped me to express my inner feelings so that I could say how I felt and not just report what happened. She never gave up and always remained positive. Without her I would never have finished.

Foreword

READERS OF THIS book should understand that the story is told from memory. If you were there it may have been different; memories become rose-tinted with the years. Three incidents have deliberate misinformation to avoid identifying individuals and some names have been changed. Most surnames were avoided for reasons of security.

Fighting Scared conveys how I felt at the time. If I was proud of my violent behaviour then, I am not now. If I disliked or resented an individual then, it is unlikely that I feel the same way today.

First Kill

THE TWO MASKED men had forced the lock on the back door of the red-brick terraced house and entered through the kitchen. It was 3 a.m.; the house was still and quiet. They knew the way to the main bedroom – all these Belfast two-up, two-downs were the same, and it didn't take a Ph.D. to figure out in which bedroom the adults were sleeping. They crept up the creaking stairs and slowly opened the door. The man sat up in bed. Believing it to be one of the children from the other room, he asked, in a calm voice, 'What is it?'

The two men fired together, one with a sawn-off shotgun, the other with an automatic pistol. The bullets and shot spread blood across the sheets as their intended victim rolled onto the floor and lay still. As the firing stopped, the penetrating sound of a baby crying filled the room. The gunmen were gone, down the stairs and out through the back door to the waiting getaway car.

In the house, the children screamed as their father lay beside the bed where he had fallen, half wrapped in the blood-smeared sheets. Their mother hadn't moved since the door had first opened: the shotgun had blasted straight through the blankets and killed her as she slept. The baby standing and howling in the cot he shared with his sister had no idea how lucky he was not to have been hit by the ricochet that tore open the little girl's head and left her lying motionless at his feet.

The car took the corner fast. It was just three minutes since the attack and now the terrorists needed to get out of the area before the security forces got their act together. As the vehicle rounded the corner, the driver saw the Land Rover blocking the road and panicked.

The car's speed and the reaction of the driver immediately alerted us; we cocked our weapons, high-velocity self-loading rifles (SLRs), capable of killing a man at 1,000 yards with a round that travels at 2,300 feet per second. As the car slewed to the left in an abortive attempt to turn round, a Thompson submachine-gun opened fire from the rear right window. Any automatic weapon fired from a moving vehicle needs an expert hand to achieve any semblance of accuracy; thankfully, the firer in the back of the car was no expert and the .45 rounds struck the brick wall high above our heads.

The car reversed across the road, still trying to change direction. We dropped to the ground and returned fire. The noise was deafening; although I could hear shouting, I felt cocooned in an invisible shell that separated me from the voices. My eyes and mind were totally focused on the turning vehicle. My rifle sights were silhouetted in the lights beyond the car, and I could now see the vehicle beginning to move away. Heads bobbed in the seats in front of my eyes as I consciously breathed out and squeezed the trigger: four, five, six, seven times. There were no obstructions, no parked cars or civilians to get in the way, so we let rip, firing continuously into the car until it smashed into a lamp-post and came to a violent and sudden halt. It had been hit more than twenty-five times.

The silence was disturbed by the hiss of a cracked radiator as it spilled its contents onto the ground. Steam rose like smoke into the midnight air. We moved carefully towards the car, hugging the shadows and reloading our weapons while the opportunity was there. Now was the time to be frightened: now we had time to think. A wounded man is a deadly creature, and a dying man has nothing to lose.

From about ten feet away we could see that there were four men in the car. The driver was dead – the front of his face was a big hole, so there was no guesswork needed there. He was slumped back against the seat with his head protruding from the shattered side window. The front-seat passenger was moving, breathing noisily. Two of us moved in closer while the other two covered the street, watching for other dangers. As we got to within four or five feet of the car, there was a sudden movement on the rear seat. Our rifles exploded simultaneously – whoever had moved would be moving no more. Now they were all dead.

I've withheld some details of this awful incident to avoid identifying the families of the victims and these particular gunmen. But 'freedom fighters' or 'terrorists', Protestant or Catholic, it made no difference to me. They were the enemy, and today they had lost the fight.

CHAPTER 1

No Place to Hide

I WAS BORN on 23 March 1957. My mother worked in a hospital laundry while my gran and granddad looked after me in their little three-bedroomed semi-detached house in a small village called Weybourne in the South of England.

My only real memory of my granddad is of me standing looking up at him over the rim of the dining table on a Sunday morning. Granddad was the only one to get a cooked breakfast, and I would stand next to his knees and ask for the bacon rind to chew. He would cut it off and give it to me, and I remember feeling very contented with this largesse from his plate.

My mother was a beautiful woman; tall and slim, with dark locks of curly brown hair around a captivating face. She had warm, smiling hazel eyes and a gently turned-up nose. The sixth child in a family of seven, she had been blessed with a good brain and a wild, romantic and independent nature that determined the course of her life from an early age. The year after she left school at the age of seventeen, I was born, putting an abrupt end to any career plans she might have cherished.

While she was pregnant she married Bob, a known thief and safe-breaker who was not clever enough to stay out of prison. He spent most of their married life inside. Mum tried desperately hard to support Bob, and her marriage, but after several convictions, she gave up. I never knew him well enough to recognise him; his only legacy to me was the insecurity of growing up without a father.

By the age of seven I had a sister and a brother and my mother was in the process of filing for divorce from my father. I recall writing later in my schoolbook that my mother was getting married to Geoff Horsfall the following Saturday. The headmistress, Mrs Monday, wrote 'again' next to my sentence – she was concerned that people would think I was a bastard.

The man I came to know as my father, Geoffrey Granville Horsfall, the only child of ageing parents, was born in Leeds in February 1929, not long before the Second World War began. He spent his teenage years dodging German bombs and by the time he was sixteen both his parents had died, leaving him an orphan, with no close family. He joined the Army in 1948 as a mechanic driver in the Royal Army Service Corps, later to become the Royal Corps of Transport. The Army became his family, and he saw active service in Palestine, Malaya and later in Cyprus with the United Nations.

Mum married Geoff Horsfall when she was twenty-five and he was nearly thirty-seven, a corporal in the RASC, attached to the Parachute Brigade. A tall, narrow, balding man with a bony build that belied his great physical strength, he had a long hooked nose and large blue eyes which gave him the appearance of a hawk. His huge, digger-bucket hands had fingers like salami sausages, which were constantly lined with oil from his mechanical labours. He was really my first father, but we never formed an affectionate relationship. It was probably hard for me to accept a man in my mother's life, and equally tough for him to take on a woman with three children. Geoff had no patience with me; his staring eyes and loud voice would leave me frozen to the spot like a petrified rabbit whenever he spoke.

In 1965, after their wedding, we moved into married quarters in Napier Square in Aldershot, a three-bedroomed flat that for the first time allowed my sister to sleep in a separate bedroom from my brother and me. The accommodation surrounded a large tarmac square filled with rotary washing lines and bricked-off dustbin areas. It was standard practice to adopt all the other parents as aunties and uncles and to use their houses as if they were your own: wherever you happened to be at teatime, you ate there, and the same applied to their children. The school was five minutes' walk away and I had many friends. I found myself in a secure and comfortable environment and began to enjoy my childhood.

That year my grandfather died in his sleep from a heart attack. He was only fifty-seven. The following year, in February, Mum gave birth to my brother Wayne, and shortly after this we were posted to Dortmund in West Germany, where Dad was to serve with the British Army on the Rhine. The next three years were the most stable and happy of my childhood. Our first house was across the road from huge cornfields, with a farm at the far end: an idyllic playground and a scrumper's dream. We were bused to and from school every day by the Army. The British Army schools were excellent, with small classes and good teachers, and I thrived in this well-disciplined and happy environment. The usual punishment involved walking out to the front of the class, touching your toes and receiving a big slap on the bottom. It might not have hurt for long, but it worked, and I never resented it.

I HAD MY first experience of bullying when I was nine. In all groups of children, there is always one individual who is either the oldest or biggest; in ours it was a lad called Robert. He was ten, pushing eleven, we had played together once or twice before, and I liked him. One day we were playing with some toys at the back of my house when he suddenly jumped on me, pinned me down and punched me in the face. I just lay there and cried – not because it hurt particularly, but because his attack didn't make any sense. We hadn't had an argument; there had been no warning. I was simply shocked into submission by the unexpected. Sadly, this set a benchmark for future incidents. It hurt my sense of dignity, I hadn't been able to do anything, and I didn't have anyone to run crying to. Even at that age I felt ashamed not to have done more.

Geoff still hadn't been able to connect with me, and my most dominant memories of him are of the beatings he gave me. One summer evening, when I was nine, he kicked me up the stairs for being late home. Being hit by his big hands was bad enough, but when a person kicks your arse it is degrading, even for a child. My fear of him grew into an intense dislike, which he obviously sensed, and that of course made matters even worse. I took every opportunity I could to avoid him, and never spoke to him unless I was spoken to first.

In spite of the problems with Dad, I loved living in Germany. For the first year I went to a junior school in Dortmund, and later to Mulheim, an old mansion that had originally been owned by the famous Thyssen family and had been taken over by Hermann Goering as his headquarters during the Second World War. Set in a dark forest, it was remote and exciting. Inside, the high ceilings and dark panelled walls allowed the imagination to run free. With no access to English-language television, we found many more activities to pursue than most modern-day children. I was already finding my feet as a runner: the forests were great for cross-country races; the winding muddy paths through the trees were a wonderful challenge for a nine-year-old discovering his physical abilities. The school even had its own T-shaped swimming pool, graced in the middle by a statue of a kneeling naked female washing her hair, and it was here that I first learned to swim, finally achieving the enormous distance of twenty-five yards.

At eleven I was at my best: made head boy, I was gaining good results in all my subjects. I took and passed my eleven-plus exam easily, and was looking forward to going to Hamm Boarding School for Boys – but unfortunately Dad was now called home to England: at the age of forty he was coming to the end of his military career and was due to retire.

As is often the case with Army children, my whole pattern of life changed. We returned to England and went back to my grandmother's house, while Dad finished his Army service away from home.

I attended Farnham Grammar School, but though I felt privileged, and was very aware of the fact that I was the only boy from the village not to go to the local secondary modern, I was not prepared for the effect this would have on the local boys, who now came to regard me as something of a snob. I didn't quite fit in at the grammar either – my rough Army-brat manners and lack of preparation for the school left me out on a limb from the beginning. Mum and Dad had borrowed to the limit just to get me the required uniform and sports clothes, but I was just not ready for middle-class Surrey. Once a secure, bright and popular boy, I suddenly found myself alone.

My parents had their own problems to deal with, like finding a suitable house. Gran's house was not ideal for a boy with two hours of homework every night. The only heating was in the living room, and of course Gran and my three younger siblings all congregated there in front of the fire and the TV. My schoolwork started to deteriorate, and with it my self-esteem. As long as I had been able to prove that I was as good as the next boy I had held my own at school, but now the rot began to set in.

I started feigning illness to avoid school, and I became a regular visitor to the doctor's. I think he understood and was sympathetic, but of course my results got worse and worse. Finally I pretended to have appendicitis, and I was so convincing that the doctors decided to take my appendix out. Great, I thought, lots of love, attention and sympathy. However, I got more than I bargained for – I developed septicaemia and almost died. My temperature went up to 108 degrees Fahrenheit and I spent a month recovering. By the time I got back to school I was hopelessly lost. The attention I had received when I was sick encouraged me to develop even more illnesses, and I began to miss more and more school.

We did finally get our own home, a four-bedroom house in a village called Heath End, just outside Farnham. I made one final effort at school, deciding that I would work hard and try to catch up. For the next six months I didn't miss a day. I completed all my homework and put my heart into everything. I felt better for it; my confidence was growing. Eventually Parents' Evening came around. I knew I had worked hard and I expected Mum to come back full of praise for me. Instead, when she did get home she told Dad that the French teacher had said that while there had been some improvement it was nowhere near enough. All my hard work over the past months summarised in those few words: I had been hoping for a pat on the back and instead I felt as though I had been kicked in the balls. It was not what I needed, and I thought, Sod them, what right do they have to tell me how to lead my life? From now on I would make my own decisions.

Dad had no sympathy for my cause. As far as he was concerned, I shouldn't have been so big for my boots in going to such a posh school in the first place. We argued and I got battered, usually after running upstairs to hide. He would simply follow me and dole out the punishment. Finally, aged twelve, I figured out that there was no point in running from him, because he would get me anyway. My dislike had turned to hatred, and instead of fleeing when he approached with his hand raised, this time I turned and faced him. I glared at him as he knocked me to the floor, and I refused to cry. As soon as he stopped hitting me I stood up and glared at him again, my hatred obvious. Perhaps in despair, he finally walked away.

That evening I penned a letter describing my feelings for him. I wrote, 'I hate my step, step, step, step, stepfather,' and left it where it would be found. My mother told me later that he had indeed found it. I felt guilty, but he never hit me again. Looking back, I imagine he had a lot to contend with: a wife and three kids, all the security of twenty-two years in the Army gone, no qualifications, a low income and me making him feel inadequate. I don't envy him.

BY THE TIME I was thirteen, I was the school delinquent. Although the teachers thought I was bright, I no longer had the desire to succeed. I wanted to hide from the responsibility and the shame of failure at school, and I found the ideal place. I went fishing every weekend, holiday and truant day, disappearing on my bicycle, loaded down with about fifty pounds of camping and fishing gear. I would stay by one of the many local ponds until I had to return for food or bait. The other, older boys in the street would sometimes camp with me. I learned to be self-sufficient out of doors and I became fit from all the cycling – sometimes I travelled as much as ten miles each way. My favourite hiding place was the closest pond, at Badshot Lea, a large gravel pit with high reeds, woodlands and islands, an ideal setting for many a weekend adventure.

My Uncle Peter was a first-aider in the St John's Ambulance Brigade, and he encouraged me to become a cadet. I joined with some enthusiasm, initially so I would be able to get into football matches and motor racing for nothing, but I grew to love first-aid, and completed four hundred hours of voluntary service in two years.

Late one night in the winter of 1970, when I was thirteen, I sat by the steamed-up window of a double-decker bus, waiting for it to take me home. I had been on first-aid duty at an Aldershot football match. Some of the fans from the match came up the stairs; they were all dressed as skinheads in cut-off blue jeans, T-shirts and ankle-high Doc Marten boots. The leader was about sixteen years old with a piggy nose and a bald, round Charlie Brown head. I kept my eyes on the darkness outside. Charlie Brown walked up to my seat and sat beside me. I continued to look through the window. My heart was pounding in my chest: I knew I was in trouble, but I didn't know what to do. The skinhead spoke softly to me: 'Were you at the football?' As I turned to look at him, his forehead crashed into my nose. The shock numbed my brain and sent me sliding to the floor between the seats. By the time I had recovered, he was walking away, laughing, with his friends. My nose began to bleed and my eyes filled with tears. While I lay there, they left the bus.

The skinhead's name was Robert Wilkinson; he lived by my local pond in Badshot Lea. He never fished, but he used to walk the banks of the pond, looking for mischief. Having identified me as a weak target, he now took every opportunity he could to make my life a misery. My favourite hiding place was safe no more. To avoid him, I went further afield, but his cruel smile and demented laughter continued to haunt me. Once I saw him tear the legs off a live duck. He laughed as he watched the poor creature flap around on the ground in its death throes. I wished he didn't frighten me so much. I wanted to beat him to death. I dreamed of challenging and defeating him in front of all of his friends, but I was too scared even to talk to him, let alone fight him.

When you're bullied at home you have nowhere to run to. If you have a secure base, where you know you're protected and loved, you can get away from whatever's going on in the outside world and run back to that safe environment; reassure yourself that you're OK, and go back into the fold. Fishing was my way of escaping the bullying at home, but in time I was to lose even that hiding place. I found myself constantly trying to run from one place to the other.

While it was at home that I first made a stand, it took me a much longer time to overcome my fear of the consequences of standing up for myself. I was constantly imagining what the outcome would be, to the extent that my imagination became the enemy. Eventually I realised that I would learn to deal with the bullying only when I learned to overcome my imagination. Lacking a father figure to guide me, it took me a long time to work these things out for myself.

Bullying is the one thing in life that still makes me angry. If I see it going on, whether it's physical or mental, I get involved.

BACK AT HOME, money was still tight, so my parents took in a lodger, a builder called Brian Blake. He was young, strong and humorous, and he was there when Dad was not.

We had not been on holiday since I was seven. When I was fourteen Mum announced that we were taking one, whether Dad liked it or not. It didn't require a mastermind to work out that Mum and Dad had not been getting on, but it was still a shock when we discovered that it was Brian who would be taking us on holiday. It didn't matter to me, though. All of us had a wonderful, wet seven days in Perrenporth in Cornwall, in a caravan.

When we got home, Geoff Horsfall had moved out and Brian moved into Mum's room. It was as simple as that, and I welcomed it, but it was too late to fill the gaps in my life.

LATER THAT YEAR I walked to the bottom of Hospital Hill in Aldershot and into the Army Careers Information Office, to join the Army.

CHAPTER 2

Indoctrination

IT TOOK A considerable effort of will to walk into the Army Careers Office alone and without an appointment. There was a sergeant behind a desk, wearing a smart brown uniform with three red-and-gold stripes on his arm. 'I want to know about joining the Army,' I said. He was very affable, and told me to sit down while he noted all my personal details. Once he had established that I was only fourteen, he told me that it would be at least twelve months before I could join up; I couldn't leave school until I was fifteen. 'No problem,' I said, 'I'll come back next year.' The sergeant said that there was a lot we could still achieve, and suggested I come back the following day at 2 p.m. I made an appointment and left, feeling like a brave man. I had taken my future in my own hands and I had been treated as an adult. Finally I would show everyone what I was made of.

The following day I was presented with all the documents I needed to join the Army, including the parental consent forms. A weekend visit to Sutton Coldfield, the large military camp where boys were assessed and pointed towards the career the Army thought they were most suited to, was arranged for me so I could take the assessment course and see which unit I might want to join. Mum and Dad didn't try to dissuade me in any way: in their shoes, considering my faltering performance at school, I would have done the same.

In March 1972 I had to attend a medical examination at Browning Barracks, the depot of the Parachute Regiment. I showed my paperwork to the guard at the gate and he directed me to the medical centre. While I was waiting to be seen, a skinny young recruit limped in and went up to the reception desk. The medical sergeant looked at him and bawled, 'What do you want?' The recruit said a nail had gone through his boot. 'Well, go and get some new fucking boots,' the sergeant screamed. The lad left the room, bewildered and dejected. This was a short but powerful introduction to the Paras: I was left in no doubt, these guys were tough.

The medical was no big deal – and yes, they do lift up your balls and ask you to cough: it's to see if you have a rupture. After taking several written tests, I was interviewed and shown some films. Later all the potential recruits were herded into a building full of show-stands to talk to members of the different regiments, who were all doing their best to promote their own units. At the end of the day, we were asked to make a list of three choices. My first choice was the Royal Army Medical Corps, my second the Military Police and my third the Parachute Regiment – God knows how the Paras got in there. Junior service in the Army ran from fifteen to eighteen years of age: the highest scorers were offered apprenticeships with Corps, the next highest the rank of Junior Leaders (as potential high achievers) and the third and lowest, Junior Tradesmen and Junior Infantrymen.

'We don't think you're good material for the Royal Army Medical Corps,' the interviewer said baldly. Then I was asked why I wanted to be in the Military Police. 'To be a dog handler,' I replied, but this was not considered a good enough reason. 'We can offer you a place as a Junior Leader in the Parachute Regiment,' the interviewer concluded. I took it. It wasn't my first choice; in fact, I had been more inclined to heal people than kill them, but at least the Paras would make me tough and stop me being bullied ever again. I imagined wearing a red beret and walking the streets while other young men looked at me with fear and respect.

MY REMAINING FEW months at school were a drag. I didn't want to be there, and the teachers had given up on me. As soon as the summer holidays came I was out looking for a job, and within two days I had one, at the local chicken factory. It was my task to stand by a conveyor belt as a line of recently killed chickens, hung up by their feet, swung past me. Various different parts of the anatomy were removed until an oven-ready bird was finally washed and frozen at the end of the line.

It was my first introduction to women in the workplace. I was young, shy and, I'm told, handsome. I had dreamed of the day when, instead of fumbling around with some equally shy girl, I would have the chance to go for it for real. Now the opportunity arose several times, but I was too scared of getting it wrong to get it right. Being unavailable only made matters worse – I became a challenge, and this drew unwanted attention my way. After only a week a tall, dark, eighteen-year-old man walked up to me and told me that he didn't like me. I didn't know the man, I had never spoken to him, but he knew me, and he was 'gonna get me'. Once again my complete lack of understanding left me vulnerable. How could I reply to a threat for which there was no reason? How could I apologise for something I hadn't done? Asking questions only elicited responses like, 'I'm warning you, any more of your lip . . .' or 'Don't get smart with me, right?' I arrived early and left late to avoid him, but eventually he pulled me aside and said, 'Meet me behind the factory tonight at five. I'm gonna sort you out. If you're not there, it'll be even worse tomorrow.'

For the rest of the day I worried myself sick, my trepidation not helped by half the girls in the factory asking me what I was going to do. I had nowhere to hide. The day dragged endlessly, and four-thirty arrived far too soon. As I left work I wanted to run home; I wanted a big brother to stand up for me. Why couldn't this guy just leave me alone? I hadn't done anything to him, so why was he picking on me, for God's sake? There was no sanctuary anywhere, unless I decided not to return to work the next day. I resigned myself to my fate and walked to the back of the building, quietly praying that he wouldn't turn up. When I reached our rendezvous he wasn't there, and for a moment I thought my luck was in. It was warm and sunny and I waited for a while on a small footbridge, watching the water flow beneath me. As I was about to leave, I recognised his large frame as he strolled towards me. He was surprised that I was there and told me so; my heart was in my mouth and my knees were shaking and I said nothing – it seemed pointless. He picked me up, turned me over and dropped me head-first onto the concrete. Then he kicked me until I was unconscious. I came to on the way to hospital, suffering from cuts and concussion. After twenty-four hours' observation I was sent home to continue my education in the grown-up world.

I never considered reporting him to the police: it just wasn't the done thing. Some fool had convinced half the nation that the police were there to oppress us, that they were, in fact, the enemy. I, like many young people, believed that calling them in was a worse option than being beaten up again.

I returned to work the next day sporting my black eye and stitches, expecting to be shunned as a weak nobody. I was also terribly afraid of confronting the bully again, but when I arrived, several young women acknowledged me in a kindly manner. I was polite but withdrawn, shy of a potential cutting remark if I dropped my guard and became too friendly. I slunk into the canteen and hid behind a cup of tea in the corner. It was no use – the cup wasn't big enough. In came my tormentor with a grin on his swarthy features and walked straight across to my table. I looked up at him, not knowing where to go or what to do. He wouldn't hit me in the canteen, but I would have to sit here and be humiliated by him all over again in front of everyone.

'I want to apologise for the other day,' he said. 'I was totally out of order and it won't happen again. Can we just shake and forget it?' He thrust out his hand. I sat motionless, looking for the trick. Would he pull me forward and head-butt me, or just laugh at my weakness and walk away? 'No fooling,' he said. 'I mean it.' The whole room was watching as I put out my hand and shook his. He turned and walked out. As he left, several girls came and sat with me. Apparently the staff had threatened to down tools and not work with him unless he apologised to me in public.

Power to the people, eh? I didn't have any more problems at the factory. I hadn't realised that by turning up to fight I was morally in a no-lose situation. I was expected not to turn up; hence I was brave just for being there. He, on the other hand, was a bully; if he won he was a coward, if he lost he was a coward. He couldn't win.

I STOOD BY the back door with my suitcase and holdall at my feet, both excited and eager. I felt like Dick Whittington, off to find adventure, fame and fortune in the great big world.

Mum fussed around me, making sure that everything was in order. Where were my tickets, money, documents? What time did the train leave?

When there were no more questions to ask, and we knew that everything that could be done had been done, we just stood for a moment, neither wishing to make the next move. She hovered in the centre of the room, surrounded by her life: baskets of laundry waiting to be washed or ironed, the floor waiting to be vacuumed, the kids' toys needing to be stashed away. The late summer sun shone through a gap in the curtains, casting a spotlight on the floating dust. In the warmth of the morning, time seemed to drag.

To avoid the awkwardness of the moment I looked away from her and out through the kitchen door. I allowed my eyes to wander down the four concrete steps that led from the small kitchen into the back yard, where many childhood memories bade me farewell.

As she moved towards me, the sun caught her face and glistened off the tears welling up in her eyes. I looked down and she held my gaze. I could bear it no longer – I stepped forward into her arms and buried my head in the warmth of her shoulder. Inside I cried, though no tear touched my cheek. I thought myself too grown-up and tough for that. We held each other for a long time until, finally, I broke the embrace and kissed her.

I picked my bags up and left home in good heart. As I walked down the gravel lane to the bus stop I felt a strong urge to go back, but a stronger force pulled me on, towards the future, whatever it should be.

I boarded the train at Aldershot and travelled to Waterloo Station in London. From there I lugged Dad's old army suitcase and my holdall down to the Underground to catch a train to Euston. I checked and double-checked my route, and even when I was on the right train I still checked each and every station to make sure. At Euston it was just a matter of catching the train to Wolverhampton, which I managed without any problems. I noticed an increasing number of boys of my own age on the train. I kept myself to myself, but by the time we disembarked at Wolverhampton it was impossible not to talk to some of the hundreds of excited fifteen-year-olds who were standing on the platform, all waiting for the same train. They came from every corner of the kingdom. I had never before heard such a diversity of accents: Welsh, Scots, Irish, Yorkshire, Lancashire, Newcastle, Birmingham, Liverpool, and many more. It was the first time in my life I heard people use 'thy' and 'thee' in normal spoken English. I couldn't understand some of the Jocks at all.

As we approached our final stop, Gobowen station, a hundred heads leaned out of train windows, as though expecting a brass band and red carpet in honour of our arrival. Instead, our eyes were met by the sight of a solitary figure, in a brown number-two dress uniform with three stripes on each arm: a Grenadier Guards sergeant, the first I'd ever seen. I would describe his face, but all I could see were two flared nostrils sticking out from beneath a shiny peaked cap. The peak was pointing down, so that his eyes were hidden; it almost touched his nose. As we moved down the short grey concrete platform, the sergeant guided us towards two large green three-ton Army trucks and two green Army buses. He gently told us to 'get our cases on the truck and our arses in the bus'. I then made the second mistake of my military career (the first was joining up): I asked an unnecessary question. 'Excuse me, Sarge, how far is it?' One second he was standing six feet away from me; the next his nose was almost touching mine. His hot breath blasted across my face. 'Don't call me Sarge, call me Sergeant.' The volume almost knocked me to the floor. I looked up his nose, squeaked out, 'Yes, Sergeant,' and got on the bus.

PARK HALL CAMP in Oswestry was a huge place, covering about nine square miles of countryside. The whole area was a mass of wooden barrack blocks, tarmacadam parade squares and huge open, metal-roofed sheds. The only visible disruption to the local landscape was an old Saxon hill-fort that rose one hundred and fifty feet to the north of the camp.

Once the laborious process of entry administration was completed, we were divided into our various platoons of thirty to thirty-five boys and handed over to our respective platoon sergeants. Each platoon belonged to a regiment or division. Mine, of course, was the Parachute Regiment, with three Light Infantry boys to make up the numbers.

Our accommodation was old wooden huts, built in the fifties, each consisting of six long rooms, joined in the centre by an ablutions area which held toilets, showers, baths and washrooms. In spite of having only six rooms leading out from the centre, they were referred to as spiders. My platoon was housed in three of the rooms belonging to one spider. The other three rooms were occupied by a platoon formed from the Guards regiments. In the other spiders, platoons from the Scottish regiments, the Light Division and the county regiments were housed. These five platoons were the building blocks of Z Company, the lowest of the low, and comprised the youngest boys in the battalion.

Altogether the camp held about two thousand boys, all between the ages of fifteen and eighteen. Our platoon sergeants were Sergeants Duncan and Murphy, the former from the Queens Regiment and the latter from the Royal Irish Rangers. Duncan, formerly of the Parachute Regiment, was a fit, athletic man, with broad shoulders and a narrow waist. Standing six foot one, he had a full head of black hair and a swarthy complexion. Murphy was his absolute antithesis: short and stocky, close on forty, with mashed-potato skin and fair, reddish hair. Their appearance was always immaculate; their boots shone like black glass and their green fatigue trousers were shiny with being pressed so many times. They even had creases in the shoulders of their heavy green wool pullovers.

Duncan had formerly served with the Paras, and wasted no time in letting us know that we were going to have to be tough to get past him and into the Army for real. For the first six weeks we were confined to camp, after which those who survived would be allowed to leave the barracks and go to town on Sundays.

We were allocated a set of bed springs and a mattress, blankets and sheets. A plastic Army mug and a knife, fork and spoon rested on top of the sheets. We then lined up in three ranks outside our room to 'march' to dinner. The cookhouse was about a mile away. En route we passed the parade ground, the football pitch and the cricket field, before coming to a lone hut, outside which stood a gargantuan man wearing a tam-o'-shanter beret and a Black Watch kilt. The hut was the guardroom and the man was 'Black Mac', the provost sergeant, the ugliest and most feared man I ever saw. He stood a proud five foot ten and looked as square as a block of concrete. His dark Black Watch tartan kilt stood clear of hairy knees and thick socks holding ceremonial dirks. He was 180 pounds if he was an ounce, and the fact that he wore glasses made him even more intimidating. As we marched past he stood stock still, and we all averted our gaze until we had gone safely by. I didn't need to be told that if I could get through two years of this place and never speak to that man, I would have achieved a great deal.

The cookhouse was huge and divided into several eating areas. Z Company had its own queue and eating area. The other areas were for junior privates, junior NCOs (non-commissioned officers) and permanent staff. The food was good. Most of us had never had a choice of what to eat before – at home you got what you were given and pudding (dessert if you were posh) was something you had at parties and sometimes on Sundays.

As we ate, we watched the older boys across the hall. They were well-built and confident, and they didn't even give us a curious glance. We must have looked very untidy and scrawny to them. I wanted to be just like them, confident and tough, and I believed that if I could stick it out here, the Army would make me like them. All I had to do was stay the course and I would never have to be scared of anyone ever again.

Our first evening was spent learning how to dress, how to press our clothes and how to make a bed and bed block. An Army bed had to be made in the correct military manner: sheets folded back to the regulation length, blanket line dead centre, and corners at the required forty-five-degree angle. When the first day was over, some still-excited lads chattered endlessly into the night until they were tipped out of bed in order to let the others get to sleep. It was strange sleeping in the long, airy room with twelve other boys turning and snoring.

At 0600 hours the double doors at the end of the room burst open and a dustbin flew down the aisle between our beds. 'Get up, you horrible lot, get moving, get moving.' Duncan launched boy after boy out of his warm bed and sent him rolling across the floor with his upturned mattress and springs following behind. At 0630 hours we were washed and dressed in our new uniforms, our bed blocks were on top of our lockers and we were ready to march to breakfast.

At 0800 hours we stood by our beds ready for inspection. By 0815 hours every bed was overturned and every bed block was airborne as Duncan rampaged through the room like a mad bull in a Chinese laundry. Half an hour later, beds remade to Duncan's exacting standards, we set off to the quartermaster's stores to collect and sign for all our military equipment. The rest of the morning was spent alternatively standing in a long queue or waddling back to barracks like a two-legged tortoise, weighed down with trousers, vests, boots, socks, pouches, water-bottles and endless other items. Even Y-front underpants came in regulation Army green.

We were also issued with our berets. Every film featuring soldiers I have ever seen has one great failing: nobody tells the star how a military beret comes to be the nice snug, folded-down item that appears on a real soldier's head. Instead, the likes of Roger Moore, Richard Harris and Richard Burton are seen running around with weird upside-down L-shaped pork pies on their heads; no genuine soldier could ever take them seriously. The unique shape of an Army beret is achieved by spending hours dipping it into scalding hot water to shrink it and then, as soon as it cools, fastening it onto the head and shaping it by stroking it down to the right-hand side, then it is plunged into cold water; the whole process is repeated until at last it reaches the desired shape.

We wore green canvas belts that were coloured daily with a green substance confusingly named blanco – blanco means whitener, except that *our* whitener was green: typical military logic. Footwear was spit-polished by a method known as bulling one's boots, which only worked with Kiwi boot polish (bloody New Zealand has a lot to answer for). Late at night we were often taken by surprise by random changing parades, which meant having to be outside the barracks, dressed, in three ranks, in whichever uniform the sergeant desired. Once on parade, five minutes was allowed for changing into an alternative dress: PE kit, number-two dress, combat dress, fatigues, and so on. After every item of uniform had been worn and creased, the rest of the night would be spent getting it ready for inspection the following morning.

As time went by I was gradually indoctrinated into a system designed solely to break a personality down and rebuild it. In the process, the question 'why?' and the answer 'no' were eradicated from the soldier's vocabulary. Blind obedience and a total commitment to the orders given were the prerequisites for success as a non-commissioned soldier. Total commitment I handled easily, but the question 'why' remained in my vocabulary: my Achilles heel.

CHAPTER 3

Hangman's Noose

BIG MICK WAS the biggest and most physically mature boy in my room, and thanks to a combination of my big mouth and my *naïveté*, he was the cause of yet another miserable period of my life. In our second week of training, I was sitting on the end of my bed, offering opinions on the world according to Rob. Mick, who was opposite me, quietly told me to shut up. I ignored this and carried on with my verbal diarrhoea. 'Do you want me to make you shut up?' he asked. 'Yeah, OK,' I said, without carefully considering the implications of his question; I had no idea that this was fighting talk, as the whole exchange had taken place without raised voices or posturing.

Mick walked over to where I was sitting and punched me in the mouth. I fell back onto my bed and looked up at him as he stood there, waiting for my response. I didn't know what to do. 'I told you to shut up,' he said. 'Now, do you want some more?' 'No,' I replied, as I wiped my swelling lip. Mick turned and walked away.

He never made a big deal out of the incident – I had obviously been mouthing off far too much for my own good and he had put it to rights. The other boys saw it in a different light: I hadn't fought back, I was a soft touch – perhaps they could get away with it as well, especially if Mick was their friend. Suddenly I felt isolated again; I had failed my first personal test. Once again my self-esteem hit rock bottom, and as usual, there was no one to tell me how to recover. What I should have done, to protect my dignity and show other potential adversaries that I would not be an easy kill, was to have got stuck in, win or lose. With the right advice I might have laid into the next person to bother me, but I didn't. His name was Bill, and he had been very friendly towards me up to this point, but he turned like a hungry dog and became the next one to offer to fight me. I declined, and so the pattern continued: I became a recognised whipping-boy; everyone was allowed to insult and threaten me without fear of retaliation. My self-worth faded to nothing and the joy went out of my life. I began to understand the saying 'life without honour is no life at all'.

SO I BURIED myself in my training and education. My days were filled with endless hours of drill, weapons training, map-reading and continuing schoolwork – English, arithmetic, history and geography. Three afternoons a week were spent playing sport.

It was only when the organised day was over and the sergeants had disappeared that the intimidation started. Fortunately for me, I was not the only victim of barrack-room bullying: there was a small, fair-haired boy called Whitecross, who was soft and very immature. He was fifteen going on thirteen, and someone had made a mistake sending him into the Army. One night after training he was manhandled onto a chair to face a hangman's noose tied to the cross-beam in the centre of the room. He was summarily tried for failing to come up to the standards required of our glorious platoon, found guilty and sentenced to be hanged by the neck until he was dead. He stood on the chair with his hands secured behind his back, a quivering bundle of fear. Tears ran down his face. When one of the boys stepped forward and placed the noose around his neck, no one except Whitecross believed he would really be hanged. I felt for him: he was frightened and crying, and I wanted to help him, but I was too scared to intervene. I would become the object of the others' derision instead of Whitecross, so I kept my silence, and my shame, and watched as a boy named Ken kicked away the chair. As Whitecross fell, the noose suddenly tightened around his neck. The strands of sewing cotton that were all that held it to the beam parted and Whitecross hit the floor in a crumpled heap. Hoots of laughter filled the room as the 'joke' sank in.

I was relieved it was over. It was over for poor old Whitecross, too. He cashed in his cards and went home the following day – junior soldiers could change their mind and leave without penalty at any time during the first four weeks of service. I was sorry to see him go, not because he was a friend, but because he kept some of the flak away from me.

IN WEEK FOUR we were given a fitness test to decide whether we were worth keeping for the next two years. Anyone who failed to make the grade still had time to leave without penalty; once the first four weeks were over, the Army would want to be compensated for its time and expense, and those wanting to leave after this stage would be required to purchase their discharge.

The test involved a ten-mile march in boots, denims and T-shirts to the top of the Wrekin, a hill surmounted by a memorial known as Rodney's Pillar, a monument to the great eighteenth-century admiral. The forthcoming climb grew to epic proportions in our imaginations: if we failed, we would go home in shame.

The climb was gradual, undertaken at marching speed, and should not have been too hard for any fit young person, but before we had gone more than two miles, a few were lagging behind, and in spite of our encouraging words they fell out. When we got close to the top an air of relief spread over us – we knew we were going to make it; the down-hill stretch would be easy. Duncan's voice boomed out: 'OK, I want to see the last one to the top.' We were off, full of pride and joy at the prospect of conquering this great obstacle. Legs that moments before had felt as heavy as lead now bounded forward with renewed vigour.

We were all euphoric: few of us had been sure of success, and now we regarded ourselves as selected, special individuals who could do anything that was asked of us. We sat resting for a while, and then set off back to the trucks at the bottom, singing paratrooper songs all the way down. In spite of my problems, I started to feel a part of the platoon at last. It was only when we returned to the trucks that we quietened down. There, on the back, looking lost and forlorn, were those who had dropped out on the way up. We didn't speak to them, because we didn't know what to say. The next day they were gone, and then we abused them terribly. It made us feel better than them, more important. I hoped I would never be sitting on a bus going home like that. The idea frightened me even more than being beaten up.

Duncan enjoyed his position to the full. He was really a full corporal acting as a sergeant because he was serving with a boys' battalion. Every morning we would stand by our beds, lockers open, ready for room inspection. Duncan would stroll down the room with a silver-topped swagger stick tucked under his arm. 'What are you?' he would shout to each individual as he faced them. 'I'm a paratrooper, Sergeant,' was the expected reply. Then he would strike the individual square on the top of the head with the bulbous, silver end of his cane. Sometimes, for a change, he would punch one of us in the stomach and watch his victim curl up at his feet in agony. He was a bully of the highest class: it takes nothing, after all, for a man in his twenties, with the authority to imprison soldiers for any insubordination, to beat up a fifteen-year-old recruit.

One morning he asked a boy named Mills what he was. Mills was very small, and was one of the two remaining Light Infantrymen in the platoon. 'I'm a Light Infantryman,' he shouted. 'Oh yes, so you are,' said Duncan as he brought his cane down on Mills's head. Mills's knees gave way and he fell to the floor unconscious. The momentary panic on Duncan's face was a picture. He crapped himself, knowing he had gone too far. Fortunately Mills was revived, and unfortunately Duncan got away with it, but he left his stick in the office on all future inspections.

Our pay was nearly ten pounds a week, not a bad wage for the time – I had earned twelve pounds in the factory, and there my food wasn't included. We drew only two pounds a week, though; the remainder, after tax and national insurance, was saved for our leave. Two pounds was quite enough for boys who had little or no time to spend it. We had to buy our own boot polish, so the remainder would be spent on cigarettes and chocolate.

Almost all the lads, including me, smoked – it was a way of being grown-up. Tuesday was pay-day, so on Tuesday we would smoke

Rothman's King Size, thirty pence for twenty. By the following Monday we were down to shouting 'Two's up' at anyone that lit a ciggy: the shout entitled the first caller to smoke the butt-end of the smoker's cigarette when he had finished it. Then Tuesday would come around again.

After about eight weeks of training and smoking heavily, I developed bronchitis. Going sick as a recruit was no better in Oswestry than it had been in Aldershot. The doctor was on the other side of camp, about two miles way; I would have to collapse before I could go sick. Also, because I was not held in the highest regard by my colleagues, I refused to give anyone the chance to label me a weakling or a malingerer. At the beginning of November I was walking to and from breakfast coughing up large lumps of yellow phlegm; I felt as weak as a kitten. On the eighth I had to take part in the weekly five-mile run. Unusually for me, I was not in the front group; instead, I was lagging behind, coughing my guts up. As Duncan stopped the group, I caught up. I pulled out a packet of ten No. 6 cigarettes, tore them up and threw them away. I never smoked again.

It wasn't easy, even at that age, to stop. I had smoked since the age of thirteen, and the first weeks were a nightmare. I didn't know what to do with my hands, and everyone else I lived with was smoking. Some lads lit up as soon as they woke up in the morning. Four weeks after I quit smoking, I rose in the middle of the night, went to my locker, took a packet of cigarettes out and sat on the bed and smoked one before going back to sleep. In the morning I was disgusted with myself. I had failed yet another personal test. A moment later I realised that I didn't have any cigarettes in my locker. I had dreamed the whole episode.

I was developing fast. The training was making me strong, but I still couldn't find the courage to fight the other members of the platoon who were being hard on me. It wasn't that any individual was particularly bad, but given that I was unpopular and scared, no one was afraid to put in their pennyworth, and it all added up. I took every taunt seriously, instead of just laughing it off. The more I responded and showed my aggravation, the more frequent the taunts became. One of the favourites was, 'Is your mother a wog? I bet she's a Paki. That's why you're dark with curly hair.' There were very few members of any ethnic minorities in the battalion, and they were never, to my knowledge, abused, but because of my fear, I found out what it was like to be segregated by bigots.

Once again, I felt completely alone, with no one to talk to; I was too ashamed to phone Mum. Only one thing kept me going: my refusal to be proven wrong. Before I left for the Army, my mother had told a friend about my plans; she said that I wasn't the type for the Army, and that she didn't think I would last. It might have been just a small comment, but there was no way I was going to prove her to be right.

I tried to mind my own business, and I avoided all conflict and communication with the others. I worked hard, kept my kit clean and went to bed early. I also read a lot, sometimes three books at a time. It was another hiding place, but it didn't help. One night, as I hid under my blankets, my full suitcase was pushed from the top of my locker onto my head. It hurt, but not as much as the laughter that followed. Now I had no choice but to stay awake. Once a dart was thrown at me from behind, hitting my lower leg and sinking in up to the hilt. The thrower refused to identify himself, and the dart gave me impetigo, a vile disease that leaves scabs all over the body. I still refused to go sick.

I had let the situation deteriorate to the point where I could take very little more. I thought that if I stood up for myself now, the others would join in on the side of whoever I fought. If I answered anyone back, they would all support him. I was at rock bottom; I was actually thinking seriously about leaving the Army. One day, finding myself alone in the room with 'Saddlebags', I told him I was thinking of leaving. He was always sound and fair, and his reply pulled me back from the brink. 'You're not as bad as they make out, Rob,' he said, mature words from a fifteen-year-old, and they meant a lot to me. They were my candle in the dark.

A few days later a lad called Philip gave me some abuse and, for the first time, I answered him back. As I opened my mouth, I resolved to follow this through, no matter what. My heart pounded and I started to sweat. I wanted to run, but I knew that this time I wouldn't. He threatened me and I hit him. We fought and fell into the usual unskilled bundle of arms and legs that most schoolboy fights are. First I was under him, then he was under me. I gave as good as I got until we were eventually pulled apart. It wasn't much of a fight as fights go, but to me it was a tremendous step. I could fight, I could be brave: maybe I wasn't a complete wanker after all. I had conquered my fear; I had discovered – yet again – that what I was afraid of was nothing compared to what my imagination had created. I could take a punch and carry on; the pain wasn't so bad if you ignored it. My reaction – for the first time – finally put an end to the physical bullying.

Of course, I didn't suddenly become 'Mr Popular' overnight; I never would. And there were a few more people to stand up to before I could hold my own. A reputation can be established in seconds; to rebuild a reputation from scratch can take years. I wanted to be tough, and I carried this desire into every situation. Having been unpopular, I now assumed that everyone disliked me, and this insecurity made me dislikeable even to those who didn't care one way or the other. I accepted their dislike and comforted myself with the knowledge that I could do my job better than they could, but this chip on my shoulder was to weigh heavily for the next ten years.

IN MY THIRD term I was promoted to Junior Lance-Corporal, my first step up the Army career ladder. I had my own room to command and was settling down into military life. I did well enough in most areas – I passed my Certificates of Secondary Education in all subjects, I was in the battalion rugby team as a left wing, and in the fencing team too. I loved any form of physical training, especially when it involved travelling long distances, and I loved map-reading. Whenever there was training to do in the mountains of Snowdonia, I was always eager to volunteer.

Every year there was a competition called the Welsh 3000s, a military race over all the peaks over three thousand feet high in Snowdonia. The junior soldiers' course was the last two-thirds of the course, about twelve miles over seven peaks. I was selected for the training, and every weekend from April to July we travelled to the Ogwen valley in North Wales and ran over the peaks. When July, the time for the race, came, I was sixteen, and so fit that I could run up the mountains. It would take our four-man team about three and a half hours to complete the route, which included about twelve thousand feet of climbing.

Snowdonia separated the fit from the unfit. Some of the most rugged and beautiful countryside in Britain, it has always offered the greatest challenges. I loved the mountains. They were wild and untamed, the great slabs of granite looming over wet green grass and dark heather. The tops were sodden and peaty, with bogs that sucked your legs down and wouldn't let go. The view when the sun shone was magnificent; you could make out the sea in the distance.

The weather was the big one: getting through the cloud on a compass bearing, with nil visibility, and being exactly where you wanted to be; plodding through mud and rain and bogs, and then plunging downwards across rocky boulders like a mountain goat; drinking from the mountain streams, walking through thunderstorms and feeling the power of the wind as it tried to thrust you back whence you came: when the day was over and my lungs were bursting, my legs so tight that I wouldn't dare bend them lest they cramp up, I was always euphoric. I had pushed myself hard, and I loved it.

The week before the race was spent at Blackrock Sands on the North Wales coast. After a day in the mountains, we would retire to our tents on the beach, swim in the sea and relax. When we didn't go to the mountains to train, we ran along the beach, six miles one way along the dunes and six miles back along the edge of the surf. In the evenings we rested and listened to Suzi Quatro on the radio. 'Devil Gate Drive' was her big hit at the time, and whenever sex came into the conversation, our teenage dreams centred on Suzi.

On the day of the race, one member of the team, a little Welshman, had an off-day, and we had to push him all the way to the finish. It took us three hours and forty minutes, and we came second. I was happy with what I had achieved: I had proved I could bounce over these hills as if they were trampolines. Every slope encountered in my life, every stairway and walkway, became a personal challenge to see how fast I could get up it. I began to enjoy pushing myself harder and harder; it allowed me to be unquestioningly better than the others at something, and no matter how unpopular I felt, no one could take that away from me.

As my physical prowess developed, my self-confidence should have as well, but in spite of the fact that I could now fight, I still spent most of my time avoiding conflict. If someone gave me a hard time, I would never take up the gauntlet unless there was no other way out of it. It seemed pointless, and I was still scared. If I could walk away, why on earth shouldn't I? Why get hurt?

IN NOVEMBER 1973 I was officially promoted to full Junior Corporal (two stripes). I had worked hard for the promotion, kept myself out of trouble and performed all my duties well. It meant more money and an expectation of passing out as a sergeant at least. The promotion was published on Part One Orders, which made it official. The stripes were always given out at the end of term, so I had a few weeks to wait. I was very pleased that all my hard work had been rewarded at last.

Three days later the adult company sergeant-major sent for me. He told me that there were too many corporals being promoted and I had been taken off the list. Then he sent me away. There was no promise of future promotion, no apology, and apparently no comprehension of the huge disappointment he had just dumped onto my young shoulders. I was devastated – not gaining promotion was one thing, but to get it and then have it taken away was another thing entirely.

It was a Wednesday, and I went to town alone. By ten o'clock I was in a pub, as drunk as a skunk, with a chip on my shoulder the size of a Canadian forest. I sat down across the table from a young girl, and asked her name. No sooner were the words out of my mouth than a heavy object caught me smack on the side of the face and almost knocked me off my chair. I knew I had been hit, but I didn't know who by, or what with. My right hand shot out in self-defence and caught my assailant in the face. As my victim hit the floor, I realised it was another girl, who then accused me of calling her friend a slag. I was no Romeo and I was shy, but calling girls slags was not my favourite opening line. Two men in the pub took me outside and beat the crap out of me for hitting a woman. I really didn't care that much – I was still too busy feeling sorry for myself.

By the time I got back to camp, the girls had phoned up and reported the incident. My kit was waiting at the guardroom and I was under close arrest. I wasn't charged with assaulting the girl, but with drinking under age, which is against Section 69 of the Army Act: 'behaviour unbecoming of a member of Her Majesty's Forces'. I was given twenty-eight days' restriction of privileges and reduced to the ranks. So I was promoted and busted in the same day.

Word went around that I'd struck a woman, and no one cared for my side of the story. None of the Regimental Policemen who monitored my punishment were in a frame of mind to make it easy for me. Restriction of privileges meant a parade at 0600 hours in number-two dress (best uniform) every morning, cleaning duties at lunchtime, and parade at 1800 hours for more extra duties, such as cleaning prison toilets or painting stones, or even cutting the guardroom grass with nail scissors. Then parade again at 2100 hours in number-two dress and off to bed. Hours would be spent bulling boots to a gleaming shine for each parade. The provost would take great pleasure in standing on the toecaps at the end of inspection so that the bulled-up polish cracked and I had to spend several hours repolishing the boots for the following morning. If I was late or found at fault in any way, the duty officer could award extra days of restrictions. I was not allowed out of camp, or to pursue hobbies. I could only work and eat.

After the twenty-eight days I had been given eighteen days of extras and I was cracking up. I went to the sergeant-major in despair and told him that I couldn't do any more than I was already doing – as it was, I was getting nowhere. He could see I was desperate and put me back on normal duties. I never told anyone why I had been in the pub in the first place; it felt like a waste of breath, but with hindsight it might have aroused some sympathy.

The final twist came at the end of term. My name was still on the list for promotion, and the colonel called for me to collect my stripes. The RSM (Regimental Sergeant-Major) informed the colonel that the promotion had been cancelled.

ONE EVENING BEFORE going on leave, I was lying on my bed when from the door a corporal in my platoon told me there was someone outside to see me. I asked him who, but he wouldn't say. When I stepped out into the darkness I was confronted by two Black Watch privates. They were eighteen and had passed out at the end of the summer term. They knew the girl I had hit and were there to teach me a lesson. Rumour had it that I was a soft touch, but they didn't give me a chance to get scared – they just attacked. I managed to hit the first one a few times as he went for me, but I was finally wrestled to the floor by the second, who jumped on my back. As I fought him on the floor the other man stood up and fired kicks at my head. I didn't give in, and I frustrated their poor attempts to sort me out – in fact, I gave as good as I got. As I lay there getting kicked, I looked up and saw three members of my own platoon watching and doing nothing to help. That hurt more than anything.

I walked back into the block dirty and dishevelled, although certainly not beaten up, but I nearly cried in frustration. I would never have let two outsiders attack a member of my platoon, even if I hated him. I would have stood by him, because he was in my family. The next day the adult platoon sergeant, a Para, heard about the incident. He sat the platoon down and spoke to them about loyalty and backing each other up. I don't know whether it shamed them – probably not. These loyalties were to develop later for most of the boys, when they were in fear of their lives and they needed every bit of help they could get.

IN NOVEMBER 1974 my time at Oswestry was up. I was at the end of the seventh term and ready to pass out. Infantry Junior Leader Battalion (IJLB) Oswestry had also had its day, and was to close down when we left; the unit was transferring to Deal in Kent. I had achieved high marks and was passing out to become a paratrooper, my one burning ambition. I hadn't been promoted again, but it didn't matter – this was the start of a new life as an adult. I was strong, fit and confident. I had climbed mountains, lived in shit, fought back from the depths of despair, and now I was raring to get to my new base: Parachute Regiment Depot, Browning Barracks, Aldershot, only two miles from my mother's home.

CHAPTER 4

Knowledge Dispels Fear

MY FIRST EXPERIENCE of the Paras was when I went for my medical, aged fourteen, and my only exposure since had been when I visited the Junior Parachute Company at Malta Barracks, Aldershot, during boys' service, to practise on the tranasium (a contraction of 'training gymnasium').

The tranasium was a formidable test of a young man's courage. It consisted of a series of metal bars, seesaws, ropes, wires and ladders that were suspended in the trees anywhere between twenty and sixty feet above the ground. We had to run, crawl or otherwise manoeuvre our way across all the obstacles, without any safety measures whatsoever. Dressed in an airborne helmet, green denims, boots and a red T-shirt, I just went for it, praying that I wouldn't fall off.

The hardest test of all was the parallel bars: two four-inch-thick, twelve-foot-long metal bars that stood sixty feet up amongst the trees. Halfway across were two raised metal clamps that we had to get over. An initiate would shuffle to the first clamp, arms outstretched, and step over, then shuffle to the second, step over, and finally shuffle to the end and climb down.

When my turn came I shuffled forward as described, my legs shaking, up to the first clamp, and stopped. I couldn't lift my right foot. I began to tremble and, in spite of all the encouragement from below, I couldn't move. Tears began to well up; I wanted to crawl off to die.

Suddenly the Physical Training Instructor (PTI), a man called Mick, climbed up the opposite side and walked out to the centre, facing me. Standing only inches from me, he said, 'Come on, son, you won't fall, come on.' I lifted my foot over the clamp and shuffled forward as Mick walked backwards across the bars in front of me. When I was across he sent me around to do it again alone, which I did.

This memory has stayed with me ever since. I knew that I had lost it, but with the right leadership and instruction I overcame my fear and became – for want of a better word – brave.

My image of paratroopers before arriving at Aldershot was tinged with reverence: everyone knew they were the toughest, hardest men in the Army. With examples like Mick to look up to, I wanted nothing more than to be one of them.

WE ARRIVED AT the depot on 19 December 1974 and stayed just long enough to sign out our kit and go on Christmas leave. Amongst the new equipment that we signed for were our Dennison smocks: sandy-yellow and brown camouflaged parachutists' jackets, issued only to paratroopers. When we wore them, we had a special identity, separated from the rest of the British Army. I had waited two years to get my hands on one. Wearing it felt great.

At the start of the new year we returned to Browning Barracks to take advanced Brecon training at the Parachute Regiment Battle Training School at Derring Lines, in Brecon, South Wales – the wettest place in Britain. For the next four weeks we were not allowed to walk outside the barracks: we doubled everywhere. The training was similar to that which we had been through as boy soldiers, but the levels of fitness required were higher, and the amount of abuse we absorbed was horrendous. For us, as experienced soldiers, it was tough; for the new recruits, with only three months behind them, it was harder still.

All the training was battle-oriented: live firing section attacks, weapons handling, platoon battle drills, digging trenches and living in them, marching longer and longer distances day after day, and sleeping while soaking wet and cold: nothing many of us hadn't done before, but now we got less rest. Every time we thought it was over, we would be forced to draw upon our reserves and go on even further, even longer. We were pushed and pushed until the cracks started to show, managing to hold ourselves together only with the buddy-buddy system. We were taught that we were totally reliant on one another, and that each one of us was as important as the rest. We ate the same food, shared the same cup, and split the last biscuit into equal-sized bites. If a man went down, we carried him and his kit. There were never any men left behind. The strong supported the weak.

We became the ultimate team. We didn't necessarily like each other, but our differences were internal: if an outsider intervened, he'd find six hundred brothers facing him. And the harder we struggled as a team, the closer we became. We were not allowed to have psychological weaknesses. If you had a smooth face and a soft voice, you were a poof; if you were dark, you were a nigger; if Irish, a thick Paddy. Jocks, Jews, Catholics, Proddies, Slant-Eyes, Dinks, Wops: there was no hiding place; we were insulted day and night. If you took offence, it just got worse. Fortunately, I had already learned to laugh whenever I was called a wog, a prick, a bum bandit or whatever – by then it was water off a duck's back. Other lads took umbrage and cracked, which was a weakness. In my time in the Paras I rarely encountered true prejudice. We took the piss out of everything and everyone, so that no one could tell the difference. As one of the corporals said, 'No one can call me prejudiced, 'cos I just hate everyone, including all you white honkies.'

What surprised me most of all during training was the unofficial attitude to violence. It was actively encouraged; it was almost a required part of your psychological make-up. If a man had a problem, he sorted it out immediately with his fists. There was no room on the battlefield for deep-seated, festering resentment – it undermined the buddy-buddy system. Fighting was not punished.

The four weeks at Brecon were hard, but my fitness stood me in good stead. I often carried the weight for others, and that boosted my self-esteem. From the original forty, we were now down to thirty-one, and we had lost only one former junior soldier, which left only four of the lads who had joined as adults. Now it was time to go to Abingdon, to the Parachute Training School.

AT ABINGDON, all training was run by Royal Air Force Parachute Jump Instructors (PJIs). Dressed in air force-blue overalls and carrying the rank of sergeant, these guys were the experts. Their motto was 'Knowledge Dispels Fear'. They spent their working lives teaching young men to do something totally against the instincts of normal human beings: to risk their lives deliberately by leaping out of a perfectly serviceable aeroplane at eight hundred feet in order to float to the ground on a piece of cloth packed into a canvas bag by persons unknown. This great leap of faith was achieved not by belief alone, but by educating students in the technical operation of all the equipment, in the finest possible detail: how the parachute operated, how the aircraft created a slipstream, how to steer, how accidents happened, the likelihood of their occurring, how to avoid problems. This instilled such an in-depth knowledge of the equipment that one began to trust it. Then they made us practise time and time again on artificial parachute harnesses, during which all the normal and emergency drills were repeated endlessly until we all knew instinctively what to do next. Through such training I came to understand the system so well, and had such confidence in it, that I believed in it completely and overcame my fear of making a mistake or of the equipment failing.

As with any phobia, it is the unknown and misunderstood which creates the greatest fear, not that which we know and understand. Big cats frighten laymen, but not their trainers in a circus – not because the trainer is especially brave, but because he has a deep knowledge of his charges' behaviour and reduces the risks to a minimum. When I arrived at Abingdon, the monkey of fear was already perched on my shoulder, and he stayed there, but the training made him lighter as the day of my first jump approached.

The standard-issue parachute was a PX4. Adjusted to fit each individual, it was hooked up to a wire inside the fuselage of the aeroplane. When you leapt out, the static line that attached the wire to the parachute would pull the chute from the pack in which it was contained. Then a final tie, with a well-defined breaking-strain, snapped and released the parachute and parachutist, allowing him to float safely down to the ground. The maximum wind speed allowed was thirteen knots – any faster and your lateral speed would be as great as your downward speed. Hitting the floor at fifteen miles an hour and moving sideways just as fast is not a very forgiving situation where bones are concerned.

We practised landing and rolling endlessly, from all possible directions: backwards, forwards and sideways. This exercise is the most efficient way of developing stomach muscles I have ever known – after three or four hours my stomach was aching with cramp.

There are several common accidents that occur with parachutes. The first is to have your air stolen. A parachute falls on a column of air that is allowed to escape slowly through a round hole in the top. If someone steers across your column from below, they steal the air that is holding up the parachute, the chute collapses and you fall past the intruder before the chute reopens. This takes about two hundred feet of drop. God help you if you are only two hundred feet from the ground. To avoid air-stealing, you keep a close watch around you and steer away from any danger by pulling down on the rigging lines. This spills air out of one side of the canopy and drives the parachute in the opposite direction.

Another danger is a blown periphery. In this case a rigging line crosses over the top of the canopy and creates a cleft in the centre. This in turn reduces the lifting ability of the parachute and consequently, the parachutist drops at twice the normal speed. In this situation you pull the reserve parachute that is on the front of the harness. If it inflates, you know you needed it.

The only accidents I ever witnessed were when troops were leaving the aircraft from both sides at half-second intervals, one from port and then one from starboard. If the timing was wrong they would sometimes collide in the slipstream beneath the aircraft and become entangled. I saw this happen twice: on the first occasion, the men cut themselves free before landing; the second time, the collision knocked one man unconscious, although he managed to land without serious injury and recovered later in hospital.

FINALLY THE BIG day came. We drew our parachutes from the store beside the drop zone (DZ) at Weston on the Green and checked them thoroughly for any damage, then we adjusted them to our own size and tightened them up. A loose harness would not come off, but it could slip under a testicle in the slipstream and ruin your year. Once both chutes were on back and front, each soldier's was double-checked by his buddy. Then, helmets on, we moved out across the flat grass field to where a huge grey barrage balloon swayed on its cable above a square cradle with a doorway cut into the side – our first jump would be not from a plane, but from this silent monster's low-swung box.

The first four recruits walked forward and we wished them well. The PJI directed one into each corner and clipped their static lines to the centre of the cradle. Then he lowered a metal bar across the door. 'Up eight hundred, four men jumping,' he shouted, and the metal winch started to unwind. Every two hundred feet a flag was attached to the cable to indicate the height until finally three flags were fluttering in the breeze. We sat on the grass and watched the cradle sway from side to side until it settled in the wind. Would anyone refuse to jump? Would we see an accident? God, I hope I can do it. What if I lose it? I looked at the others. Most of them were smiling and talking, and looked completely calm. Weren't they scared like me? Why was I the only one shaking like a leaf? I was petrified.

A loud murmur rose from our group as we saw the first man leave the balloon cage. As he fell, feet and knees together, we watched the parachute leave the pack and develop above him. He was almost next to the first flag, two hundred feet down, before his canopy was fully open, about four seconds of falling. We were ecstatic: one of our group had made it. As the other three followed, we gained confidence from their success. As soon as the first four had landed, the cage descended for the next four. I was number three of the second group. Up eight hundred, four men jumping; I thought, I hope that's true.

The sound of the winch engine died as the balloon rose into the sky. I looked out at the horizon and refused to think about what I was about to do. The PJI smiled and offered a hundred pounds to anyone who could show him a hard-on. I smiled back weakly and felt sick. The balloon jerked to a sudden halt and the wind whistled in my ears. I fixed my eyes on the PJI and kept them there. He was my mother and father and best friend, and at that moment I needed him to reassure me that it would be all right. 'Number one, step forward,' he ordered, and Nigel stepped into the doorway. The bar was raised. The PJI yelled, 'Red on,' and Nigel's hands slapped the top of his reserve parachute. 'Go!' I saw Nigel disappear over the edge. Number two disappeared in the same fashion. 'Number three, come forward.' I staggered from the back corner of the cage to the door and instinctively looked down. As I did so, I lost my balance for a second and almost toppled forward. My knees were shaking, and I hoped they wouldn't give out beneath me. 'Gooo!' I jumped forward into space, and before I had fallen three feet, I thought, I've done it, I've done it!

I looked up and watched as in almost slow motion the canopy began to develop above my head. Once it was full I parted my legs and checked beneath me, and then steered away from the balloon cable. I watched the people on the ground and heard the instructor's loudspeaker, but I was too elated to listen. I put my feet and knees together and got ready for a forward landing. Nothing during training had prepared me for the speed at which the ground was rushing towards me. Thump – I was down and alive.

Every man that day sported a grin like a Cheshire cat's, which stayed fixed for at least an hour. The worst was over: we had faced death and survived. We were Paras – well, baby Paras; we had jumped, and we knew now that we could do it . . . only seven more jumps before we got our wings.

The second jump was from a Hercules C-130 transport aircraft. The C-130 could hold sixty-four Paras with equipment and drop them all in less than forty seconds. Our first jump was as a single stick of eight from one side of the plane only. The noise was tremendous, and as the door opened we watched the PJI stick his head out, looking for the drop zone. 'Stand up,' he shouted, and we stood and fixed our own static lines to the cable above. Each man checked the chute of the man in front, and then we sounded off from the rear, each man indicating that he was OK and ready to go. We shuffled forward to the door, as close to one another as possible, and watched the lights above and beside the door.

The aircraft banked as it turned for the final approach, and as it did so, from my position as number two, I realised how close to the ground eight hundred feet actually was. I could see people and cars. The plane levelled out and I heard the engine tone change as she slowed to 130 mph. The red light came on. 'Red on.' A pause. 'Green on. Gooo!' It was like a fast conga, each man following the one in front, and suddenly I was flying at 130 miles an hour along the side of a large camouflaged aeroplane at eight hundred feet. Less than two seconds later I watched my chute develop above and behind me before its braking effect swung me underneath and past it as I continued to try to follow the C-130. It was so quick, much faster than the balloon, and much easier. 'Steer away,' someone shouted. I pulled down on my rigging lines. Soon I was on the ground and ready to go again.

For the remaining jumps we left from both sides of the aircraft simultaneously. The last jump was a night jump. This was the best of them all. It had been described to me as jumping from nothing into nothing, and this was true. It was my first jump as number one, and as I stood by the door of the aircraft, although I had no doubt that I would go, I was still nervous as I watched the bright white and yellow lights of Oxford beneath me. As the aircraft banked, I was looking straight down at the ground and the lights were directly in front of me. The only thing keeping me inside the aircraft was my left hand, which was holding on to the side of the starboard door.

Although I was apprehensive, I wasn't frightened – I knew what I had to do, and I knew the risks. I smiled, and realised that I was actually enjoying the sense of danger and having fun. I saw the red light go on, the PJI shouted and my hand automatically fell across my reserve. Now I was staring at the black night air with the slipstream trying to suck me forward. Endless seconds ticked by. 'Green on. Goooo!' I felt the familiar sensation of the parachute deploying above me – even at night you can see it open clearly. I was the first one out, so I knew there was no one below me. I released my container of equipment from the clips that held it to my chest and felt the line that it was hanging on go taut.

All I had to do now was prepare to land. I heard the container hit the floor and then, kerthump, I was down. Eight jumps completed: I had earned my blue parachute wings, and the right to join my battalion.

Before we could join our units, there was one final exercise to be undertaken, on the island of Guernsey in the English Channel. The intention was for us to parachute onto the island; in the event, the weather prevented us from doing so, but while we were there we took our milling test. Milling involved the unit commander lining up all the men in two ranks, facing each other; the man you were facing was your opponent. A small square of men was then formed, and each pair in turn donned boxing gloves and entered the square. They had to fight each other until a set of metal mess tins was rattled together. The halt would be called only when both men had shown the required level of aggression. If a man was hammered by his opponent without showing due courage, he was put back in with someone else until he came up to the mark. If he failed to come up to the mark with every opponent, he would be transferred out of the regiment.

There were three guys I would rather not have faced: Big Blackie, who was a heavyweight boxer, Steve, who gave everyone the willies, and James, who was twenty-four years old and had a boxer's nose. I got James. He was a big bloke, and six years my senior. I avoided looking at him right up to the time that the mess tins were banged for us to start. I knew I was going to get pasted, but I threw my insanity switch on and launched myself across the square. My right hand landed straight on his nose and blood streamed down his face. Left, right, left, right: I hit him again and again until he was at my feet in a bloody mess. I was determined not to give him the chance to hurt me. I was pulled off him completely unhurt.

I walked away, shaking with rage. It was a strange feeling, a mixture of elation and shock: I had just pummelled the living daylights out of a man who had never said an angry word to me, and I felt terribly guilty. Many of my peers congratulated me on my effort, but I felt no joy. If I was tough now, I still didn't feel it. My only satisfaction was that it would deter future aggression from others who heard about it. I never apologised to James – that would have been regarded as an insult to him – but I felt bad and spoke to him as soon as I could, to reassure myself there was no ill-feeling.

Milling was intended to confirm that a Para would fight, and it did that. Something had changed inside me, though. In a fighting situation I had always been afraid of being hurt; now I did my utmost to completely destroy any aggressor first, to ensure my own safety. I had no rules when I was scared – just win, and don't get hurt. I had changed, and I wasn't sure that I liked what I had become: aggressive, proud, violent, and very insecure. But I could fight, and I needed that to survive in this military world.

When the day came to pass out to the band of the Parachute Regiment playing the regimental march, 'The Ride of the Valkyries', I had conquered several levels of fear, but I still regarded myself as a bluffer. I had done everything that had been asked of me, and done it well, but I couldn't help feeling that I was a fraud: I was the only one who had survived the course and yet had still been scared. I wasn't a tough guy yet.

CHAPTER 5

The Front Line

IN AUGUST 1975 2 Para – the 2nd Battalion the Parachute Regiment – was sent to West Belfast in Northern Ireland. West Belfast holds most of the predominantly hard Republican, and therefore Catholic, areas. It was regarded as the only place in Belfast worth going to as a soldier. At this time the province was still experiencing violence on a daily basis, and with the IRA now clearly braced against the British government, the poor British soldier was placed firmly in the front line, against an enemy who had all the advantages. The IRA terrorists enjoyed the support of the local population, they had no uniform, and they were therefore invisible. They could choose the time and place at which to mount an attack, and were then able to hide behind the safety curtain of the British legal system that they so detested. They weren't our only enemy – there were also Unionist terrorists led by fanatical bigots who used religion and fear to cement their power.

It is not now common knowledge, but when British soldiers first appeared on the streets of Northern Ireland, the Catholic community welcomed them as a bulwark against the Protestant community. It was only in 1972, when the British government removed the Catholic barricades and started interning their people without trial, that the IRA grew in strength. Then the British soldiers really began to get the worst of it.

I had never been racially or religiously indoctrinated as a child. I didn't really understand what was going on in Ireland. My training had taught me to shoot anyone illegally carrying a weapon who was endangering life, most importantly mine. The terrorists were bad guys, and I was a good guy. If I shot one, it didn't really matter to me which side they were on.

So in October 1975, at the age of eighteen, I climbed aboard the ferry at Liverpool to sail to Belfast. I joined D Company in Flax Street in an old cotton mill on the edge of the Ardoyne, a tough Republican area. I was immediately struck by the bleakness of the city. It was cold, damp and grey; the streets consisted of endless lines of red-bricked terraced houses, many of them bombed out. All the main roads had red-and-white metal barriers across them in an attempt to control terrorist movement. Flags indicating the affiliation of the residents hung from poles mounted outside upstairs windows. Everywhere there were troops patrolling, on foot and in vehicles. Some of the vehicles were heavily armoured with Browning .50 calibre machine-guns protruding from turrets on the top. I felt excited to be there, but also frightened. I had heard the stories and read the papers; I expected to be driving through riot-filled streets, hearing bombs going off. Of course, the reality was completely different; at this time the province was experiencing a relatively quiet period.

Flax Street Mill stood about five storeys high. It was built in red brick and was surrounded by armoured watchtowers, known as sangars, built of concrete or brick. They were surrounded by fine-mesh wire to stop rockets and grenades from penetrating to the walls before they exploded. The viewing slits were lined with sliding steel-plate shutters, to reduce the size of the hole an enemy sniper could shoot through. Inside, the bunk-bedded accommodation was laid out on the ground floor. Each platoon area was sectioned off with thin board. Thirty men lived together in close proximity and without respite for the entire four-month tour of duty. There was no natural light and the ceiling was about thirty feet from the ground, making the billet cold, dark and noisy. It was said that the toilets were haunted by a young lad from 3 Para who had blown his head off in there with a pistol after receiving a 'Dear John' letter from his wife.

No sooner had I arrived than I was sent to Ballykinler on the east coast, for three days' build-up training with the Northern Ireland Training Team (NITAT). It was their job to ensure that latecomers understood the law and the routine on the streets. They also highlighted the dangers of doing something stupid, like handling a strange package. A great deal of emphasis was placed on the current IRA practice of booby-trapping everything, especially attractive items that a soldier would tend to pick up. We were issued with yellow cards which told us in detail when we could and could not open fire, and what one had to shout first. All this was practised, and then ignored. We all knew that if we had a chance to kill a terrorist, we were not going to waste it.

The last day of NITAT training was spent with a different unit to practise patrolling. I was sent for twenty-four hours to the Black Watch. When I arrived I immediately recognised many of them from my time in boys' service, and I was made very welcome. I was surprised they were so happy to see me, but it was instantly apparent that any old resentments were forgotten. I like the Jocks, and especially the Black Watch: as paratroopers do, they say it as they see it. They removed my red beret and Dennison smock and dressed me like one of them, in a tam-o'-shanter beret and combat jacket. At 0400 hours the next day I would be gone; between now and then, anyone I hit would identify me as Black Watch. No ID parade would ever be able to locate me.

Before I left for my first foot patrol, we loaded our weapons under the sangar at the front gate. It had been patched together after being hit by a rocket attack. 'Was anyone killed?' I asked. They told me no – the soldier who was inside got out in one piece, and then found himself in prison for opening his big mouth. When the sergeant-major had commented on how lucky he had been to survive, the soldier had replied, 'Aye, sir, if I hadna been asleep on the floor I would ha' surely bin kilt.' That night was fun. I didn't hurt anyone, but I did find my feet very quickly. I was sorry to go back to 2 Para the next day.

Back in Flax Street I was introduced to Rooster, my first section corporal. He gave me a bunk and told me to dump my kit and settle in. I knew some of the others in the platoon from boys' service and Para depot, Mac and John amongst them. Later, as I left the room to go and eat, a lance-corporal called Paddy walked up to me and asked me my name. 'Rob Horsfall,' I answered, and stuck out my hand. He punched me smack in the face, and as I hit the floor arse-first he said, 'I've heard about you and I don't like you. Any of your lip and you'll get some more.'

Once again I was stunned. I thought I had left this kind of stupidity behind with IJLB. Sadly, I was wrong. The boys at IJLB had been selected as above-average; now I was back with the average, and it was mind-numbing. Why would someone who had never met me attack me because of what he had heard? I sat on the floor and did nothing. I wasn't frightened or even hurt, just bewildered. While I was trying to work it all out, Paddy walked away. He wasn't even in my platoon. I had believed that as I moved further up my career ladder, older people would behave better than the youths I had been used to before. It was a shock to find out that the shallow-minded childishness I had experienced earlier was to be exaggerated tenfold in adult service. Obedience and the ability to be just like the rest were what were required. Enquiring minds were not needed, and a quiet, thoughtful man who was unable to conform without understanding why was, to some extent, an outsider. I felt this distance without seeking it. I did what everyone else did, and in Northern Ireland that involved working hard as a soldier.

Most of the official patrolling drills that I had been taught by NITAT went out of the window and in came the unofficial modus operandi, as designed by veterans of earlier tours: the iron fist of the Parachute Regiment – don't take any lip, stop and search everyone, including babies, hit anyone you don't like, make the locals think you are totally insane and would kill them for the slightest reason. If you are fired upon, return fire in the general direction the shots came from, whether you have seen a target or not.

The enemy's losses had to be greater than ours. In fact, the Regiment's losses had been low in Northern Ireland from the start. Partly this was because of our methods; the IRA tended to move their main operations outside our areas until our tour was over. Four months wasn't long to wait for us to leave, after which they could carry on much as before.

Two weeks before I arrived, Flax Street had been mortared: four bombs, made from oxygen gas cylinders, had been fired from the back of a lorry in the Ardoyne. They had gone through the glass roof of the mill and landed on the concrete floor inside the accommodation area. Nobody was killed because all the bombs failed to go off on impact.

I was told when I arrived that the area where we were patrolling was quiet; it was unlikely that anything would happen. The area we were covering included Ballysillen Park, the Crumlin Road and Ligoniel, a mixed area ranging from hard Protestant to hard Catholic. In the 'Proddy' areas we would whistle Republican tunes and in the 'Cat' areas, Unionist marches. We wanted them all to hate us, and we revelled in being feared.

One cold morning during my second week, at about 0530 hours, my patrol was driving slowly down a lane in Ballysillen Park; I had my head stuck out of the top of our reinforced Land Rover in the freezing cold. A blast-proof mackeralon cover on the rear of the vehicle and wire-mesh grilles on the front were effective for stopping stones and petrol bombs, but that was about all. The pale dawn light was just starting to reveal the blue sky of a winter's morning. I was looking forward to a fried-egg sandwich and a warm shower when a high-velocity bullet cracked past my head, followed by the bang of a rifle. I spun in the direction of the bang and cocked my own rifle, but saw nothing except three large, grey, oblong blocks of flats. I ducked down from the roof hatch and propelled myself out of the back of the vehicle and onto the road. The Land Rover was still moving at about ten miles per hour. As I landed, I rolled into the side of the road, preparing to give covering fire. I heard the final words of Lee's (the patrol commander's) question: '— fuck was that?' It had all happened in the time it took him to say 'What the—'.

Lee sent a contact report and we moved up into the area of the flats. The shot could have come from anywhere, but I had a good idea which block we should be focusing on. We sealed off the area as well as four men and a driver could and waited for the Quick Reaction Force (QRF) to show up. The QRF commander, a full corporal, decided to search one of the blocks of flats. I, the man on the ground who had been shot at, pointed out that I thought he'd chosen the wrong block. 'Shut your fucking mouth and do as you're told or you'll get your face sorted,' he said. He found nothing, and after a couple of hours we went home for breakfast. He might have had information about that block and a baddie who lived in it; he might have had a good reason for searching where he decided to search, but I was left feeling aggrieved because I thought my opinion was valuable, even though I was a new boy. He, of course, did not.

It was lunchtime when we got back. Our patrol was over, so I went to the recreation room for the two cans of beer that we were allowed daily. I sat down and, as I raised the can to my lips, I noticed that my hand was shaking. I swapped hands, but the other was no different. Adrenalin was still running through my system and the effects had not yet worn off. At the time the incident happened, I hadn't been aware of my fear: my training had taken over; I hadn't been given time to think the worst. I didn't feel brave or special, but I did feel good about myself. I had done my job well, and I relaxed.

I'd joined the tour late, and it was over in three months. In that time I saw a great deal of Belfast. Our company tasks had mainly involved mobile vehicle patrols, which gave us the opportunity to tour up through Ligoniel and out to the hills looking down on the city from the north. I saw both communities, and dealt with both in the same way, but the Catholic community, which was generally poorer, seemed less friendly.

We sailed for Liverpool. It was a calm day: the Irish Sea was a gorgeous blue and the sun shone, warming the deck of the transport ship. I stood on deck for hours, watching the water and having my photo taken with my patrol. It was good to be going home, but I had enjoyed Ireland and looked forward to returning soon.

My mother had just got out of hospital after having a breast removed. Still only 35-years-old, she had not been well for some time. Home on leave, I carried on as if all was well, but one day Brian took me aside and told me that Mum had terminal cancer and was unlikely to live more than another year. I took the news calmly, and then went away to think about it, but I didn't think for long. Instead, I subconsciously pushed it aside, denying to myself that it could happen: Mum looked well and was in good spirits. I was happy doing my thing, there was nothing I could do for her, and anyway, maybe it wouldn't happen – a childish response to an uncomfortable situation. It frightened me, so I ran away and hid inside my own mind – a bit like pulling the blankets over your head and hoping the burglar will go away. Brian and I didn't get along. He probably saw me as an obnoxious young nuisance who interfered with his relationship with my mother. So in spite of the fact that I lived locally, I started staying in camp and paying visits home. This made things easier for Mum as well.

IN 1975 THE Parachute Regiment was selected to represent the British Army in an international march-and-shoot competition. Taking part were all the countries in CETO, the Central European Treaty Organisation: the USA, Britain, Turkey, Pakistan and Iran. The competition was to take place in Turkey at the end of the summer. After a brief shooting test I was selected to be in the squad from which the team would be chosen but I didn't make the final team that time. The following year I was selected again, and on this occasion the competition was to take place in Iran, which was still under the rule of the Shah. This year, 1976, was one of the hottest and driest years on record, and most of the British Army presence ended up supporting the fire services, putting out forest and bush fires.

We in the shooting team spent our days marching and shooting. The competition involved each team, a section of ten men, including a machine-gunner, marching five miles in battle order, completing an assault course, and immediately engaging electronic targets at ranges of up to five hundred yards. I ended up being the machine-gunner, not because I was the best shot, but because I was very fit. After the march and assault course, the ability to breathe slowly was an important factor in accurate shooting.

After several months' training, the team prepared to go to Cyprus so we could acclimatise ourselves to the heat we would encounter in Iran. A week before departure, my best friend at the time, Taff, and I set off for our usual weekend jaunt to the coast. We would spend our time hunting girls, dancing and drinking, and then sleep in our sleeping bags on the shingle by the sea. On the Sunday we would hitch-hike back to Aldershot.

On this particular Sunday we arrived back early enough to have a drink in town in our regular haunt, the South Western. Within a short space of time we were sitting with two young ladies, enjoying the evening. Taff went off to take a leak, but when he came back, a stocky man was sitting next to 'his' girl, giving her a line. Never one for pretty speeches, Taff just picked the guy up and punched him in the mouth.

I was happy just to sit back and watch the show, but the man's friends were not – they decided to pile in and offer assistance. What could I do? I had to help. In no time at all the bar was in uproar, with chairs, tables and bodies flying everywhere. It was just like in the movies, except the chairs were hard. I saw one man swing a bar stool and hit Taff straight between the legs. Taff paused for a second and then grabbed the man's shirt and head-butted him to the floor.

The fight could only have lasted a few minutes, but it felt like much longer. Eventually the bar went quiet and I found myself standing quite alone, with a large man with a very hard head tucked in a headlock under my arm. While I had been trying to punch him senseless, everyone else had left. He was bleeding, but no matter how many times I hit him, he would not go down. I looked around: there were bodies everywhere, but no Taff, no stocky man, and none of his friends who had joined in the fray. Two or three men were starting to close me down when a gravelly Scots voice to my left said, 'D'ye need a hand there, Bobby boy?' I looked round and saw Harry from 2 Para. He was about five foot eight with broad shoulders and a face like a bulldog chewing a wasp, which was handsome for a Glaswegian Para. 'Cheers, Harry,' I said, 'hold this.' I passed him the bleeding man and picked up two beer mugs and began edging my way to the exit. The doors were swing-doors like in the old western movies, and just as I got to them they burst open and two sets of arms grabbed me from behind and dragged me out. Oh shit, I'm nicked, I thought, but it was the boys. They had realised that I wasn't with them and had returned to the rescue.

We split up and ran. Taff and I made our way back to his house, where his wife, Tina, patched us up. We both needed stitches from glass wounds, but we couldn't go to the hospital – the police would be looking for us – so Band-Aids and disinfectant had to do the trick instead.

The next day every Para unit in Aldershot was lined up on an identity parade at 0830 hours. There was no way anyone could get out of it. We knew we would be identified and charged, so we went to our sergeant-major and came clean. He looked ready to rip our heads off; he had spent four months building up this team, and now he was about to lose two of us. We were ordered to fuck off up to our rooms and stay there. He covered our arses, and we had every reason to be grateful to him. It turned out that twelve victims of our fun night out had ended up in hospital; we were lucky not to go to prison.

We were in town twice more that week, and on each occasion saw people running off to call the police. Otherwise we laid low until we flew out to Cyprus and anonymity.

WHEN WE ARRIVED, we were billeted at Dekhelia Barracks, a British Sovereign Base Area on the south-east coast. It was beautiful. We did one march and shoot each day, and spent the rest of our time swimming and touring.

The country had been divided into two halves since the Turkish invasion in 1975 and the south was now full of Greek Cypriot refugee camps. We drove past them every day and I wished there was something I could do to help. They were well fed and the weather was warm, but this didn't change the fact that they had lost their homes.

In the evenings we would drink in the George Club, a posh name for the NAAFI (Navy, Army and Air Force Institutes). I still wasn't much of a drinker, although I enjoyed a couple of beers. Getting drunk always made me feel sick. I usually went back early and complained about the loud, drunken bums coming in later, after they had had a really good time. I wished that boozing was as much fun for me as it was for them, but it never was. They called me 'Two-pint Bob'.

A FEW DAYS before we were due to leave for Iran and the competition, I went to bed early as usual. I was awakened by a sudden violent pain in the back of my head. As I turned over, the pain came again as a wooden shaft of some sort struck me on the side of the face. As I raised my arms to protect myself I realised there were two men striking me with long wooden broom handles. I curled up under the sheet and tried to roll off the bed, but as I hit the floor, I became entangled in the linen. I lay still in the hope that the beating would eventually stop, but it didn't: the attack was frenzied and relentless. I felt the wooden poles breaking my fingers as I raised my hands above my head to shield myself. Gradually I sank into unconsciousness, only to come to some time later on the floor of the tiled shower room, soaking wet and bleeding. Two grinning faces were waiting for my eyes to open; feet and fists ensured that they closed again. I tried to shout, but found that my jaw would not move. My two attackers dragged me back to the room along the third-floor balcony, and then cut me with a razor and shaved off some of my pubic hair – to humiliate rather than injure me. I tried to get up, but the fists and boots piled in once again. I struggled onto my hands and knees, grabbing hold of one of them and pushing him aside. I staggered towards the door and out onto the balcony, swinging wildly at anything that I could see through my bruised and rapidly closing eyes. One punch in the right place was enough to finish me off.

How I ended up in bed after that, I will never know. The beating must have lasted more than twenty minutes. I was found some time later by one of the corporals, who couldn't sleep because of my noisy breathing. He pulled back the sheets to find a bloody, bruised, unconscious man. He called an ambulance and I was taken to Dekhelia Hospital. I was intubated and then transferred to Akrotiri Hospital on the west coast of the island.

Two days later I came to. I knew I was awake, because I could hear people talking in the room. At first I thought I was blind, but when I raised my hands to my eyes I could feel the swelling, and realised that I couldn't open them because they were swollen shut. I painfully prised my eyelids apart to let in a little light. My fingers were taped together, and when I tried to speak, only a rasping grunt came out. I heard someone calling for a nurse, and finally a woman came to speak to me.

The nurse told me that my jaw was broken on one side and had been dislocated on the other, some of my ribs and fingers were broken, and my throat was swollen from the bruising where it had been hit. My eyes were OK, but I would have to wait for the swelling to go down before they would open. It took another three days for them to open sufficiently for me to be able to walk to the toilet unguided. When I looked in the mirror, all I could see was a round red-and-blue puffball, covered in stitches, with red teeth (my lips were still bleeding through the stitches). I couldn't have been uglier if I had had two heads.

It was three weeks before I could get out of hospital and fly home. The two men who had attacked me had been arrested, charged and sentenced in my absence. One was a Para, who was sent to Netley, the military psychiatric hospital; the other was a cook who fabricated a cock-and-bull story to his superior officer, accusing me of trying to beat him up and then claiming he had only been defending himself. He got busted to private and fined.

Why did they attack me? I spoke to the Para when he was released from hospital six months later. He apologised, sincerely. He seemed so remorseful that I felt sorry for him. He told me that they had been drunk and wanted a fight, nobody was available, and when they found me asleep in bed they decided I was a suitable target. Pat, the cook, had started the assault, and he had joined in – once started, they didn't know how to stop.

Pat was another story entirely; he bragged about beating me up. I saw him in Aldershot on several occasions over the next year, but there were always other people around. I would wait – a lifetime, if necessary. One evening eighteen months later I was at a party in the medical corps men's quarters with my girlfriend Elaine. I left the room for a while, and when I returned, Pat was talking to her. I stood by the wall and watched. Eventually Elaine caught my eye and walked over to me. Pat shat himself: he walked over with his head down like a cowering dog.

'Sorry, I didn't know she was with you,' he said.

'That's all right, don't worry about it.'

'I hope there are no problems about that incident.'

'No, that's all in the past. Forget about it.'

I watched him closely throughout the evening. Eventually I saw him walk out through a fire door and I followed. He was having a piss against the side of the building. I punched him in the side of the head. He fell to the floor and I proceeded to kick the hell out of him while he curled up into a ball, screaming, 'Give me a chance!' Yeah, I thought, the same fucking chance you gave me. My friends finally pulled me off and I left him to be taken to hospital. He had just left the Army, so the incident was a civilian matter. The medics and nurses kept the police off the scent and nothing ever came of it. I had learned patience, and I had had my revenge.

After that beating in Cyprus, I was never again afraid of getting punched or kicked. I had been hurt more than I thought it was possible to be hurt, and I had survived. My face didn't look too different, so I could safely assume it would always recover. I vowed that I would never let it happen again; that if anyone started on me, I would retaliate immediately, without warning. This may have been the first time that I was a truly frightening human being, and it wasn't because I was tough, it was because I was so frightened of getting hurt that I wasn't ever going to give another man the opportunity. I became a psycho, for want of a better word: if someone was looking for it, I gave it to them first. If they were staring at me, I hit them; if they were talking a fight, I hit them. I switched from being quiet, frightened Robin to being 'Bad Bob' the troublemaker.

After that I appeared to be forever fighting. One night I was in the Globe Trotter pub in Aldershot having a beer when a Muhammad Ali lookalike walked over and elbowed me away from the bar. Discretion being the better part of valour, I moved away and hunkered down where he couldn't see me. When I went to the toilet, who was there but this good old boy? He wanted my space at the urinal and moved me aside to take it. I know that pissing can mark territory but this was not on – I was marking my own desert boots.

I walked back into the bar, cold, controlled and angry. I spoke to Jimmy, my best mate. 'There's gonna be a fight tonight,' I whispered.

'Oh yeah, who's gonna start it?'

'I am,' I said, 'with that big fucker over there.'

Last orders were called – the signal to let loose. I was talking to the landlord when suddenly I turned to my left and planted a right hook straight into the face of Muhammad. I followed him down and punched him until he couldn't move. The whole bar had split into two groups: 2 Para on one side and the black community of Aldershot on the other. Blood began to spread across the floor, and visions of a military prison swam through my head.

The barman, a monster of a man with muscles growing from his earlobes, heaved his big frame over the bar and strode purposefully towards me. As he came within range I let out a scream of pure hatred and launched myself at him. All hell erupted. The last I saw of Jimmy were the soles of his boots as he leaped through the air and into the fray.

I was punching and kicking my way across the room when I felt a thump in my back, followed by a strange grating feeling in the area of my shoulder blade. It burned like hell and I couldn't move my right arm. It took me a couple of seconds to realise that I had a knife stuck in my back. I dropped into a crouch and made my way towards the door and ran up the stairs. I could feel the knife inside me – the pain burned into me every time I moved. As I reached the top of the spiral staircase the knife fell out and bounced away down to the bottom of the stairs and out of sight.

I walked around the back of the pub and tried to assess the damage, but I couldn't see a thing. Blood was running down my back and creating a warm sticky feeling all the way down to my waist. If I went to the military hospital, the MPs (Military Police) would get me. If I didn't get help, I might die. Oh shit, I'm right in it now, I thought. How could I get out of this one?

I walked for a bit, then got a taxi to Farnham Hospital's casualty unit, about five miles away. It was a purely civilian environment and so it was possible that the police wouldn't get involved. I didn't tell the taxi driver that I was bleeding all over his seat. Instead I told him that a friend of mine had had a serious accident and I was going to see him.

I got out of the hospital at about three in the morning. My arm was in a sling and my back was stitched up. I had been lucky. The knife had hit my ribs and slid sideways under my shoulder blade, severing some muscle, but not getting through to the lungs. The doctor had wanted to admit me, but I had declined his offer and signed myself out of his care. Then, with no money left, I walked back to Aldershot.

I'd broken my nose some years before playing rugby; now I broke it for a second time, while having a piss. I was in the toilet of the Globe Trotter pub when someone walked up behind me and simply thrust my face into the wall while my eyes and hands were concentrating on the matter in hand. I lost that fight before it started.

I didn't realise at the time quite what a reputation I was developing as a nasty, aggressive brute, a reputation that then became very hard to shake off. It's like being a prostitute in a small town: no matter how much you reform your life subsequently, you'll always be a prostitute to everyone else. The result of being bullied as a child was that I had always tried not to voice an opinion unless I was sure it matched everybody else's; I tried desperately hard to conform. Ironically, this didn't help, because people despised me as a wanker for trying to be like everybody else. I couldn't see any escape: no matter what I did, however agreeable I was, nobody was going to like me, so I might as well be nasty.

CHAPTER 6

Ballymurphy

IN OCTOBER 1976 I was back with 2 Para, and back in Belfast. This time we really got the plum area: the Ballymurphy, one of the toughest and poorest Catholic areas in Belfast. The Murph was a warren of flats, back streets, alleyways and high walls, interspersed with patches of open waste ground. Moyard Park, our base, was on the Springfield Road. It was a small outpost about two hundred yards square, surrounded on all sides by twenty feet of steel and concrete, with watch-towers on each corner. Each tower was surrounded by anti-rocket wire. The camp looked down over the tightly packed housing estates where many convicted terrorists, and many internees who had not been convicted, lived. The streetlights rarely worked, which was to our benefit.

Inside our compound was a series of Portakabins, each with rooms that would normally be suitable for two men. Fitted out with bunk beds, each room now held eight men, or two patrols. One building was set aside for sinks, toilets and showers, and another for laundry. Some of the houses that we had to search were so filthy that the search teams would have to strip off in the laundry room, put their clothes in the machines on a hot wash, and then scrub themselves with anti-parasite shampoo before being allowed to enter the living accommodation. Lice, crab-lice and scabies were a common problem, and if they got into such confined areas, they would spread like wildfire.

One morning I was guarding the back door of a suspect's house while the search team went inside. It was so cold that I pushed the door open to take advantage of a little of the heat from the kitchen. The smell that hit me was so putrid and foul that I had to close the door and freeze as an alternative to vomiting. Some of the two-bedroom houses held families of up to twelve individuals, and search teams regularly found faeces, used tampons and condoms, full nappies and other similarly disgusting items in the worst houses.

We took over from the Light Infantry, who had been having a rough time of it, having taken a few casualties during the last four months. We adopted four-man patrols and maintained twenty-four-hour cover, going out for two hours and coming in for four, then out for four hours and in for two, then out for two hours again. During the four-hour break we would wash off the camouflage cream, but if we washed on every change-around, our faces would have become even more dry and cracked. Oil of Ulay was my skin's best friend on that tour.

On our arrival in the Murph we expected the Provisional IRA (PIRA) to test us, and on the second night they did just that. I was on the front gate with a lance-corporal named Jed, who had toured the Murph in '73, and knew the place well. It was around three thirty in the morning and he was telling me the old, old stories when suddenly three shots hit the tower up to our right. An extra patrol was on the streets in seconds, launching out of the front gate and into the dark ground across the road. They moved quickly into the area where the shots had come from and linked up with the other men already on the street. They were careful not to charge into an ambush, and slowly sealed off the area until daylight.

As soon as it was light enough to see, the patrols found empty cases from three .22 rounds. The intelligence section located the nearest known hardline PIRA house and sent in a search team. By 0700 hours a rifle and ammunition had been found, and several arrests were made. PIRA had grown soft, and this response came as a big surprise to them. They would have to plan more carefully in future: the Paras were back.

By 1976 the troubles had been going on for six years and PIRA had organised themselves into quite an efficient body, raising funds through their propaganda campaigns in the USA, by extortion and through robberies. They had developed an intelligence network second to none amongst the world's terrorist organisations. In the Catholic ghettoes they had the support of the majority of the people. The British politicians as usual were slow to respond, and when they did, found their hands tied by the criminals using their own laws against them. If a terrorist was shot, the policeman or soldier involved was immediately investigated to determine whether he had committed murder. If a prisoner became violent and was injured while he was being restrained, it was always a case of police brutality. The law never seemed to be weighted against the criminal; it always leaned on the good old soldier or policeman who was out there, in the firing line.

I have travelled to the USA many times since, and it never ceases to amaze me that the British never mounted their own propaganda campaign there. Telling contributors to IRA funds the truth about what was, and still is, going on could have made a vast difference. Many Irish-Americans still believe that Ireland is one nation under British occupation; they still believe that Nazis are walking the streets of Belfast, murdering women and children and arresting people on trumped-up charges. Citizens of this democratic nation are not aware that the partition of Ireland was agreed by both sides to allow the Protestant majority in the North their own state, which remained within the United Kingdom – rather like the Tamils in the north of Sri Lanka wanting their own nation today. Of course, the killings in Northern Ireland have been carried out by terrorists on both sides. My sympathies are mostly with the Northern Irish Catholics, but not with the killers who, supported by foreign money, blow up pubs full of blameless people and kill indiscriminately.

Whenever something obvious happened in our area, we always looked for the hidden agenda. If there was a warning of a bomb, we would be careful not to rush straight in and move innocent people into an area where there was a second, larger bomb waiting. If a car crashed, we would be looking for snipers. If an attractive item was left on the street, it would instantly be regarded as a booby trap. We were always trying to out-think the enemy. Attacks were common, and the battalion was fired upon almost daily. On one occasion a patrol was dismounting from an armoured vehicle when a Russian-made RPG-7 rocket hit the rear door as it was being opened. The rocket ricocheted off the door and exploded against a wall alongside. The occupants of the vehicle were very lucky.

Street riots were less common in the Murph, so when a small crowd of women gathered to protest one day, we were sent to investigate. Other patrols spread out to determine why the disturbance was taking place – perhaps some weapons were being moved, or a known baddie was getting out of the area by car. As we approached, we stopped and questioned every suspicious person we saw.

I was interviewing one man when a woman came out of her front door and began to scream abuse at me. The man I was questioning told her to shut up; she was apparently his wife. Unable to control her anger with me and her husband, she waddled her two hundred pounds of freckled flesh and black teeth over to me and proceeded to tell me what a fucking cunt I was and how I was abusing her husband's civil rights. I calmly continued to question the man while under this continuous fire of obscenity. The husband was now seriously embarrassed; the tirade of abuse was endless. I asked the man whether he could shut his wife up. He shrugged his shoulders and said, 'Sorry, no,' so finally, like any well-disciplined British paratrooper, I put my notebook away and swung my gloved left hand across her mouth. She fell backwards and almost somersaulted to her front door. 'Thank you, soldier,' the Irishman said gratefully, and we moved on down to the disturbance. A complaint was made, of course, but it was one of hundreds received daily. If fewer had been made, they would have been taken more seriously. All knowledge of the incident was denied, and I don't suppose the husband was very supportive of his wife's cause anyway.

When we reached the disturbance we found some hundred women blocking the road and chanting slogans. Our job was simply to observe the group until they grew tired of shouting. We were spat at, and the occasional missile flew at us from the back of the crowd or from behind a wall, to little or no effect. In front of the women were five or six small mongrel terriers, barking and growling in support. Every now and then one would rush forward and take a snap at our ankles before running back in between the women's legs. In response we would swing a kick at the dogs and miss, much to the amusement of the baying crowd. Suddenly I felt a sharp pain. My boot had been penetrated by a set of canine teeth – the little bastard had come at me from behind and bitten straight through my boot. The women howled with laughter as I limped away, trying to look dignified. I walked slowly into a back alley and worked my way around the rear of the howling crowd. I then started to shoulder my way through them to the front. As I broke through, I spotted one of the terriers retreating into the sanctuary it thought it had at the back. Thwack! My right boot swung up between its back legs and launched it about six feet into the air. It turned head over heels, crashed down onto its back and lay motionless, probably dead.

This was the regimental system. Everybody was expected to behave this way, to go in with the iron fist, to be as mean and hard as possible. I needed to show that I was one of the guys, as tough as the rest of them.

Dogs were a continual problem: they were trained to hate British soldiers, and were often let out just to attack us. They barked whenever we came past a garden or front door. At night they were often a source of ammunition for those who wished to drop their shit down from the tops of flats. It was pretty hard to arrest dogs, and the rules of engagement in Ireland were very strict, so we couldn't shoot them. Every round of ammunition we carried was counted and the batch number was noted, so rounds couldn't be switched. If a shot was fired without due reason – due reason being 'if your life is in danger or the life of someone it is your duty to protect' – then the firer was in deep trouble.

In a hard area, we always hard-targeted. If we were moving, we moved fast, especially across open ground; if we were waiting somewhere, we bobbed and swayed; and if we were stationary we took cover, either lying down or kneeling behind something solid, something a bullet could not go through. This made a hard target; it also made us positive and alert. At night we wore camouflage cream and helmets, but this made us look so aggressive that the locals complained. Eventually we were told not to wear the cam cream, so we went out without it and came back in wearing it.

One night in late November my patrol was hard-targeting back towards the front gate of the camp when the silence was shattered by the sound of gunfire. If we were running before the shots had been fired, we were sprinting now. About ten yards from the gate my ankle twisted under me and I fell to the ground in considerable pain. Two members of the patrol grabbed the shoulder straps on my equipment and within seconds had dragged me the remaining few yards into the safety of the front gate.

The firing stopped and I lay in agony on the floor, looking up at the cold winter sky. 'Where have you been hit?' asked one of the guys who had just dragged me in.

'I think I've twisted my ankle,' I groaned.

'Oh, is that all?' They were profoundly disappointed and strolled away, leaving me on the wet floor like an unwanted garbage bag. Within a few minutes an armoured Saracen ambulance arrived and I was lifted into the back on a stretcher, ready to be dispatched to Musgrave Park Hospital. Once the doors were closed a medic who could see how much I was suffering gave me gas and air to relieve the pain, and then cut away my boot and trousers.

'I thought you had twisted your ankle,' he said.

'Yeah, so?'

'Well, there's a hole here that says you've been shot.'

I looked down. My lower right leg was coated in blood. Oh well, at least they can't take the piss out of me for that, I thought.

When I got to the hospital I was taken straight down to theatre. I woke up in Recovery with my leg swathed in bandages and hurting like the blazes. The pain was continuous, and I let out a shout which brought a nurse (male, unfortunately) to my side. He gave me an injection of Fortral, a painkiller. It worked quite fast and I dozed off to sleep. Two hours later I woke up and was given another shot, which induced mild waves of euphoria – I watched the nurse walk away with a yellow-and-red aura emanating from his body.

By breakfast-time I was in pain again, but this time my pleas were to no avail. 'You've had the maximum dose,' I was told. 'Have an aspirin and suffer like a real paratrooper.'

It turned out that I had been shot in the lower right leg with a .22 low-velocity round, which had stopped when it hit the bone. This had knocked me over and caused me to twist and severely sprain my ankle, and it was the sprain that was causing most of the pain. I was told that when the wound had closed up I would need to have my leg in plaster. 'No need for that,' I said. 'It'll get better quickly enough.'

'Now, now, Private Horsfall, if you want to go home for Christmas you will have to have your leg in plaster.'

'Ah, well, in that case I think I need my leg in plaster after all.'

Home for Christmas, eh? It was almost worth getting shot for.

As I lay in hospital that night I heard three bombs go off, and began to appreciate just how much was actually going on out there. Thank God I didn't live here, like all those other poor beggars.

I FLEW HOME on a military flight to RAF Lyneham in Wiltshire. I was met by car and taken to Wroughton RAF hospital for one night. The following day I was dumped – suitcase, crutches and, fortunately, uniform and all – to make my own way home from Swindon railway station. It is not easy getting on an Intercity express on crutches with a suitcase: British Rail porters were no better then than they are now. Fortunately, a kind gentleman actually got down from the train to help me board.

I didn't go home. I went to London to stay at the Union Jack Club, a soldiers' hotel in London, with Elaine, my first long-term girlfriend. She was a nurse in the QARANC (Queen Alexandra's Royal Army Nursing Corps) and at twenty-two, a year older than me. I played the wounded soldier and got lots of sympathy and love of the best kind. Elaine went home to her family for Christmas Day and I cut off the plaster with a bread knife and went back to the barracks in Aldershot. I intended to visit Mum, but I had to find her first: Brian had married her in my absence, she had sold the house in Farnham and they were now renting a place in Bracknell. I popped round to see how she was. She seemed in good spirits, and healthy enough, but I was too frightened to ask, or to look any further into the matter.

ON 4 JANUARY 1977 I rejoined 2 Para in the Murph. I was placed on light duties, whatever that meant, but found myself on patrol after two days. Four days later, my patrol was moving across some waste-land at the junction of Springmartin Road and Whitecross Road. We had to cover another patrol that was going into Kelly's Bar, a fierce PIRA hangout. It was dark and I lay down behind a mound of earth, next to the side wall of the post office. As I pointed my rifle at the pub, I rested the magazine on the grass. Instead of coming to rest on soft turf, it scraped a metal surface. I pulled away the grass to discover a galvanised builder's bucket, half buried in the ground, with cardboard taped onto the open end. It was buried sideways in the mound of earth on which I lay, and was pointing towards the wall of the post office. It was a claymore mine, a directional bomb which, when it exploded, would send its shrapnel towards the wall, killing anyone standing there.

I crawled back, keeping low in case anyone was waiting to fire it, then I scampered around the corner of the building and reported what I had seen to my patrol corporal, Pete, who radioed in the news. The operations officer at the time had received the same training as we had before deploying to Northern Ireland. He had seen the photos of bodies blown to bits by bombs, of headless corpses and butcher's slabs of meat. He had been taught that if a suspect device was found, it should not be touched. Yet his first command to Pete was to go and take another look, to make sure.

Pete looked at me, and I told him that I was sure of what I had seen – I was definitely not going back. Being a sensible lance-corporal, he agreed, told the ops officer that he trusted my judgement, and requested FELIX, the code name for the bomb disposal Ammunition Technical Officer (ATO). The patrol in Kelly's Bar had heard the report and came over to assist. They were led by an officer who 'bravidly' (a cross between brave and stupid, with the emphasis on stupid) crawled over to the device and tied a piece of string to it. He then hid around a corner only ten yards away and pulled. The bucket hardly moved, so he gave up and called in FELIX himself. If the device had gone off, he would have been killed needlessly, just because someone didn't want to be seen to have made a mistake and wasted the ATO's time.

We cordoned off the area and the stand-by platoon was called out to assist. It was by now about three in the morning. Ice was on the ground and it was drizzling with rain. It was bitterly cold and unpleasant and we couldn't even walk around to keep warm. One of the corporals on the cordon, a Welshman named Mi, came up to me and told me that there was probably nothing there except an empty bucket and we were all wasting our time freezing our bollocks off. When we got back, he said, he was going to cave my face in for keeping him out all night. I told him it was a bomb and to leave me alone. As I stood there in the cold, it dawned on me that I had answered him back without fear of retribution. In the last six months I had been shot and almost beaten to death. I wasn't particularly worried about his kind of threat any more. I had changed.

That morning, as soon as it was light, a reconnaissance aircraft flew over and took photographs from above the device. By lunchtime they had been developed and showed a clearly defined line from the bucket travelling about three hundred yards to the boundary of our area with the Turf Lodge; this showed where wires leading from the device to the firing point had been buried.

When the bomb was disarmed it was found to contain an electrical detonator, two ounces of Frangex (a high explosive) and ten pounds of Co-op, a home-made explosive. Packed on top of this was a pile of steel fragments from a scrapyard. If it had gone off, it would have wiped out a patrol. Proceeding along that dark-walled side of the post office had become normal routine – in such a small area it was difficult not to cover the same ground regularly. It was lucky that I had found it.

Mi never said a word to me, but the sergeant in charge of the machine-gun platoon actually said well done. I thought about how stupid Mi had been. What if it had turned out to be nothing? What if he had berated me or attacked me afterwards for wasting his precious time? What would I have done the next time I found something suspicious – kept my mouth shut, out of fear of being wrong again? Who knows?

Just before the end of the tour, support company was delegated to provide the Quick Reaction Force (QRF) for West Belfast: a selected group of about thirty men had to stand by for twenty-four hours to support any emergency in the city. On this occasion, an emergency did occur. Another regiment was trying to quell a riot in the New Lodge area of the city, but the riot had escalated to the point where we were called in to offer support and act as a snatch squad – such squads were used to charge a crowd and nab the ringleaders and bomb-throwers, then arrest them. The only equipment a snatch squad member usually had was a soft wooden baton and his steel helmet. The batons were so useless that a big drunk could have snapped one in half, or simply ignored it while he punched you in the face. We, to even the odds, would drill out the larger end and fill it with molten lead, then glue the shavings onto the top and, hey presto, a truncheon.

When we arrived in the New Lodge our sergeant went off to liaise with the commanding officer while we hid behind our short perspex shields and tried not to get hit by petrol bombs. In front of us the troops were taking a pounding from the rioters. Bricks and petrol bombs filled the air and bounced off their shields. Petrol flames were doused by soldiers dashing back and forth carrying fire extinguishers. Over the troops' heads I could see the fires from overturned cars lighting up the night sky. The sound of the crowd was deafening: dustbin lids were being crashed against walls and the ground, bottles were breaking and the fires were roaring. Angry voices released blood-curdling screams as the rioters grew in confidence and advanced closer and closer to the waiting shields. The occasional bang would make us all duck our heads in case it was a gunshot. The flanking soldiers were firing rubber bullets at the ringleaders to hold them back, but the situation was starting to deteriorate.

Our sergeant came back and called us into a huddle to give us our brief orders. Then, as soon as we all understood what was going to happen, we formed up in three ranks, ten abreast, holding only our short shields and batons. The sergeant hit his shield twice with his baton, ba-bam, and we answered, ba-bam. We kept it going until a rhythm was established: ba-bam ba-bam, ba-bam ba-bam.

We were lined up about twenty yards behind the soldiers to our front, and as our rhythm increased in tempo, the noise of the crowd quietened as they tried to work out where the sound of the drums was coming from. At this point our sergeant shouted, 'By the left, quick march'. We advanced to the beat of our batons on our shields, louder and louder and faster and faster. As we closed up on the line of soldiers in front of us, they peeled off to the sides. We dropped our shields and exploded through the gap in a screaming, raging torrent of blind, wild, unstoppable aggression.

The rioters at the front of the crowd saw our Para smocks and helmets and realised instantly who we were. 'Paras, they're fucking paras!' They tried to run back through the mob behind them. We waded into the mass, shock troops doing what they do best: attacking superior forces with surprise and aggression. I hit everything that moved, using my boots, my helmet and my baton and fists. I was on a high in the midst of battle. I felt unbeatable – no one could put me down. Across to my left I saw one of my comrades with the back of his flak jacket on fire, punching his way through a group of rioters while another soldier with a fire extinguisher tried to catch up with him to put the flames out.

I brought my baton down on the shoulder of a man in front of me and felt a satisfying crack as his collar bone fractured. Someone grabbed my left arm in an attempt to pull me away from him, and I spun around and rammed the rim of my steel helmet into his face. As he fell, my boot caught the side of his head and flipped him over. To my right a fleeing rioter ran straight into my baton as my right arm swung back. His head stopped, but his feet kept going until his head connected with the ground. I could smell the enemy's fear; the taste of blood was in my mouth. It was sheer bloodlust: I could feel my lips curled back over my teeth and feel, rather than hear, the growls and blood-curdling yells that were escaping from my lips. It was glory with a capital G. I had no fear – with these raging Furies beside me I knew we could not lose. I knew that they would not leave me if I fell, and that I would die rather than leave them. We were a small, united, highly trained team; we trusted each other with our lives. For the first time I knew why no reward could ever replace the bond that exists between men who have faced danger together against superior odds.

The military don't tell you to go out there and be as violent as you like, because you're still answerable under the law. A soldier isn't a killing machine, but someone who kills when he's in the right situation – he's violent when the situation warrants violence. But when you find yourself in a scenario where your mates are getting shot, where you're getting abuse on the streets and you have an excuse to use violence, you use it. It's a great release. You're on a high and you feel totally powerful, totally alive, utterly fearless – you want to destroy everything in your path. You're a small group against a mob and you know you can trust your comrades implicitly. And it's what you've been trained to do. You don't have to think, your training guides you. The instant imagination kicks in, you've lost it. Samurai warriors always accepted that they were going to die, and that way they could fight to their absolute maximum without worrying – as far as they were concerned, they were already dead. Only afterwards do you start to think.

Within seconds the throbbing crowd had fled through doors and down alleyways and into the darkness of the night. I heard someone behind us shout, 'Stoooop! Move back!' As we turned around, we could see that we had advanced about a hundred yards over the burning barricades and beyond. Many of us could not remember leaping through the flames and over the burning rubble, myself included. The ground was littered with the bodies of rioters we had knocked down during our charge. They were all being arrested and loaded into vehicles to be taken to the local police station and formally charged.

When we got back, we sat around eating fried-egg banjos (sandwiches) and talked endlessly until someone told us not to get big-headed about it because it was nothing compared to the old days. Twenty-four hours later we were back on patrol.

There were a few more contacts throughout the tour, during some of which soldiers escaped death by a hair's breadth, but we didn't lose anyone, either seriously wounded or killed. We all returned home in one piece.

This time I got the nickname 'Half-tour Horsfall' because I had been late out on the first tour and had gone home for Christmas; by now I had enough of a sense of humour to laugh it off. We returned home in March and looked forward to Easter leave before the battalion prepared to go to Berlin for two years.

CHAPTER 7

Compassionate Leave

BACK HOME IN England, I had one thing on my mind, but unfortunately, Elaine had been posted to Rinteln in Germany. I planned to hitch-hike across and visit her.

Mum, meanwhile, had undergone another operation. I went to visit her in Frimley Park Hospital. When she saw me, she rushed up and hugged me. Why hadn't I told her I'd been shot? Why hadn't I written more letters? I couldn't understand what all the fuss was about. She held me really tight. I was embarrassed – this very open display of love and emotion was unusual. Once again, I told myself she was fine and carried on with my life.

Because I'd been away in the Army for so long, I did not have a particularly close relationship with my brothers or my sister. We touched base when I visited, but my appearances had been few and far between. I visited them at their new home (Brian had by now rented a different house in Bracknell). I found my seventeen-year-old sister Virginia keeping house and looking after four-year-old Tony while Brian went to work. We talked about Mum and the other brothers, Christopher, aged fifteen, and Wayne, aged eleven. Brian showed up at the end of the day, driving a new Mercedes and wearing a nice suit. He'd made a fortune from the sale of Mum's house but it never occurred to me to ask where the money had come from. Wayne had started spending most of his time at my grandmother's house with Geoff Horsfall. Chris was continuing at school and making the best of it.

Three weeks later Mum was transferred to a hospice in Guildford. I didn't know what a hospice was, or that people were sent there to die. I thought it was just another type of hospital. Before I went on Easter leave I visited her. For the first time I realised how ill she really was. She was clearly glad to see me, but when she smiled the skin was drawn back over her bones, making her look skeletal. Her face had an orange hue to it, and every few minutes she would vomit into a bowl. She didn't know how ill she was – Brian had decided that it was best not to tell her. I don't remember how long I stayed, but looking back, it wasn't long enough. I went back to camp and requested a transfer to another unit so that I wouldn't have to go to Berlin. I told them my mother was dying and that I had to stay in England.

THE ARMY TRANSFERRED me to the Vigilant Platoon (Vig). Vig was a special guided-missile anti-tank unit, drawn from all sections of the Parachute Regiment and operating as a separate, independent force. It would attach itself to every exercise it could find, with any regiment that could use it. Vigilant itself was a large, heavy missile; it needed a Land Rover to transport more than one at a time. It also needed a well-practised controller to have any chance of hitting a tank. Each man in the platoon was a driver and a medic, and was trained to be a controller. All had more than three years' service. I moved my kit across to Vig just before the complete unit went on Easter leave. I just had time to dump my stuff and depart on leave myself.

My trip to Germany was fun: exploring by day, drinking in the evening and sleeping in the nurses' quarters at Rinteln overnight, but after two weeks I was running out of cash, so I borrowed my fare home from Elaine. I still had a few days' leave remaining, but I chose to return to my only true home: the barracks in Aldershot.

As I strolled across Queen's Avenue outside the barracks, one of my friends waved and told me there was a message for me at the guard-room. I walked over to see what it was about. 'Got a message for me?' I asked. The lad behind the desk knew me and replied, 'Only the old one from a week ago, about your mum dying.' The guard commander, Harry, was a friend of mine. He looked at me through the glass partition and realised immediately that I hadn't known.

I stood staring at my reflection in the glass. My body and mind were frozen in time. She was gone; it had happened. A cold emptiness started to grow in my stomach and gradually forced its way up to my throat. Harry came out and put his arm around my shoulder and I buried my head in his neck and burst into tears. I didn't well up, I didn't sob, I just let this terrible feeling of sudden loss empty out of me. I wept with grief.

Harry sat me down after a while and told me that 2 Para had been searching for me for the past two weeks, but I hadn't filled in my leave documents properly so no one could find me. I told him that I wasn't in 2 Para any more, that I had been transferred to Vig. They had my documents there. He phoned the Regimental Sergeant-Major, who had asked to be informed when I returned. After speaking briefly to him, Harry handed the phone over to me. The RSM then began to bawl me out down the phone about my leave documents; he seemed unable to understand the simple English I was using to tell him that I had been transferred out of his battalion. Finally, I told him that I had just been informed that my mother was dead and I didn't want to talk about it any more. I put the phone down, thinking at least that had sunk into his thick skull.

My Uncle Peter (my mother's brother-in-law) came up from Aldershot to collect me. He told me that they had broadcast all over Europe on the radio for me, but to no avail. Mum had died the week after I left; they had cremated her three days later. They had done all they could.

When I got to my uncle's house I went to bed and cried myself to sleep. In the morning Brian turned up to take me to the crematorium. He laid the guilt on thick and fast: he told me that I should have been there and that she had asked for me at the end. He emphasised the terrible pain she had been in and kept repeating that I should have been there. Finally, with nowhere to hide, I knelt down and cried over the plaque dedicated to her memory.

I was granted compassionate leave. It took about two weeks for the emptiness of my grief to wear off. I lived in the barracks and visited my sister and brothers. Brian was planning a holiday with his new girl-friend. While Mum lay dying, he'd been carrying on with his new woman and I wondered what would happen to my family. Virginia was seventeen. She moved in with her boyfriend of long standing, John, who has been her husband now for twenty years. Christopher lived with our gran until he was old enough to join the Army at sixteen. He followed my advice and kept away from the Paras, where he would have learned no trade, joining the Royal Electrical Mechanical Engi-neers and becoming one of the youngest warrant officers in the Army. Wayne was eleven and was taken under the wing of Social Services, who helped Geoff, his father, get him into Midhurst Grammar School as a boarder. I wrote to him constantly and later, when I moved to Here-ford, he spent all his holidays with me until he went to college. He is now a leading scientist with a German electronics company. I'm very proud of them all.

Brian took his son, my youngest brother, Tony, along with all the money from the sale of the house, and vanished from our lives. We never saw a penny from the estate.

Fortunately, given what we all achieved later, we never needed it.

NOW I TRULY had only one home, the Army. I spent all my holidays in camp and rarely left Aldershot. At Christmas I would volunteer for duty to let those with families go home. At New Year I would get drunk and go home to my bed in camp. Elaine was posted back to Aldershot and I found great solace in her company and in her bed. It took a long time to get over the death of my mother. I didn't talk about it to anyone. I put it away in my angry young mind for another day.

I STILL HAD a chip on my shoulder from the years of bullying. The insecurity stemming from being bullied by my father, bullied as a boy soldier and bullied in barracks left me very cynical. I trusted no-one, regarded other peoples' actions in the worst possible light and basically assumed they would dislike me and treat me in the way I'd become used to. If you're that insecure, you can cause the very problems you're trying to get away from: it's an awful vicious circle. But Vig was a great place to be. We spent so much of our time out on exercises that we never had time for duties or parades or other such bullshit. It was the greatest period of continuous soldiering I ever had, with the best soldiers in the world. I felt an established part of the platoon.

WE LIVED ON the Sennybridge training area in Wales, or on Salisbury Plain, and when we weren't in the field, we were preparing to go into the field. We were young, fit and very happy to be soldiers. We had our own vehicles, and when we had nothing to do we would borrow them without permission and set off to wherever we fancied, care of HM Government. It was common practice to ask a girl at a disco if she would like a ride in a three-litre Rover convertible. When she got outside, the door to a green Army Land Rover was opened for her.

Towards the end of 1977 we were told that the Vigilant guided missile was to be replaced by a far superior system called Milan and the battalion support company's anti-tank platoons would be trained in its use. We were to be disbanded, but not before another trip to Northern Ireland. Prior to that we were asked to decide where we wanted to go to when the unit closed down. Most of us had been in the infantry for several years and were older and more aware of our prospects than we had been before. If a man served twenty years with the infantry, he would still have no useful civilian qualifications. Many of us asked to go to units where we could learn a useful trade. I asked to join the Royal Engineers. I had seen the skills they acquired and knew that all of them were useful in civvy street. The Army were not impressed, and turned down all our requests. 'You may go where you like in the Paras,' they said. OK, I thought, there was no harm in trying. I decided to go back to 2 Para mortars. All the others wanted to return to their original parts of the regiment.

THE NEXT TOUR of Northern Ireland was to be different from my last two. We were going to South Armagh, 'Bandit Country', the toughest and most dangerous area of rural operations in the country. We were to be attached to the 1st Battalion, the Parachute Regiment

(1 Para) as an extra platoon. It was 1 Para's first tour of Northern Ireland since the Bloody Sunday killings in Londonderry in 1972. Adapting to the battalion's strict discipline after the relaxed affair of Vig came as something of a shock to us all, and we didn't like it.

Before we departed for Armagh we were told that when the tour came to an end we would all be absorbed into the different rifle companies of 1 Para instead of returning to our old units. I was not amused. I had been in special parts of the regiment since I had joined. I had probably forgone promotion because I was serving with older, more experienced men, and now I had to go back to the strict regime of a rifle company, with less experienced men in charge of me: back to room inspections and cleaning parade grounds. I couldn't bear it.

I had heard about a unit called the Special Air Service and had been to one of their presentations. It had been interesting to learn about special forces patrols and how they operated, but the points I remembered most were: 'If you're not over twenty-five years of age, forget it, you don't have a chance of passing selection', and 'If you apply, you cannot be refused the chance to take the selection course'.

In spite of the fact that I was still far too young I applied. I went for it, not because it was something I particularly wanted to do, but because it was a way of not doing what the Powers That Be were trying to force upon me. I was cocking my snook at authority, and they couldn't do a thing about it. It was March 1978, and I had just reached the age of twenty-one.

IN MAY, VIGILANT Platoon set off to Northern Ireland for its final mission before disbandment. We were stationed in the small town of Bessbrook, in another old cotton mill. Our platoon was given a windowless room at the top of the building: twenty-four men coming in, going out, switching on lights, farting, wanking and occasionally sleeping in the same airless room. Lovely.

Our platoon commander had convinced the B Company commander that we would be best suited to duties out of camp, in the field. We were very rebellious about having to join the battalion, and this resentment was best expressed away from the barracks. We were put on field duties almost continuously, patrolling the fields and hedgerows of the border between Northern Ireland and the Republic of Ireland. When we weren't patrolling, we were mounting observation posts or watching a house or some other point of interest. It was summer and the country was at its best: rolling green pastures lined with hand-built stone walls, small woodlands and streams full of fish.

We would be taken out of camp and deployed in Royal Navy or RAF helicopters – it was too dangerous to leave by vehicle. With only a few roads leading to and from the camp, it was just too easy for a terrorist to lie in wait with a radio-controlled mine. Loaded up with four days' rations, we would patrol up and down the border, looking for any signs of PIRA. We would sleep in the woods or bushes, and sometimes, on fine nights, on the tops of hills in a defensive circle. After four days we would call in a helicopter, resupply, and have our rations restored for another four days. It wasn't unusual to be out for two weeks at a time, moving from one task to another.

This sort of patrolling made movement very hard for PIRA, because they could never tell where and when we were going to appear. We had almost no contact with the local community, except when we set up a spontaneous vehicle checkpoint to stop cars and search them.

I carried a light machine-gun, a 7.62mm magazine-fed version of the old .303 Bren gun. It was a great weapon for Northern Ireland, accurate to over a thousand yards and relatively light compared to the General Purpose Machine-Gun. My number two on the machine-gun was an eighteen-year-old lad called Shane Scott, Scotty to us. He was from London, and was probably the most likeable soldier I ever had the good fortune to meet. He loved his job and everyone liked him. He was humorous, handsome and, most importantly, a good soldier. In the Paras the biggest insult that could be levelled against anyone was to accuse them of being a bad soldier. Every man prided himself on being one of the élite, and tried never to leave himself open to such a comment. He could be wet, queer, thick, an idiot or any number of other things, but he could not allow himself to be called a bad soldier.

I got very close to Scotty. I was the old sweat, aged twenty-one, with two tours under my belt, and I had to guide him and show him the ropes. On one patrol we had a single shot fired at us from a long range. I, as the gunner, ran about fifty yards to some high ground and prepared to cover the others if they decided to go forward. As I lay down and cocked the gun, Scotty appeared next to me, smiling, trusting my decisions and following my lead. He was always ready to learn, and he placed his complete trust in me when things were difficult.

Halfway through the tour, 'Half-tour Horsfall' earned his nickname once again. The B Company commander came to me when I was on guard duty on top of Bessbrook Mill and told me that my application to go to the SAS had come through; the selection course started in August. I was surprised. I hadn't expected to hear from them so soon. The major tried to convince me to stay with 1 Para. He offered early promotion and pointed out to me the problem of my youth. Finally, in good humour, he relented, and told me that he would send me home early from Northern Ireland so that I would have time to get ready for the selection course.

So in the middle of July I said my farewells to the platoon and went home. I owned an old bottle-green Vauxhall Viva, which I never drove faster than fifty-five miles per hour in case a wheel came off. With all my belongings in the back, I set off for the Black Mountains in South Wales.

CHAPTER 8

The Regiment

FOR THE FIRST time in years I was totally alone. I had no one to answer to, nowhere I had to be, and no comrades to talk to.

All I knew about the SAS selection was that it involved long marches with heavy weights over the Welsh mountains. I found a little campsite in the Black Mountains in a small village called Cym Du. With my little two-man tent pitched, I set about climbing the hills above me every day. I carried about thirty-five pounds of equipment, including my sleeping bag, emergency rations and waterproofs.

It was a wonderful feeling to be free. I could go where I wanted, when I wanted. I spent every day walking from one point on the map to another; I tested myself on my ability to come out exactly where I wanted to, despite the fog and rain. Within a very short space of time getting to the top of the first peak was about as stressful as walking to the corner shop.

I met a lot of people on the hills. The great thing about hill-walkers is that they always stop and talk, and if they are eating, they share what they have; it's like an unwritten code.

I had never lost my love of the mountains: the wild, open expanses of grass, the summer colours of green, red, yellow and brown, the wild ponies with their long, shaggy manes, and the streams of sparkling clear water. Even when the rain and wind set in, I loved it: the challenge of conquering the next ridge line, of reaching my next target, of pushing myself harder and harder, was both a pure physical and a mental joy.

After a week, however, I started to feel lonely. It was great being dedicated, but I longed for a little company. Elaine was in Woolwich, in East London, too far to go in my little car, so I set off down to Newport in Gwent to find my old fighting buddy, Taff.

Taff had bought himself out of the Army, but he had given me his address when he left. One afternoon I turned up there and was welcomed with open arms by his wife Tina and her mother, but there was no Taff: after leaving the Army, he and Tina had got divorced. They didn't know where he was and they weren't particularly interested. I, on the other hand, was treated like royalty. I was fed and pampered and invited to return the following weekend. This was great – I had some company and some home cooking and it was close to the training area.

THIS TIME I went up to the Brecon Beacons, a bit higher and wilder than the Black Mountains. I spent the week covering longer and longer distances, building up to twenty miles a day. I began to meet other soldiers training for the same selection. They told me that I could get accommodation at the SAS camp in Hereford as well as free rations, and that I would be offered any help I needed with the test routes. This sounded interesting so I decided to give it a shot, but not before another visit to Tina's.

I drove into Hereford on a Wednesday evening. I thought I had missed the town: it was so quiet and sleepy, like something from a Constable painting. I wandered into the centre and found a pub called the Grapes; I'd heard that this was the local hangout for SAS soldiers – they had their own little bar at the end of the building that no one dared enter unless they were known. I had by now built up a picture of these supermen in my mind: big, strong, muscular, hard men, who stared at people they didn't know; men who asked straight questions and were frightened of nothing. I wanted to be just like that picture in my head, a tough guy.

It was impossible to be sure who was a soldier. In Aldershot I had known exactly who was who: short hair, jeans and desert boots said paratrooper; if you had a beer, you kept your back to the wall while you drank it for fear of getting jumped. It was tense and exciting, always waiting for the next violent incident to happen. Hereford, on the other hand, was Sleepy Hollow, and there was certainly no violence. The women were chatty and friendly, and when I told them that I was planning to take selection they took it as an everyday occurrence, no big deal at all. They all knew people in the SAS and they wished me the best of luck. The term SAS was never used in Hereford, and to turn it into one sound – 'sass' – was sacrilege. It was referred to as 'The Regiment' by anyone who had actually been a part of it.

The next morning I discovered Bradbury Lines, a small turning off a side lane leading out into the countryside. To the left of a red-and-white barrier stood a light-and-dark-blue sign with the flaming sword of Damocles emblazoned upon it: the now famous winged dagger. Above it were the words 'Bradbury Lines' and underneath, '22nd Special Air Service Regiment'.

I showed my ID and parked my car on a patch of grass set aside for people attending selection. The Ministry of Defence policeman on the gate had directed me to the training wing to check in. I strolled around the old wooden spider-type buildings, identical to the ones I had lived in as a boy soldier. I saw a few people in uniform, but none wearing SAS berets. I wandered into the training-wing block and down a long, dark corridor, looking for the office of Major (retired) Jerry. There I gave a middle-aged female secretary my details. Behind her sat a small, white-haired man wearing thick glasses, a white shirt, tie and black trousers. At his feet was a small white Scottish terrier.

'Ah, yes,' said the secretary. She turned to the man behind her and told him, 'Major Jerry, this is Private Horsfall reporting early for selection.' I stood to attention as the major stared at me through his glasses. This was the man in charge of training-wing administration. If you wanted to get to Hereford, this was the man you had to convince. His power was tremendous, and his word was law. He was miserable and unfriendly, but there was no doubting his determination to get the best possible men for 'his' regiment.

He told me a little about selection and arranged accommodation for me while his dog growled and sniffed around my feet; memories of other dogs I'd met in Northern Ireland floated into my head. By the end of the day I was billeted in one of the barrack rooms and had been issued with all the kit I would need for selection: an SAS-style bergen, waterproofs, maps, compasses (Silva and prismatic), emergency equipment, and so on. The other soldiers who had checked in early introduced themselves and showed me the layout of the camp.

As we left our spider-building, they pointed out a large tin-roofed building, the cookhouse. Inside, it was divided into two halves, one side for selection students and the other for SAS soldiers and permanent staff attached to the regiment, such as signallers and drivers. Close to the serving areas was a long table surrounded by chairs, the SAS soldiers' table, where you sat at your peril. There were only about sixteen places, which surprised me – I thought there would be more for a regiment that totalled two hundred and fifty. I found out later that most of them were never in England, let alone in camp for meals.

Leaving the canteen, I walked through a gate and into the Pal-udr-inn Club, the building that operated as the NAAFI where, during breaks in the day, food and drink could be purchased. But on Wednesday and Saturday nights, it became the best nightclub in town. The booze was cheap and the club was open until 2 a.m., later than anywhere else in Sleepy Hollow. Each man could sign in two guests – usually girls – so the club would always have enough 'goodwill' to go around. Alongside it was a large building about the size of a small aircraft hangar, known as the Blue Room because of the colour it had been painted on the outside. This was the one place where the whole regiment could assemble for briefings. Further up the road was the medical centre, the pay office and, surrounded by an extra fence and barbed wire, the Regimental Headquarters. It was a small, old-fashioned military camp, completely unpretentious; it took less than ten minutes to walk from one end to the other. It was personal and effective, and I immediately felt comfortable.

I spent the last few days before selection walking over some of the routes in the Brecon Beacons that I would soon have to do for real. One of these routes was forty-five miles long.

ON 20 AUGUST 1978, 127 men from all units of the British Forces lined up outside the training wing at Bradbury Lines. A tall, red-headed sergeant-major in SAS uniform strolled from the barrack block. Following him were six SAS corporals. We fell silent and waited to be called to attention. The sergeant-major strolled over to where we were standing, waiting in perfect silence. He said, 'OK, lads, just answer your names if you're here.' We all answered, the names were checked off and we were marched around to the Blue Room for a briefing.

First, the sergeant-major stood up and introduced himself as 'Lofty'. Then he told us about the rules and discipline of the regiment. Permanent staff instructors would be referred to as 'Staff'. This made all ranks on selection, whether they be officer, warrant officer or just plain private, junior to the SAS corporals during training. All men on selection would be equal, no matter what their rank in their own units. Minor breaches of regulations (late on parade, not shutting gates in the field) would be punished by making the perpetrator donate five quid to a fund that would be used for a piss-up at the end of selection – hard luck if you didn't make it. Any serious misconduct would result in the soldier concerned being returned to his unit (RTU'd). There were only two ways to fail the first stage of selection: the first was to withdraw voluntarily, which included pulling out because of injury; a man could withdraw at any time without incurring shame. The second was to fail to make the times allowed for completing a march during the test phase of week four. You could attempt the course up to three times but selection only took place twice a year.

Major Jerry, the training-wing major, then took over, telling us what was needed to join the SAS. For the first three weeks we would take part in a gradual physical build-up, starting with a standard battle fitness test over three miles, to get rid of no-hopers. On day two everyone would take a fifteen-mile hike over the highest peak in the Brecon Beacons, Pen-y-fan, twice: up and down, then up and down again. The maximum time allowed was four hours.

Map-reading and gym work with local training runs would complete week one. In week two, we would be divided into small groups of ten to fifteen men to spend our days walking over the Brecon Beacons with a member of staff, practising map-reading, carrying on our backs just a light bergen of around twenty-five pounds. In week three, we would spend every day in the Elan Valley, covering longer distances and working in pairs, carrying thirty-five pounds of equipment.

Week four was test week, starting on the Monday. The times expected of us would depend on the weather but as a guide, three and a half kilometres per hour would be the minimum average time allowed for a C-grade pass, for which three points were allocated; four kph would gain a B pass and four points and five kph, an A pass and five points. Everyone who totalled twelve or more points from the first four marches would qualify for the fifth march; those with fewer than twelve points would fail.

The first march in test week was eighteen kilometres, carrying thirty-five pounds; the second twenty-two kilometres with forty pound-bergens; the third twenty-seven kilometres with forty-five pounds; the fourth eighteen kilometres with fifty pounds and only a sketch map to guide you. For the successful candidates, the fifth 'endurance' march was sixty-five kilometres carrying fifty-five pounds; between eighteen and twenty-two hours would be allowed for the final march.

SAS candidates would not be encouraged or pushed by anyone. The minute they withdrew, they would be off the course and sent home. All test-week marches would be carried out as individuals; routes for anyone leaving from the same start point would be varied, so it was pointless to try to follow anyone.

Those of us who passed test week would then go on to continuation training, first in Sennybridge in South Wales to learn SAS tactics and weapons, then into the jungles of Belize for four weeks. After the jungle period, we would be assessed again. Those who passed would go on to combat survival training and counter-interrogation; following which, those who successfully completed this stage and who were not already trained parachutists would go to Brize Norton in Oxfordshire to learn to parachute.

If you got through all these stages, you were a graduate.

An SAS graduate would then join his SAS squadron on probation for six months, during which period he would be required to learn his troop skill. Each SAS troop specialised in a particular field, so you'd either be learning boat-handling, mountain-climbing, free fall parachuting or astro-navigation/mobility skills. Within the troop, each man also had to learn his personal patrol skill, as either a linguist, a paramedic, a signaller or a demolitions expert. It wasn't just a case of being successful in these elements of training; he also had to gain the acceptance of the experienced members of his troop – but if he succeeded, he would be in the SAS for the remainder of his three-year tour.

When his first three years were completed, he would again be assessed, this time for a second tour of duty. Everyone who passed SAS selection was only on secondment from his parent unit and could be returned at any time, either of his own volition or because he was no longer required.

The worst transgression any man could commit was to mess around with another man's wife while he was abroad. This would result in an immediate RTU.

Major Jerry then wished us all good luck and we watched a film about the Regiment, showing all aspects of the training. That afternoon we went out to do the battle fitness test, which was easy, and we relaxed in anticipation of the mountain march on day two.

There were men from many units in my room of twelve, and all of us were united in our cause. None wished to fail, and each would assist the others in the knowledge that the only help one would get would come from one's colleagues; the staff would simply stand by and watch us fail. It was a great feeling to be part of such a determined group of men, all striving for such a high target. I already felt special. I would collapse and die to get into this Regiment. Nothing would stop me.

On day two we got off the truck at the foot of Pen-y-fan and marched in a long line to the top, then down the other side and along an old track. After checking in, we returned up the slope over the top, and back to the start point. About halfway up on the return journey I started to have trouble with my left knee. It ached unceasingly, until I was finally forced to sit down for a break – but when you sit on a painful problem, it only gets worse. I watched several men pass by; they all asked whether I was OK and then moved on. After about ten minutes

Z Company, IJLB (Infantry Junior Leader Battalion), September 1972. My first choice was the Royal Army Medical Corps, my second the Military Police and my third the Parachute Regiment – God knows how the Paras got in there.

The Welsh 3000s, 1973: a military race over all the peaks over 3000 feet high in Snowdonia. I was sixteen, and so fit that I could run up the mountains. They were wild and untamed, the great slabs of granite looming over wet green grass and dark heather. The tops were sodden and peaty, with bogs that sucked your legs down and wouldn't let go. The view when the sun shone was magnificent; you could make out the sea in the distance.

LEFT The tranasium: a formidable test of a young man's courage, it was a series of metal bars, see-saws, ropes, wires and ladders suspended in the trees up to sixty feet off the ground. We had to get across without any safety measures whatsoever. I just went for it, praying that I wouldn't fall off.

ABOVE Me on the 7.62 mm GPMG (General Purpose Machine-Gun) with Big Mick as part of the shooting team.

BELOW 'Up 800, four men jumping'…The balloon jump at Queens Parade, Aldershot, 1976. My first jump would be not from a plane, but from this silent monster's low-swung box.

OPPOSITE TOP Y Vigilant Platoon, South Armagh, 1978. This was 'Bandit Country', the toughest and most dangerous area of rural operations in Northern Ireland.

OPPOSITE BOTTOM Me in South Armagh during my second tour in Northern Ireland. We were attached to 1 Para as an extra platoon during its first tour there since 'Bloody Sunday'.

TOP On patrol in Belfast during 1975. Note the massive early model night sight on the SLR (self-loading rifle).

I joined D Company at the age of eighteen, based in Flax St, Belfast at an old cotton mill on the edge of the tough Republican Ardoyne area. The city was cold, damp and grey, the streets just endless rows of red-brick terraces, many houses burned out.

The area we were covering included Ballysillen Park, the Crumlin Road and Ligoniel, a mixed area ranging from hard Protestant to hard Catholic. In the 'Proddy' areas we would whistle Republican tunes and in the 'Cat' areas, Unionist marches. We wanted them all to hate us, and we revelled in being feared. This is Ballysillen Park where I was shot at.

BELOW Captured terrorist weapons, Ballymurphy 1976.

The bomb I lay on, now safely dismantled, Ballymurphy 1976.

RIGHT Omeath VCP (Vehicle Check Point) at South Armagh, 1978.

On exercise in Denmark with Vigilant Platoon, 1978.

LEFT My number two on the machine-gun was an eighteen-year-old lad called Shane Scott, 'Scotty' to us. He was from London, and was probably the most likable soldier I ever had the good fortune to meet. On his nineteenth birthday he was killed in a parachute accident on Hankley Common.

Mortar platoon, 2 Para, Ballymurphy 1977. Happy Days!

BELOW Me at Pravassian Camp on SAS selection, Belize, 1979.

I got up, carried on to the top and ran down the other side to the finish. I was easily inside the four-hour limit, but I took to heart the warning about succumbing to pain and sitting down; we had been told that it made getting up and continuing much, much tougher. My knee still ached, but the first hurdle had been overcome. Fifteen of the one hundred and twenty-seven starters had already gone home.

During week two, we got to know some of the permanent staff a bit better. My instructor was black, with a Caribbean accent. He was a phenomenal athlete: he could clear ten miles an hour running cross-country twice a day without any effort at all. His name was Bart, 'Black Bart', and his favourite saying was 'I want your maximum'. One soldier told him that he was giving his maximum; he was told, 'Well, your maximum ain't good enough, man.'

Week two was fun. The weather was good and I found the map-reading easy – it was familiar ground we were working across. I took it all in my stride and comfortably got through to week three. I had been thinking when I started training that I was a little overweight, so I tried not to eat too much in the evenings; I believed that if I were lighter, I would be fitter.

There were some super-fit guys on the course: some were physical training instructors, who made sure that they came in first on all the marches. I tried to do the same, but every day they outclassed me.

On week three I was paired off for the first three days with a guy called Jacko, who was from the Guards. We had been boy soldiers together, and also team-mates on the Welsh 3000s. The Elan Valley is a high, flat, boggy area, even in summer. Where it is dry, large clumps of grass grow up from the peat, leaving dangerous gaps in between. On day two, Jacko turned his ankle. When we examined it, we saw that it was swelling badly, but he hobbled to the finish and, much to my surprise, was still limping around the course the next day.

On the Wednesday we finished the day march and then started another march when it got dark. This time I was paired with Max, a tall, fit, dark-haired man of about twenty-two. The night march went through terrain covered with these large clumps of grass; we called it elephant grass because each clump was about the size of an upturned elephant's foot. In the dark, marching on a compass bearing, we would take two or three steps and then fall over. We went on for about five kilometres, constantly picking each other up from the ground. It was soul-destroying; alone, it would have been very testing indeed. Together we made it through.

By this time I had been back in the UK for about two months; 1 Para had returned from Northern Ireland, enjoyed some leave and returned to Aldershot to take part in a night parachute training drop onto Hankley Common in Surrey. I heard through the grapevine that a young paratrooper had died during the exercise: it was the night of his nineteenth birthday. As he left the aircraft, his rigging lines somehow wrapped themselves around him and collapsed his parachute. His arms had been pinned to his body so that he could not pull his reserve parachute. Scotty fell from eight hundred feet and died instantly.

It had all happened a week earlier. Vig had held a piss-up in his honour. I felt his loss very deeply: I had guided him through the first three months of the tour of Armagh. It was the first and last time I ever shed a tear for a lost comrade.

AT THE START of test week we had seventy-five men left; a third had gone already. The weather was good, so the times were going to be fast. The only problem was water: we would have to carry extra, and this added greatly to our bergens – all food and water were additional to the statutory weight that each man had to carry. Every day, at one checkpoint, a member of staff would have scales waiting. If any of us were found to be underweight, we would be loaded up with more, or simply failed. It wasn't a risk worth taking.

I finished the first test march in the maximum time allowed to gain three points, but I was starting to have trouble with rub sores on my back: where the metal frame of the rucksack came into contact with my lower back, the skin was starting to blister. No matter how much I padded the bergen, the weight of it bouncing up and down only made matters worse, especially when I ran. My right shoulder was also starting to play up from where it had been dislocated and fractured the previous year playing rugby.

The third march was called a point-to-point, and took in seven different peaks. By the end of this I had acquired nine points – I needed only three the following day to qualify for endurance. That evening my body was in agony: the sores on my back were beginning to ulcerate, and the thought of putting another five pounds on my back and shoulders was almost unbearable. All the students were bursting blisters on their feet, but I viewed those problems as minimal compared to my own pain. I began to brood about the next day; this was the beginning of the erosion of my morale.

Day four was the sketch-map march, only eighteen kilometres in distance, but carrying fifty pounds. However, the official distance was an illusion, because we ended up walking many more kilometres trying to make sense of the drawing that passed as a map. I was one of the last to set out, and this had a negative effect on me: I wasn't going fast enough to catch anyone up, and there was no one behind me to catch me up. I came into contact with no one except the staff on the checkpoints, who told me bluntly I needed to speed up.

By the penultimate checkpoint I was in agony. Every step sent burning pains down through my shoulder. The bergen felt like it was chewing large holes in my kidneys, like a hungry rat taking a small bite at every step. Then another hungry rat started to eat at my brain. If it's like this now, it said, how will you feel tomorrow? More weight, and sixty-five kilometres. You'll never make it. With only four kilometres left to the finish, I sat down on my bergen in the rain and looked out over the endless expanse of elephant grass in front of me. Even with the bergen off, my body was racked with pain. I couldn't touch my back – it was too painful. My breathing was shallow and fast; I was exhausted. If someone had passed by and said, 'Come on, Rob, not far now,' I would probably have finished the march, but as it was, my desire to stop overwhelmed my desire to succeed.

I turned around, believing that if I had to march again the next day I would fail anyway. I retraced my steps for a kilometre back to the last checkpoint and voluntarily withdrew. After I had taken off my bergen, a medic helped me remove my shirt, which had stuck to the sores on my back. He had to use water to prise it away from the scabs that were beginning to form. The blood from the sores had run across my buttocks, down my legs and into my boots; I had felt it, but thought it was sweat. He dressed the wounds and gave me a cup of hot sweet tea.

With the bergen off and the warm tea inside me I began to feel better and started to wonder whether I had bottled out. It hadn't been so far to the end, but I had failed. I shouldn't have started thinking about the next day: all that effort for nothing. Now I would have to go back to Aldershot where all the 'told you so' people would be waiting to rub it in. I would have to watch all the other students going out for the endurance march tomorrow, wishing I was one of them.

It wasn't long before the truck I was waiting in set off for the final checkpoint to take the students who had finished back to Hereford. When we had picked them up, Bart came up to me and asked why I had withdrawn – he had expected me to do quite well. I said simply that it was too much for me and left it at that. The others looked at me with some sympathy.

The next morning, at 0300 hours, they were leaving the room for the drive back to Brecon. By 0430 hours they would be setting off on the final march, sixty-five kilometres. I pulled the blankets over my head and went back to sleep. Before breakfast that morning I packed all my kit in readiness for the return to Aldershot and 1 Para. The Regiment didn't keep you for one second longer than necessary; withdrawals were usually on their way the following day. After eating a meal that I had no stomach for, I reported to the training-wing office to get my orders. Major Jerry asked me how I felt about the course. I told him that it had been a tremendous challenge and that I hoped to try again as soon as possible. He had heard about my bergen sores from the staff and asked how they were. I raised my shirt and showed him the bloodstained dressings covering my lower back. The major told me that, from time to time, a few students were asked to stay on in Hereford, to try again on the next selection. Their duties would be to help the training-wing staff with the menial tasks involved in coaching those students who had passed test week and were going on to continuation training – taking meals to the ranges, putting up targets, driving the ambulance, and so on. Any spare time could be devoted to personal preparation for the next course. Would I be interested, he asked, in staying on for four months and taking selection again in January?

Would I? I was a drowning man who had been thrown a life-raft. There was no way I wanted to go back to 1 Para with my tail between my legs; to be offered a second chance was a God-given opportunity. Four others were kept back with me in what was called 'Demo troop': Paul, Ray, Stu and Daniel. We were housed in a Portakabin and for the next couple of weeks we recovered from our trials and took food to the ranges. The successful students (there were about forty of them) departed for Belize in Central America to take the jungle-training phase. Once they had gone we were given a Land Rover, food and ninety per cent free time to prepare for January 1979.

All members of the Regiment had to be able to swim a thousand metres with equipment. I wasn't a very strong swimmer: a hundred metres was probably the best I could manage. So every morning at 0700 hours I went to the local swimming pool and started to swim up and down as many times as I could. After this I went back to camp for breakfast. An hour after eating I would run eight miles cross-country wearing boots – this would take me out over the green hills surrounding the town and back in about fifty-five minutes. Then two or three of us Demo troop men would set off for the mountains and spend the afternoon walking one of the selection routes, practising our map-reading. This was the routine four or five days a week, unless we were needed for other duties, which was rare. I loved training, and pushed my fitness to the limits. My left knee still ached sometimes, especially going downhill, but I ignored it.

On Wednesday nights I had access to the SAS club and the right to sign in two local girls, and in a short space of time I had acquired a local girlfriend named Sue. I was still in touch with Elaine in London and with Tina in Cardiff, so during the week I would enjoy myself with Sue and then, when the weekend came, I would set off for London. I would spend Friday and Saturday nights with Elaine, Sunday night would be with Tina in Cardiff and Monday morning would see me making the final one-hour drive back to Hereford. I was like a pig in clover and I couldn't get enough. I was single, so why not?

AFTER TWO MONTHS of this routine, I wrote to Elaine telling her that I was looking forward to seeing her that Friday; I then wrote a similar letter to Tina about Sunday. I set off as usual on Friday and met Elaine in Woolwich. Things had been difficult between us for a while – I really wasn't mature enough for her and we were frustrating one another. That day it blew up into a big row and we decided to end it once and for all.

Instead of going to Cardiff on the Sunday, as usual, I set off a day early and arrived at Tina's house on Saturday evening, but I didn't get the welcome I expected. Tina had seen the imprint from my first letter on the front of hers and had highlighted it with a candle and ink. The implications were undeniable, and with the proverbial egg all over my face, I set off back to Hereford.

It was still early when I got back, so I went round to Sue's house to console myself. When I arrived, there was music blaring from the windows and it was obvious that a party was going on inside. Great, I thought, just what I need. I strolled through the open front door only to be confronted by the sight of Sue wrapped in a passionate embrace at the bottom of the stairs with a B Squadron guy called Morris. I couldn't really complain, given that I'd been three-timing her myself, so I walked across and tapped her on the shoulder, enjoying the shock on her face as her eyes opened. 'Hi, Sue,' I said. 'Bye, Sue.' And I went back to my car and drove home.

The next Wednesday I arranged a date with a local girl in Hereford. She never showed, so after waiting for a bit I took off to another pub called the Ulu Bar. It was owned by a former SAS man called Frank and was famous for its lounge bar decorated to look like a Malayan jungle village. Just across the room I saw this very attractive girl waving in my direction. She was small and slim with olive skin and big brown eyes. 'Hmmmmmmm, I like her', I thought and set off without hesitation to give her my best line.

'Hello, what's your name?'

'Gertrude', she replied. Usually I would have given up and left but there was a little twinkle in her eyes that made me hang in there.

'I was waving to the guy behind you', she said. I laughed and we got talking. She was called Heather, she was twenty years old and separated from her husband. She had two daughters, Danuta and Natasha. Tonight she wanted to go to the SAS club disco. Well, I was her man.

THOSE ON THE selection course had returned from the jungle looking like victims of starvation. I had never seen such skinny soldiers; they were all at least fourteen pounds underweight. They told horrendous stories of the training in Belize. Ten of them were RTU'd (sent back to their units), leaving only thirty to face combat survival and interrogation.

I drove the unit ambulance throughout the combat survival session. Being on the ground during the training, I got a pretty good idea of what to expect. I knew the distances we'd have to cover, what clothing was available and what the terrain was like. I knew the weather too and, above all, I understood what the instructors expected of us because I'd sat there listening to them. Three men failed on the last day, during the interrogation phase. It was hard to believe that with only twenty-four hours left to go, anyone would have given up. Out of the one hundred and fifty-seven men who started, only twenty-seven went on to the squadrons; many of those were to be rejected later. This was considered a high pass number, and it elicited the usual complainants saying the course must have been soft to pass this number. From where I stood, as a not totally impartial bystander, the course had been as tough as hell. Perhaps this was just one of those courses with a lot of high-quality people on it.

CHAPTER 9

Second Chance

ON 3 JANUARY 1979, I returned to Bradbury Lines to prepare for my second attempt at SAS selection. Winter selection was reputed to be much harder than the summer course because of the terrible mountain weather. Only fifty-seven students arrived on the first day, and five of us were Demo troop.

It was a very different picture from the summer selection. The Welsh mountains are treacherous at the best of times, and this year was to prove exceptional. Several men had recently died during military exercises in Wales, and the coroner in Brecon was beginning to create waves, no doubt fed up with conducting autopsies on fit young men who had died of hypothermia, otherwise known as exposure. This was the biggest risk in the mountains: during test week you were on your own, and a student suffering from exhaustion could sit down, lost and alone, and never stand up again. He would simply feel tired and, as his body temperature dropped, he would fall into a coma and die.

My kit was very different for winter selection: two sets of waterproof clothing, one light and one heavy; two pairs of gloves, one thin with fingers and one thick pair of mittens; a thick woolly hat under a hood; snow gaiters attached to boots and rising to the knee, with several pairs of socks underneath; thermal underwear that went all the way from neck to ankle, and snow goggles. The weights and distances were to be the same; the only concession was that in very severe weather more time would be allowed to complete the courses.

I had learned the error of my ways from the summer. Every morning I coated my feet with leather grease meant for horse tack, a very useful tip from the instructors. This kept the water out of the skin and stopped blisters; layered onto boots, it helped keep them waterproof and also prevented them from freezing solid. My back was now fully recovered, but every morning I strapped absorbent paper towels to it, held on with paper tape, which would form a gooey mush beneath the tape to protect against the rubbing of the bergen.

I realised that while I was working this hard in the mountains, I needed all the fuel I could get; in future I was going to consume as many calories as I could, starting with breakfast, when I would eat as much as possible, then grab a couple of sandwiches to take along for the truck ride. Everything I could carry and eat during the march, from sandwiches to Mars bars and Kendal mint cake (and anything else I could think of), I took with me. At the end of each day, no matter how tired I felt, I would walk down to the local chip shop and eat two pies with chips and then follow this with two pints of Guinness: the more carbohydrates, the better. I carried water mixed with Gatoraid, a high-sugar drink, although this had a tendency to freeze in the water bottle. On the day selection began, the snow was already falling, and by the first week of February, when test week was due to start, the weather had deteriorated to the point where every item of clothing we had with us was being worn all day just so we could survive.

The night march in week three was a short distance from the main Merthyr Tydfil road from Brecon. The short route took us over one ridge-line and down to some woods, a distance of about ten kilometres. We set off in threes for safety; with me I had Ray from the Demo troop and a signals squadron corporal called Scouse. Both were shorter than me, which became a problem when we got to the top of the ridge, where the land flattened out into what in summer would have been a boggy plateau. Now it was covered in about three feet of snow, and where the dips and hollows were, the snow was drifting up to about four feet. We were wading through snow that came up to the middle of my thighs and was waist-high on Ray and Scouse. As we plodded on at a snail's pace, it became apparent that Scouse was tiring fast. Finally, with about five kilometres to go, he collapsed.

Ray and I knew that there was no way we could bivouac up here and hope to save Scouse. The wind was gusting to about forty knots and the snow was still falling. Even if one of us stopped and the other went on, there would be no way of finding the way back at night with a rescue team. Scouse was still conscious, but groggy. We decided to push on, with one of us carrying his bergen and the other carrying him. The extra weight made us both fall over continually, but the knowledge that Scouse would die if we didn't get him home kept us going. At one point Scouse and Ray dropped over a lip and into a drift, sinking right up to their chests.

Ray and I had prepared well for this selection, and we were both in good shape. Even so, it took us about two hours to cover the last two kilometres. Finally the slope started to drop away before us and we knew we were on our way down to the finish. There had been forty-five men walking the same route that night, but we hadn't seen any of them because of the weather.

We took Scouse over to the waiting truck, where the SAS staff put him in a sleeping bag and filled him up with warm sweet drinks. Ray and I, on the other hand, were told to go over to the trees and basha up for the night – basha is the SAS term for any form of shelter, from a lean-to made of leaves to a room in a five-star hotel. On this occasion it was a sleeping bag under a green plastic sheet. I could tell immediately who the infantrymen were: they built shelters together and cuddled up for the night, putting their boots inside their sleeping bags and hanging their wet clothes up. The forest in which we were to sleep offered some protection from the wind and the worst of the snow. I piled up layers of branches beneath my sleeping bag for insulation from the ground and then, after a mug of hot sweet tea and more food, I got into my dossbag. With only my nose exposed to the elements, I slept the sleep of the dead.

We woke with the dawn at about 0730 hours. The temperature had dropped to about minus 15 degrees Centigrade during the night, and many of the troops without good field experience had not slept well. By putting my boots inside my sleeping bag I had prevented them from freezing solid; some men couldn't even get theirs on. The wet clothes that I had hung up could now be brushed and shaken free of ice and worn – damp, but not soaking wet.

The exhausting walk the day before, followed by the night march, had taken its toll on those who had not slept well. The ominous face of the east side of Pen-y-Fan glared down on us from the north. Slow-moving, grey clouds were forming on the peak even as we watched. Our instructor, Neil, looked up at the peak and then shouted at us, 'If you're carrying on, form up over there facing that way [towards the mountain]. If not, get on the truck.' Fifteen men climbed onto the truck, some still carrying their frozen boots. We were down to thirty, and test week hadn't even started yet.

When the truck had gone, Neil turned us to the left and we went back over the ridge-line that we had crossed the night before. In the morning sun, and with good visibility, the route was fairly easy, and it took less than two hours to get back. When we hit the road we ran another two kilometres to the Story Arms mountain rescue station, climbed onto a waiting truck and returned to Hereford to prepare for test week.

In spite of the appalling weather, I was feeling confident. I had found the build-up training comfortable, I had no injuries and, with the deep snow preventing a lot of running, there were no rub marks on my back. I was as ready as I would ever be. During the weekend I ate like a horse. When I had a bath, I left my feet out of the water to keep them hard. Ian Dury was in the charts with 'Hit Me With Your Rhythm Stick' and I was going out with Heather.

A few nights after we met I was driving her home in the dark, heading south over the river Wye. It was pouring with rain, that cold winter rain that penetrates your clothes no matter what you wear. A white van shot past us at speed and I remember Heather commenting that the driver would kill someone if he didn't slow down. We followed the road to the end of the bridge and turned towards Abergavenny. Where the road straightens out we saw an old man step out in front of the van. Its brake lights lit up and the vehicle came to an abrupt halt. I pulled up, took one look and told Heather to stay in the car.

I ran up to the van to see the driver sitting stock still in an obvious state of shock. In front of the van lay the old man, equally still. I opened the van door and asked the driver if he was OK.

'Yes', he said. He started to explain what happened as if it wasn't obvious but I ignored him and told him to stay put. I took the keys out of the ignition and pocketed them: if he had driven off he'd probably have caused another accident. And if he got out in his state, he might have wandered into the road. He was in a complete daze and this was a busy route.

Other cars stopped to help so I ordered a man to slow the traffic and two others to get an ambulance. People without skills who want to help need to be told what to do. Someone has to take charge.

All this had only taken a few moments but it was crucial to make sure that everyone was safe before dealing with the old man. I knelt down beside him and cleared his airway. He had false teeth which had been broken and I pulled out all the bits and pieces I could. He wasn't breathing. I put three quick breaths of air into his lungs and felt for his pulse. Nothing. Not a beat. I started closed chest cardiac massage. Then I was joined by another motorist – a nurse. She took over the breathing part of the resuscitation: I pressed his heart five times then she breathed once into his lungs. After about thirty seconds I finally got a pulse and shortly afterwards he began to breathe for himself. I realised quite quickly that his heart was now pumping because he began to bleed profusely from the back of his head. It dawned on me that where I had been holding his head, his skull was severely depressed. I managed to stem the bleeding with my T-shirt and monitored him until police cars and an ambulance arrived.

As the ambulance crew took over I briefed them on the patient before making a brief statement to the police. Only when it was all over did I notice Heather standing by the side of the road. She had watched the whole thing. Heather said later that she was stunned at the way I'd taken charge and saved the man's life. Sad to relate, he didn't make it though. His injuries were too severe and he died in hospital.

My relationship with Heather was getting more and more serious despite me insisting that I was a professional soldier, the regiment was my life etc. and so we wouldn't last. She had fallen in love. Me? At first I didn't know the true meaning of the word. I was delighted to have a devoted beauty on my arm and we thoroughly enjoyed each other's company. But she was growing on me, no doubt about it.

THE FIRST MARCH on test-week Monday was held in the Black Mountains, near Abergavenny. The snow was thick, and on one occasion I put my bergen inside my plastic emergency bag and let it slide along the ground behind me, which was very effective when going down steep slopes. I was making good progress when I committed my first error. The map showed a large rise which I would have to cross, although there was also a footpath contouring around the side. I chose to go around. This would have been a viable option in summer, as the time gained from running would have outweighed the time lost in covering more distance, but in the snow, the detour made no difference to my speed; it only increased the distance I had to travel. I lost time and scraped in at the end with a maximum time, only just getting my three points. Lesson learned: never contour around peaks in the snow to save time.

Day two found us back in the Brecon Beacons for the twenty-two-kilometre march. The snow had fallen heavily overnight, slowing down the man in front, which caused a stream of men to extend in single file behind the leader, who was breaking trail. Only one man at a time could do this along some of the thinner ridge-lines, so the exercise became a farce, with the strongest taking turns to break trail while the rest toddled along in their wake. We got close to one checkpoint on a peak called Fan-fawr when suddenly the whole side of the mountain began to slide downwards, with me and several others sitting on top of it. A cornice of snow about two hundred yards wide had broken loose and begun to move. I looked down at several others beneath me riding on the back of our huge white toboggan. I froze as I prayed that it wouldn't turn into an avalanche. Eventually the snow stopped moving and, without a whisper, we crept carefully back up to the top, thanked our gods and moved off in a slightly different direction.

AT THE END of the march there were five or six of us breaking trail while the remainder followed on behind. This was observed by the SAS staff through binoculars. When we finished, only the first six were given a pass mark. The remainder were failed for not trying hard enough. I was in the first six, and I was mightily relieved. After the previous day's performance, I needed every point I could get.

The weather had been bitterly cold, but so far we had been spared the worst. Now all that was to change. The point-to-point was twenty-seven kilometres and started at 0800 hours in near white-out conditions. We were still marching at 1800 hours, ten hours later. Most of the day had been spent following a compass bearing; it was dark when we started and dark when we finished. The last leg of my route was back over Pen-y-fan and down to the Story Arms; out in front of me I could see the strongest student on the course, Andy. His huge Scottish shoulders made light work of everything. We had served together in 2 Para Mortars, and he had gained my utmost respect. He disappeared into the night above me as I climbed up the almost sheer east ridge of the mountain. I had resorted to counting my footsteps in fifties and then starting again, which helped to take my mind off the pain that my body was experiencing.

As I approached the summit, I almost collided with Andy coming back towards me in the dark. His face was wild, his eyes bulging, and he was stammering. This was not the Andy I knew – something terrible had happened. 'I nearly walked over the edge,' he said. 'I nearly walked over the fucking edge.' In his exhaustion he had tried to get down the wrong way, and had almost gone over the five-hundred-foot drop on the north face, straight down onto rocky ground. In the dark he hadn't noticed until he was only one step away from certain death. We made our way down to the finish the correct way and finished first after ten hours, for an A pass and five points. In the summer I had scraped a C in eight hours. When we got back to Hereford I just had time to get in my two pies and chips and two pints before last orders.

The next day was the sketch map test, the cause of my previous failure. The weather was fine when I started, but within the hour it degenerated into the worst day so far. I had on three pairs of gloves, two sets of waterproofs and three layers of clothing. My pack now weighed fifty-five pounds, excluding the extra food, and the snow was falling heavily. At each checkpoint I imagined the staff saying, 'Don't worry, lads, it's over, you can't go on in this.' But they didn't. Now it was up to me.

Once again I had reached crisis point. I started to believe that I could not go on. I got a grip of myself, forced food down my throat for warmth and energy, checked my compass bearing and set off, again counting my steps. The white nothingness gave me no sense of progress. If I had begun to think, I would have destroyed my own morale, just as I had done the year before. Ice built up on my eyebrows and moustache, and my feet felt like lumps of lead as I lifted them and crashed them down into the snow, each time hoping that I would find the depth of this step shallower than the last. At one point I dug a path up a steep slope with my rifle butt.

At the final checkpoint I walked across a road only ten metres from a three-ton truck. I didn't realise that I was crossing a road, and didn't see the truck. The driver sounded his horn and I scurried over to him and checked in. Ten yards further away and he wouldn't have seen me, and I would probably never have found him.

Before driving back to Hereford we had to dig the truck out of the snow and put chains on the wheels. This was all I needed just before the big one – more endurance.

By the end of day four I had sixteen points. I still felt good and I was raring to get it over with. After five hours' sleep we were up for breakfast. By 0300 hours we were getting on the trucks to leave, but as I strolled towards the waiting transport, I saw a new face, and asked him where he had come from. It turned out that he was a serving major in the SAS; his name was Mike Keeley. 'I'm just coming up for the walk', he said. I replied, 'Jesus Christ, boss, with the weather up there, you must be fucking mad.' He laughed and slung his bergen up onto the back of the vehicle and climbed in.

Endurance starts and finishes at Talybont Reservoir, at one end of the Brecon range. The march extends over all the major peaks to the Cray Reservoir and back. There is no staggering of start times:

everyone sets off together, and if you get back in time, you have passed test week.

It was raining when we left the truck and started up the hill. The wind, although strong, felt warmer than it had all week. In the valley a thaw had set in, and the snow was melting fast. As we climbed higher and higher above the tree line, the temperature dropped and the wind increased in velocity. Soon it was impossible to hear the man standing next to you, even when he shouted. The rain was hitting us from the left. To our right the cliffs dropped two hundred feet, and we had to lean heavily into the wind to travel in a straight line. The snow was still thick on the ground but underneath it water was running in great streams, soaking our legs and letting in the cold. The wind chill factor in such high winds is enormous. Although the temperature was probably about one degree Centigrade, it felt like minus thirty.

As I broke the ridge-line the wind hit me like a hammer. I locked my eyes on the man in front and plodded forward. After about an hour I saw three men walking back down towards me. One had collapsed with exposure and the others were taking him to safety. A short time later I saw Major Keeley shouting at two of the students. They were trying to get him into some spare waterproof clothing which one of them had been carrying. He was refusing, and I saw the waterproofs blow away over the cliffs and into the dark.

I struggled on, but the cold was beginning to prove unbearable. I tried eating and I tried walking faster, but I couldn't focus on my compass and I started to feel nauseous. I had nothing else to wear and the wind was cutting through me like a knife. Sitting down, I realised that if I didn't keep moving I would go down with exposure. I got up and stumbled on for another half-hour before I found myself alone and going in completely the wrong direction, straight towards the cliffs. I've got exposure, I thought. I asked myself whether I was bottling out again, and struggled with the choice of pushing on or accepting that I was ill and going back down. I think now that I made a good decision, the decision to live. For the second time on a selection I turned back.

When I got to the bottom, I was on my last legs. I reported to the truck, where I was met by Lofty, the training-wing sergeant-major. He simply wrote down my name and told me to get in the back. I told him I thought the weather was so terrible up there that somebody could end up dead. In the thawing valley it looked, if anything, as if the weather was better than before, but up on top it was the worst I had ever experienced in any mountains, anywhere.

I wrapped myself up in my sleeping bag and went to sleep. I was upset that this selection had come to an end, but I didn't feel that I had let myself down. I knew that my decision had been the correct one. If the weather had not been so extreme I would have been successful. A few hours later, I woke up to find the truck moving off towards Hereford. We stopped briefly and I asked Lofty what was going on. He was very concerned. It was now six hours since the group had set off, and so far not one person had reached the first checkpoint at the Story Arms. They were going to alert the Mountain Rescue Service and get A Squadron up to the Story Arms to mount a search-and-rescue operation.

We got back just in time to see the squadron departing. I wanted to go back with them but was told that I couldn't be of any help and was ordered to remain behind. The searchers were out for most of the night, but when they eventually came down, exhausted, they had found no one. It was their guess that the troops had taken shelter somewhere. They would try again at first light.

The next morning all but two were found. Only a short time after I had turned back, the remainder had decided to get off the mountain as well. They had gone down to a water pumping station and broken in. Once out of the cold, they had bedded down for the rest of the day. The roads were impassable. It was a question of survival, pure and simple.

The two missing men were Major Keeley and Simon. Apparently, when I had seen the major shouting at the men, he had been showing the first signs of hypothermia. They had tried to help him get his spare clothing on, but when they opened his bergen they discovered that instead of emergency equipment and waterproofs, he was carrying only bricks and some rations. He had pulled rank when they had tried to persuade him to go back and, as he was an SAS major, they had finally given in. A short time later he collapsed and lost consciousness. The troops that were with him dug a shelter and put up some overhead cover, then got him into his sleeping bag; they donated their own survival gear to try to keep him alive. Simon stayed with him and snuggled up to him to transfer his body heat. Now that he was unconscious, there was no way that fuel could be put into his body. He could not eat or drink; his only hope was that help would arrive soon.

A Squadron found the shelter at about lunchtime. Simon was in a bad way, but Major Keeley had died in the night, of exposure. He had been a hero at the defence of Mirbat in Oman in the early 1970s, and was highly thought of by all members of the unit. He just didn't have the kit for the terrible weather conditions we'd encountered. It was a terribly sad end to the week.

LOOKING BACK, WE had been lucky not to lose more men. Scouse could have been lost on the night march, Andy could have walked over the cliff, and the loose cornice could have turned into an avalanche. It was only with hindsight that I realised what a truly dangerous week we had all experienced.

CHAPTER 10

Jungle Training

BECAUSE ALL OF us who had qualified for the endurance test had been forced off the mountains by the weather – and had survived – training-wing decided that we could all carry on with continuation training, then complete endurance at the end of the combat survival phase. The remaining twenty-two students, including two officers – or Ruperts, as they were dubbed – prepared to leave for the small Central American state of Belize.

The SAS has probably more experience in the tropical rainforests than any other serving unit in the British Armed Forces. The modern SAS Regiment evolved from the Malayan Scouts in 1953, and it has been involved in jungle warfare somewhere, from Malaya to Borneo and Belize, ever since. The skills that have been handed down through the Regiment have been updated continually over the last fifty years. Now it was my turn to learn. I had never been to the Tropics; for me this was a whole new adventure.

While we were waiting to leave the UK, we spent the time learning SAS patrol skills, which are completely different from standard infantry skills. Infantry works in units of ten men called sections: three sections make a platoon, four platoons make a company, and four companies make a battalion. An infantryman is usually supported by about eight hundred men. In the SAS, the smallest unit is a patrol. Four men make a patrol, four patrols make a troop, and four troops make a squadron. A patrol is supported by a man at the other end of the radio.

All our drills were learned as teams of four, with the occasional grouping of five men to absorb the odd straggler. SAS patrol tasks are usually limited to reconnaissance, sabotage and laying A-type (automatically fired) ambushes. With only four men, direct confrontation with the enemy is avoided at all costs, so most of our jungle drills involved learning ways to lay down a lot of continuous fire while trying to break contact with the enemy (or running away, as it's more commonly known).

AT THE END OF February 1979 we landed at Belize International Airport and drove the short distance to Airport Camp, local headquarters of the British Army and the Royal Air Force. The camp, divided from the airport by a thin fence and some swampland and bush, consisted of a large number of tin-roofed huts of varying sizes surrounding a dry earth playing-field. The only air-conditioning was supplied by rotating fans on the ceiling, which chugged around steadily day and night. We were each given a campbed and were taken to a bare, empty hut where we were to sleep for the night. We rigged up our mosquito nets over the tops of our campbeds, then we sweated through the night until morning. The next day we moved on, not sorry to leave 'civilisation' behind us.

Belize, formerly the colony of British Honduras, was under the protection of the British government. The Guatemalans had been laying claim to the country for some time: they wanted an eastern seaboard for trade. There had been a lot of sabre-rattling and some minor incursions by Guatemalan forces, so the British government sent two battalions of infantry, a squadron of Harrier jump-jets and a squadron of Puma helicopters to keep the enemy out. One battalion was stationed in the scrub grassland of the north; the other was in the tropical rainforests in the south. The border was patrolled from north to south, including mainly uncharted territory in the Mayan Mountains.

Our first two weeks in-country were spent acclimatising and learning about the jungle. We were based in the northern part, which was sandy-soiled scrubland and pine forest – not at all what we had been expecting – and very, very hot. We practised our field craft and working together as small groups. Most of the tests undertaken in the tropics were designed to put each small team under intense pressure, so the staff could see whether students were able to control their tempers and do their share of work. Test week had assessed individual performance; now what mattered was how we operated together as a team.

The first area where we were to train was called Pravassian. What we did there was not very different from standard infantry training: we ran first thing every morning, had training sessions all day and lectures every evening. The lectures were my favourite part: we learned about dangerous animals and insects – and plants – and how to deal with them; one tree, if cut with a machete, could spurt its sap into your eyes and blind you for days. The animal that kills most people in the jungle is the hornet. We had lectures on weapons, jungle medicine, foreign military tactics, jungle survival, and what food you could find for yourself. Lofty told us that if you couldn't survive in the jungle, you couldn't survive in Tesco.

The best lecture of all was the belt-kit one, by a sergeant called Joe, a veteran of Borneo and Malaya. Joe's belt-kit was legendary; his lecture consisted of him taking his kit to pieces and explaining each article as he went along (to go through it all would take another book). The complexity of the kit was down to the aim: to carry everything you needed to survive in the jungle on your belt. The two most important items were water and ammunition, but from there the list continued endlessly – a tin of medicines, a sheet of green gardening polythene for shelter, fire-lighting magnesium and a spark-maker, scissors, knives, string, wire-saws, a sewing kit, emergency rations, water purification tablets, snares, insect repellent, string hammock, and so on. I thought, if I had his belt-kit, I wouldn't need a bergen.

At the end of each day we would relax by swimming in the local river. We were high up and the water was cold and clear. It was our only luxury.

After two weeks at Pravassian we flew out, south-west by helicopter, and landed on a makeshift platform in the middle of the Mayan

Mountains. Our new home was a clearing known as Blue Hole Camp. The helicopter pad had been built by the SAS staff on the top of a hill; they had cleared the trees with explosives and then used the wood to build a safe landing-site. As I got out of the chopper, I looked up at the huge, towering trees with large green ferns growing underneath. Some of the leaves on the ferns were more than ten feet long. At last, real jungle – this was what I had come for.

We moved away from the landing-zone and into the trees. I noticed how dark it was; very little light got through the canopy of leaves that hung two hundred feet above. The ground was brown with fallen leaves and looked to be almost a living mass of insects. Everywhere I looked there were ants and beetles of strange colours and sizes.

As this was to be our permanent base for the next three weeks we needed to be comfortable, with individual shelters from the rain. My first task was to build a pole-bed, which is constructed by cutting two eight-foot poles and passing them through a plastic sheet with two tubular holes on the sides. This creates a stretcher, which is then balanced between two A-shaped frames to hold it above the ground. Above the bed is strung a mosquito net, over which is a plastic sheet held up with rubber bungies or string to create a waterproof tent. A stick is placed outside the mosquito net, just underneath the plastic roof, with a candle on it to provide light.

Even in the dry season it rains every night, usually just after dusk as the air begins to cool. In the wet season it rains almost non-stop. We were in the dry season, so rain was not a great problem – until it came to getting water. We were on the top of a hill, the small streams had all dried up, and we had to walk down to the river every morning and night to collect our water supplies. This arduous task was shared evenly between the patrol members, and was also the first thing the staff watched, looking out for any signs of antagonism: there was always going to be one who didn't want to take his turn.

The humidity made us sweat continually, so that our clothes were always soaking wet. At night we would change into dry clothing, which was kept in a sealed plastic bag. In the morning we packed away our dry kit and put on the wet stuff again. This wasn't pleasant, but it made sense: once the dry kit got wet, there would be nothing comfortable to sleep in.

The immediate area around Blue Hole was primary jungle; it had never been cut down, but there was evidence of ancient Mayan civilisation all around us in the shape of burial mounds and hidden pyramids in the trees. These would appear as stony hills until we got close enough to see the cut edges to the stones. Where the jungle had been cultivated in the past the great trees did not keep the undergrowth down, and we found ourselves struggling to move at more than one kilometre an hour: it was like trying to move through endless miles of blackberry bushes.

We were not allowed to walk along the tracks – these were enemy ambush routes. To make matters even worse, there was a plague of large green horseflies. They would land on us, push their probosci through our clothes and feed on our blood. The bites were painful, and even if we didn't feel it at the time, we always knew when we were under attack because we could hear the change in the fly's whining tone as it began to feed. When I first arrived I swatted the horseflies endlessly, but after a week I was so fed up that I just let them take their fill of blood and go away of their own accord.

The bramble-like plants in the jungle were called 'Wait a while'. If you didn't wait a while when you became caught up, you just got more and more tangled up – another test of patience. At first the forest was like a wall of endless green: I saw nothing. Men could stand motionless only a few yards from me without my detecting their presence. But after a week I started to notice things that I hadn't seen before: birds in the trees, spiders in their holes and scorpions under roots. I could see where people had walked, and I could follow their tracks and signs to get back to base.

MAP-READING IN the jungle is not the same as it is anywhere else: it's more a case of navigating a green ocean by time and distance on a bearing. The man at the front tries to go in a straight line, while the second man keeps him straight by watching the compass. The last man counts his paces, and by combining compass and counting, an approximate position can be worked out on the map. Only rivers can be relied upon with any accuracy: they were the one fixed item in our green sea.

We weren't allowed to shave or use smelly items like soap, so that we couldn't be located by smell: in the jungle, all odours linger in the motionless air for a long time. Every week we had a fresh ration of green vegetables and meat flown in, which helped the vitamin count in our diet enormously. On these days, we all knew where the helicopter pilot was because we could smell the soap from his morning wash.

My skin became so thick and callused that the thorns no longer cut through the flesh – with one exception; the 'Bastard trees'. Bastard trees had four-inch-long spikes protruding from the bark, in circles, all the way from the base of the trunk to the branches. Whenever you were tired or slipped on a slope, you could guarantee that the tree you grabbed hold of for support would stick one of its long spikes through your hand; that's how the trees acquired their nickname.

I liked the jungle, even if I didn't enjoy the foliage and the insects. Our SAS instructor, Tony, was a rather remote man, formerly of the Royal Marines. Naïvely believing that all SAS men were jungle experts and knew all things, I asked him what a particular fruit I had seen was. He simply replied, 'I don't know', and walked on. Though my image of him was a little tarnished, I couldn't fault him for telling the truth.

Griff, my patrol partner, was another Marine: the same age as me, coming up twenty-two, although he looked younger. Tony asked him one day how old he was, then said he didn't think anyone was ready for the SAS until he was at least twenty-five. He never asked me because I have always looked older than my years – I was going grey at fifteen.

THE JUNGLE TRAINING was hard but fair. We carried heavy weights long distances and I got eaten alive by insects, but I slept well at night. In the last week we worked on hard routine, which meant that all sustenance was taken cold, including drinks. We would march for an hour, then stop for ten minutes. At night we would curl back on our route so that if we were being followed we could hear the trackers and move off before they came upon us. Once it was dark, we would sling our hammocks up between two trees on the side of a slope and sleep with our rifles within arm's reach. We would get up while it was still dark and pack in preparation for moving on as soon as there was enough light to see by. There was no smoking, washing or cooking allowed: we were supposed to be in enemy territory.

In the final days, the staff ambushed us. Our task was to escape with only our belt-kits and make our way to an emergency rendezvous. I had my survival rations and waterproof sheet, but now I would have to sleep on the jungle floor, that crawling mass of invertebrate life. It wasn't comfortable and it wasn't warm: we may have been in a tropical environment, but we were high up and the nights were bloody cold. There is one good thing I can say about Belize, though: we didn't have to suffer leeches – for some reason there weren't any – but the next morning I had to spend an hour getting the ticks out of my skin: one was as big as a penny. We would squirt them with mosquito repellent first, which made them come loose, and then pull their heads out from under our skin.

My patrol had worked really well together under the leadership of Sean, a Guards officer. No one had slacked off or argued, and we finished our training believing that we had all done enough to pass . . . but that decision wasn't down to Sean, it was almost completely Tony's: and he didn't like youth.

I flew out of the jungle at least fourteen pounds lighter than when I had gone in. The training, the humidity and my body's constant battle with disease had taken their toll and I could see every rib in my chest. When we got back to Airport Camp I had a shower and washed with soap and shampoo for the first time in a month: it was glorious. Other things I suddenly appreciated were sitting on a chair and feeling dry clothes on my body. Eating at a table with a knife and fork was a luxury to be savoured. The jungle was good, but it was great to get out and relax.

It was over. There was nothing else any of us could do to affect our results, which we weren't to be told until we got back to Hereford. We spent a day out on the Caribbean quays, soaking up the sunshine, eating lobster and steak and drinking beer. It was like something straight out of the Bounty chocolate bar adverts: white sand and palm trees with huge conch shells lying on the beach. All that was missing was the women.

We got back to Hereford on Saturday and learned that we would not find out whether we were to stay or go until parade on Monday morning. It was a nerve-racking weekend; though all of us were busy convincing ourselves – and each other – that we had done well; we all told each other how good our patrol was. I couldn't see much difference between most of the others and me, apart from the fact that I really had enjoyed the experience; I would have jumped at the chance to return to the jungle if the opportunity arose.

ON MONDAY MORNING we all lined up in the corridor outside the Officer Commanding (OC) training-wing's office. There were twenty of us (the two Ruperts – officers – would get their brief from the colonel), and I was eighth in line. Number one went in and after five minutes came out, looked along the line and shook his head. He was going back to his unit. Number two was the same, as were three, four, five, six and seven – all of them had failed. As each one left the office and walked dejectedly by me, my confidence dropped. By the time I entered the room I had already made my plans for going home. I walked into the office and saluted. Lofty was standing to the left of the OC, who sat at his desk reading from a report. I was told to sit down and then, without any preliminaries, Lofty said, 'You'll be pleased to hear that you have passed.' My face lit up in a wide grin. The OC went on to tell me that my reports had been excellent and that I should keep up the good work.

As I walked back into the corridor the remaining twelve didn't need to ask: it was written all over my face. Yes, I had done it! Many of them patted me on the back and wished me well. When I got out of the door, I ran back to my room in a high state of euphoria – I was one more stage closer to my goal – but I walked quietly and respectfully into the room. Those who had got their results before me were in there, and I felt for them. They asked how I had done and were pleased for me, but it was difficult to say much. Tomorrow they would be gone and I could celebrate properly.

Only nine out of the twenty passed, plus the two officers. Five were from Parachute Regiment: Leslie, Tony, Andy, Chris and me; Keith was a Royal Marine, and the other three, Ray, Paul and Kevin, were from county regiments. Only nine from fifty-seven . . . and we still had combat survival to go.

CHAPTER 11

Can't Crack Me,
I'm a Rubber Duck

ALL UNITS IN the British Armed Forces, including the Navy and the Air Force, send individuals on the combat survival course. Some, like the infantry and the RAF Regiment, send people so that they can return to their units and teach the survival skills there. These men do not undertake the last two days of the course; only special forces groups and fighter pilots take the counter-interrogation training.

The course consists of three weeks of living in the field, learning how to survive in the wild: which plants and fungi are edible and which are poisonous; how to build traps and the most effective ways to kill animals. I was taught how to build shelters in different climates and find water in the desert. I learned about nutrition and the way the body breaks down different food types: once you understand this, you are much better able to decide on the most effective ways of getting food in the wild. For example, building a trap large enough to kill a deer burns up a hell of a lot of calories, I might have to wait a long time for the trap to be successful, and then, if the weather was warm, I wouldn't be able to eat and conserve much of the meat before the rest went rotten. On the other hand, if I were sitting next to a termite nest, I could wet a stick with saliva and poke it inside, then take it out and eat the termites stuck to it, raw. That way I'd be able to consume a large number of calories without effort. Breaking off the bark from a dead tree in search of grubs is another very cost-effective way of finding survival food.

I learned how to light fires and keep them burning for a long time, and how to use woods that didn't make smoke. I am always amused when I watch people at campsites light fires and build them up into raging infernos, only to have them die down and go out in a few minutes. They then try to eat the blackened, still-raw meat that they were attempting to cook. If you think grubs are bad, you should try raw, frozen hamburgers in a charcoal glaze.

Finding edible plants is not as easy as it might at first appear. Very often we are standing next to a wealth of food, but we don't know it. The plants are there, but it takes time and practise to find and recognise them.

Building shelters from natural materials is another refined skill. Leaves and grasses can make very waterproof coverings, once you understand the way water runs off them – thatch is a classic example. But if you don't get it right, you get wet.

Cold and heat are both killers. Insulation can be used to keep cold and heat in or out, just as a Thermos flask can keep your food hot or cold. Survival relies on knowledge.

If we had a global catastrophe today, very few people in the developed world would have any idea how to prepare and preserve food, how to build a chimney, or how to light a fire and keep a house warm. Catching, killing and butchering game would all be alien to them – who apart from a butcher would know which parts of an animal can poison the meat? Who knows which berries you can eat and which ones will kill you? Most wouldn't even know how to grow vegetables. Without the support of food manufacturing and energy supply systems, most of us would die. Third World people still live by the skills that I learned in the SAS, and they take them for granted. If the apocalypse ever comes, Africa won't be such an uncomfortable place in which to live after all.

The countryside is also full of medicine. Even in the UK there are many remedies within hand's reach: willow bark contains aspirin and oak bark contains tannin, which can stop diarrhoea.

IN THE FIRST three weeks I digested a mass of information, most of which needed constant revision and practise to be remembered. Then we were all sent out into the hills for two days with only basic survival rations, to see what it was like to go hungry while working hard. Organised in groups of four, we had to travel long distances and find various checkpoints. Most of us were carrying not more than a packet of muesli and a Mars bar – about five hundred calories – and since an adult will consume about 2,500 calories a day just sitting around, it didn't take long to get hungry. Once I had eaten my rations I began to realise the immediate effects of hunger.

It was hard work walking across the hills on a cold night. When I sat down, I quickly got cold, so my body would burn extra fuel to keep me warm. Give me food, it started to say, I'm hungry. I had no food, and I had to get to the checkpoints. As time wore on, I could feel myself getting weaker. The empty feeling in my stomach began to disappear, but it returned every time I had a drink of water. This was only a forty-eight-hour exercise and my effectiveness as a soldier was already beginning to diminish: my hunger was affecting my thinking processes – I had to concentrate hard to map-read accurately. Always pity a hungry person. It must be a terrible thing to starve.

SINCE I HAD returned from the jungle, all my bites and scratches had gone except for one, a small bite on the side of my leg which stubbornly refused to heal: it had now grown into an itchy red spot about the size of a penny-piece. There was no way that I was going to go sick at this stage of my training, so I covered it up and carried on, hoping that it would get better by itself.

The fourth week was combat survival test week: we were all to be sent out into the cold, wet hills of Shropshire for five days. Our only possessions were to be the clothes we were standing up in: socks and boots, a pair of trousers held up with string, a T-shirt, shirt, pullover and greatcoat. We would be given a sketch-map, and we would then have to get to various checkpoints marked on the map and rendezvous with agents. That was the easy bit: a battalion of six hundred infantrymen would be chasing us constantly. We had no food or water, except what we could find for ourselves. When the five days were over, those of us on the special forces list would be taken away and interrogated for thirty-six hours.

On day one we paraded in the Blue Room to be strip-searched. I took off all my clothes and left them in a pile on the floor. The clothes were searched, then my boots, socks, underwear, shirt and pullover were returned to me. I was then bent over, to see whether I had anything stuck up my arse. I did in fact have a Sinex nasal spray tube containing a five-pound note up there, but it was too far up for anyone to see or feel it without a glove and some Vaseline and at this stage no one was going to take such extreme measures. I got dressed. My trousers were in an appalling state of repair – they didn't reach the top of my boots, and the waist was too big. Fortunately, I found some string and used that to hold them up. The old army greatcoat was thick, long and brown and it had only one button left; it might not have been the height of fashion, but I knew damn well that this would be my most important item of clothing. It was big enough and thick enough to sleep in, and when the collar was turned up it covered my ears.

Once dressed, we were loaded onto a truck and taken to a holding area for the day. We were imprisoned in an old brick bunker left over from the Second World War. It was damp and wet, and the floor was of solid concrete. Huddled together in our little groups, we passed the time until lunch in idle chit-chat. For lunch we were served a bucket of swill left over from the cookhouse. Placed delicately on top, as garnish, was a large, very dead brown rat. I, with several others, ran across to the bucket and plunged my hand down into the swill, searching for any large items of food. I came up with two fairly solid boiled potatoes, which I put in my pocket for later. Most of us weren't hungry: we'd had breakfast that morning, but I knew that in a few hours the others would be wishing that they had a potato or two to munch on too.

The day passed slowly. By the time it began to get dark, I had already eaten the spuds, although more from boredom than hunger – and anyway, they were getting furry in my pocket. As dusk fell, we were unceremoniously loaded onto trucks again and driven for two hours to God knows where. There was little to see through the gaps in the truck cover, except for the odd road sign, but I managed to ascertain that I was being taken north, towards Shrewsbury.

At a pre-planned point, the vehicle was ambushed by the staff and I was released into the dark countryside. I was partnered off with Andy, given the promised sketch-map of the local area and told to get to a certain checkpoint to meet an agent by midnight the next day. The first thing we did was get away from the ambush area – it would be crawling with Gordon Highlanders, our enemy, within minutes. Their sole purpose was to hunt us down and capture us for tactical questioning by their own intelligence people. If caught, we would be held in very uncomfortable conditions for anything up to six hours. Then, if we hadn't managed to escape, we would be released to carry on with the exercise.

By orientating my map to the stars and finding a main road, I soon managed to establish approximately where we were. Andy and I set off, using the cover of the hedgerows, in the general direction of the first agent contact point. The terrain was rolling hills, covered with blocks of Forestry Commission pine and the occasional natural wood. Lower down, the fields and hedgerows indicated farms, whose lights dotted the landscape. Andy and I soon joined up with the other selection guys. We had covered a considerable distance when one of the others wanted to go in a different direction from me. He told us that he had known which area the exercise was to be held in and had some food hidden in a cache about five miles away. 'How much food?' I asked. His description didn't exactly inspire me to walk five miles in the wrong direction and then five miles back, so I told him I wasn't interested. Andy, on the other hand, felt the detour was worthwhile, so we agreed to split up. Five of them went one way and I went the other. We had been told not to split from our partners, but both Andy and I were strong characters. I, for one, was not about to change my mind just because the majority disagreed with me.

Once alone, I could make my own decisions: I just had to rely on my brain and my training to get through. I covered as much ground as possible while it was dark, staying off the roads and footpaths, while using them as guide lines from a distance of about a hundred yards. At dawn, I was about two miles from my first checkpoint, so I knew I would have no problems getting there that night. I went into a patch of forest nearby, where the fir trees were young and the lower branches began about twelve inches from the ground. The trees were planted in lines, and plough furrows had left hollows between them. I crawled along one of the furrows for a few yards and then, using a branch, I swept behind me to eliminate any telltale signs of my entry. When I had gone as far as I could into the trees, I wrapped my coat around me and curled up in a ball. The sun was rising, taking away the cold chill of dawn. The trees kept the wind from my body, and the close proximity of the branches and the thick bed of fir needles kept me fairly comfortable. I had walked about ten miles that night and now I was tired; I fell into a light sleep.

Move at night, sleep by day: that's the rule. It was cold at night, and moving kept me warm. The dark hid me from local eyes, but not from the infrared scopes of the searchers. I woke around lunchtime and crawled to the edge of the trees. I needed to empty my bowels as soon as possible to recover my Sinex capsule and the five pounds inside it. This proved easy enough; now I had some emergency money.

I watched the road and the countryside for signs of the enemy, but I saw nothing and assumed that their search was probably still concentrated closer to the escape point. I decided to move out of the trees and try to do some scavenging. I found an old plastic fertiliser bag and cut some holes in it; it would come in handy as a waterproof jacket if the weather turned bad. At the moment it was cold – there had been a ground frost that morning – but it hadn't rained; cold and dry was easy to handle, cold and wet was a killer.

As I moved into sight of the road I saw a pub down below me. I had money and there was an almost overwhelming temptation simply to walk in for lunch. I was hungry, but not desperately so. All the local people had been briefed about the exercise and asked not to help us in any way; if they saw us, they were supposed to report us. Fortunately for us though, many of the farmers preferred being in the Resistance to helping the Gestapo.

I sat in the trees and watched the pub for hours. There were no troops inside, nor, it appeared, any customers. I finally walked up to the back door and knocked. The landlord came out; his eyes betrayed the fact that he knew exactly who and what I was. 'Can I buy some matches and some food?' I asked. He raised his finger to his lips and walked back into the building. I was worried about him phoning exercise control and was preparing to leg it when he came back with two warm pies and two boxes of matches. I offered him the five-pound note, but he refused it. We parted company with hardly a word spoken.

It was only when I swallowed the first mouthful of pie that I realised how much my walk the previous night had taken out of me. I couldn't get it down quickly enough. In spite of all my good intentions to save the other one for later, it soon followed the first.

Now I had matches, a source of heat, but they would have to be used carefully, because smoke is always a dead giveaway, and I was very close to the contact point. The inactivity of the afternoon had chilled me to the bone, so I moved back into the trees and searched for some dry wood. Pine and hawthorn are both good burners and give off very little smoke; I found both and lit a small fire so I could warm myself for a while. The activity provided something to occupy my mind while I waited.

A little later I heard a helicopter in the distance: my first sign of the enemy. I doused the fire and moved to the edge of the woods. Below me, about a mile away, I could see a line of figures spreading out across the hills, moving from left to right in front of me. About thirty were visible, so it was a fair bet that there were more; some might even be on their right flank, about to come through my position very soon.

I crawled as far back into the trees as I could. It would take a deter-mined man with a lot of time to spare to find me in here. The biggest danger was dogs, who would be able to sniff me out, and indicate my whereabouts. A sweep is designed not only as a search, but also as a driving action that can panic a hunted man into running and exposing himself. It is far easier to spot something when it is moving than when it is at rest. I stayed still and shivered until it was dark.

When it was at last time to move, it was a relief to stretch my legs and warm up my body. The contact point was the junction of a track and a road. I arrived early and watched it from as far away as I possibly could. If the agent had been compromised, then the area would be a trap.

A set of headlights broke the darkness and a car pulled up and reversed onto the track. The headlights went out. I crept closer to the vehicle and again sat and watched. The man in the front was obviously waiting for something or somebody. I waited too. After a while, a figure appeared from my left and walked up to the car. It was one of the students, an RAF pilot. He spoke briefly to the man in the car and then ran off. Now I knew that the agent was genuine I approached myself, arriving beside the car at the same time as three others, who had also been watching from the shadows. The agent gave us a dry bread roll, a drink of tea and details of the new checkpoint to get to by the following night. It was a long way off, so I decided to cover as much distance as possible now, while the night was cold.

I was hungry, but the food I had managed to acquire stood me in good stead and I moved well. I didn't want to rest then – I would get cold, and I would sleep better the next day if I was tired. I walked for about four hours, until the laborious business of keeping away from the road became a little too much. I moved out of the fields and began to move along the side of a forestry block, just to the side of the road. I had gone just a few hundred yards when, about ten yards ahead of me, an engine started up. I hit the floor and flattened out. Hidden in the trees was an Army Land Rover. I was close enough to hear the men talking inside: they had started the engine to heat up the cab, and I'd been very lucky that they had chosen to do it just then. I skirted carefully around them.

Lesson learned: I kept well away from roadsides for the rest of the course.

LIVING OFF THE land in the UK in April is not easy. Edible plant life is scarce, and three weeks of training are not enough for you to be absolutely sure of what you should be looking for. Stealing and scavenging are the most effective methods of finding safe food, but they leave traces of where you have been. I searched around in empty barns and sheds and found the odd beet or potato. I also found a pair of scissors, which were very useful. It still hadn't rained, and my greatcoat was enough to keep me warm in the daytime. The next contact was due in the early hours of day three. When I got close, I wrapped myself up in a roll of polythene I found at the bottom of a field and tried to get some extra sleep.

I woke to the sound of voices and someone kicking the polythene I was hidden in. As I shifted, the voice said, 'Fucking hell, it's moving.' I thought I had been caught, but when I rolled out I saw Andy, Tony and Leslie looking down at me in surprise. We all had a good laugh and exchanged experiences – they hadn't found the cache they were looking for, so their detour had been a wasted journey. I accompanied them to the contact point, but then explained that I was happier by myself and, with no offence given and none taken, I went my own way again.

I hadn't found anything to spend my money on: the area was completely devoid of shops and pubs. Eating nettles and old roots boiled up in a tin can was not keeping me very healthy, so I decided to take a risk. As soon as it was dark, I walked about ten miles until I was off the map. I found a shop and spent £1.30 on chocolate and a meat pasty, and then I walked all the way back to where I should be. The food helped enormously, and I made the chocolate last all day.

The next night would be the last of the exercise. In spite of eating my illicit snacks, I was becoming worn out by the distances travelled, poor sleep and the cold. Contact was scheduled for 1500 hours, when I knew we would be captured, so I had only one more night to get through.

At about two in the morning I was walking past some farm buildings when the yard lights suddenly came on. I ducked down behind a wall and watched as an unshaven young man in an old brown trenchcoat came out of the back door carrying a torch. He went into a barn and then re-emerged, quietly cursing under his breath. 'Got a problem?' I asked from the shadows. He looked across at me and asked if I was one of the runaways from the Army. I confirmed his suspicion and asked again what the problem was. He said his barn lights had failed, and he had three ewes trying to drop their lambs. One of them was stuck, and he would have to get his wife up to help. 'I'll help,' I said. 'Leave your wife to sleep.' We spent the next hour or so delivering the three lambs – all I did was hold the torch, but it was still quite an experience. Once we'd finished, the farmer asked me into the house. After four days on the run, the heat and smell of the kitchen hit me like an orgasm. It was luxury.

I was covered in mud, filthy and smelly, and I offered to take my boots off. 'Don't worry about that,' the farmer said, and he went to wake his wife. The grateful couple gave me a hot breakfast of bacon, eggs, tomatoes, sausage, toast and coffee. It was four o'clock in the morning and it was exactly what I needed – the following day I was going to be interrogated, and this meal would give me a lot of extra strength. The farmer offered to take me to my next checkpoint in his car, but I declined. I knew that if I got there early I would just have to sit around getting cold.

THE FINAL CONTACT point was next to a small village church. I found it early in the morning and hid in some trees nearby. After a few hours, a light rain began to fall and, in spite of the food I had eaten, I began to shiver violently: I needed to find shelter somewhere pretty quickly. I'd spotted a farm not far away, with a small outbuilding in the centre of a field. It offered no hidden escape route, but it had a good view of the surrounding area. As I walked through the doorway I was confronted by a huge grey goose sitting on a nest filled with eggs. She raised her head and thrust it forward, hissing at me. She was a big girl, and had every right to be angry. I knew that if she decided to have a go at me there would be one hell of a racket. On the other hand, she would deter anyone else from coming in. I edged along the wall while she watched me, hissing a warning every now and then. I sat down on some straw in the corner, about ten feet away from her, and kept still.

She did not relax once during the next four hours: every time I moved, she scolded me. I quite enjoyed watching her – it gave me something to do, and it was nice to have someone to talk to, even if it was just a large grey goose.

As this was the final contact point, I hid my map inside the rim of my coat together with the £3.70 I had left. I said my goodbyes to Mother Goose when I heard a vehicle pull up near the church. Everyone on the course turned up over the next few hours. We were loaded onto a truck and told that the exercise was over – but of course, it wasn't: just five minutes later the truck was ambushed by the Gordon Highlanders and we were captured.

NOW WE WERE prisoners. We were taken into a field and laid face down in the mud until an intelligence officer had us delivered to him for questioning. He sat behind a desk in a tent and went through the routine of asking me my name, rank, number and date of birth. These were all questions I was allowed to answer. Any other question had to be responded to with the phrase 'I can't answer that question'. I was not to nod, shake my head or sign any piece of paper. If I did any of these things, even once, I would fail instantly.

This was tactical questioning by normal infantry intelligence units. There was no subtleness about their methods, and they were easy to resist. If we looked too cold lying on the ground, the guards would run us around with our hands over our heads and make us do press-ups. It didn't make much difference to me: I shivered endlessly and waited for the day to draw to a close. I estimated the time at about 1500 hours. Only one day to go and I would be in the SAS.

I was blindfolded and taken to a helicopter. I felt it take off, and images of Vietnam war movies flashed through my head. Would we be thrown out only two feet off the ground while the helicopter hovered? It was important to remember that this was still an exercise: people weren't supposed to die on it. After a short flight, I felt the aircraft begin to descend, then, once on the ground, I was led, still blindfolded, across a field and into a building. I was spun around several times in order to disorientate me even further.

My blindfold was removed and I found myself standing alone in a small green room. In front of me were two spotlessly clean men wearing green trousers and shirts. They sported no insignia or other signs of rank. 'I am a doctor,' one of them said, 'and I want you to understand that this is not part of the exercise. It is my job to ensure that you are not sick and that you are fit to continue. Are you fit to continue?' I didn't make a sound and he repeated the question. 'I can't answer that question,' I replied. He sighed – this obviously happened all the time – and told me that he would assume that I was fit to continue.

The blindfold went back on and I was rushed to another room, colliding frequently with walls and doors. Again the blindfold came off and I was standing in front of yet another desk. A small man in glasses looked up at me. Himmler, I thought. 'Take all your clothes off,' he said. 'ALL YOUR CLOTHES!' The room was cold and as I peeled off the layers of dirty rags he turned up his nose and sneered. When I got down to my T-shirt his face changed, and his eyes showed some interest. Written in large blue letters across the front of the shirt were the words 'Raving Rob, the Roving Ringpiece'. I had had the shirt made for a laugh when I was with Vigilant Platoon, and had thought it would give the interrogators something to focus on. It was also quite funny – at least, I thought so.

My clothes were taken away and I stood naked in front of Himmler while he looked me up and down and took notes. 'Turn around,' he said. 'Bend over.' I did as I was told and made a point of not trying to cover my genitalia. It would show a weakness that they could use against me later, perhaps with a woman. When they had finished, I was given a clean, thin, short-sleeved shirt and a pair of lightweight trousers. I was blindfolded again and the guards marched me out. As I moved along the corridor, I became aware of a loud hissing noise. A door opened, and the noise swamped all other sounds in the building: it was white noise – it prevented anyone from hearing anything, except words spoken close to the ear.

I was made to sit down with my hands on top of my head. My legs were extended straight out in front of me so that I was sitting in a perfect L. My elbows were wrenched back behind my ears and I was left alone in the dark, hearing and seeing nothing. Time was now a matter of great importance. I knew that I had to hold out for twenty-four hours, which meant I needed to retain some perception of time so that I could estimate how much longer I had to suffer before the ordeal would be over.

I started to count up to one thousand: I estimated that each time I completed a count, fifteen minutes would have passed. My back and shoulders were beginning to ache, particularly my right shoulder. The old rugby injury that had resulted in a dislocated fracture prevented it from going back as far as the left. The guards thought I was relaxing my arm and continually wrenched it back, causing me considerable pain, but there was nothing I could do about it, so I bore it in silence.

After what I estimated to be twenty minutes I was taken to my first interrogation, where I was confronted by an ugly little round-faced man with a bald head and fat cheeks. For about fifteen minutes he tried to get me to say something other than the words allowed. When I answered 'I can't answer that question' he stared at me in what he thought was an intimidating manner and shouted, 'You mean you won't, not you can't. Don't you?' As he shouted the word 'won't', his cheeks puffed up like those of a bloated pig, and I began to laugh. I covered this up by pretending to cough, but I had to cough an awful lot.

A few minutes later he decided that he had given me his best shot. The guards blindfolded me and took me back to the holding area with the white noise. This time I was stood facing the wall with my legs and arms outstretched in the classic police search position; I had to hold myself up by my fingertips. Although it was uncomfortable, I found it preferable to having my shoulder pulled back in the sitting position. I continued to count the seconds and add up the time. This time the room was just cold enough to be draining and uncomfortable, but not cold enough to make me shiver. This was all part of the wearing-down process.

My next interrogator fell into my trap and started to talk about the T-shirt I was wearing. He accused me of being homosexual, which didn't bother me at all, so he changed tack and insulted my family. He asked if my mother was a whore and whether I even knew who my father was, but to no effect. I was a paratrooper, and I had been insulted by experts. You can't crack me, I thought, I'm a rubber duck.

Back to the cold-box again; I was actually starting to look forward to being questioned. The stress positions were starting to wear me down, especially the sitting one. Every time a guard pulled my shoulder back it racked me with pain – it felt as if my arm was being pulled from its socket. I had tears running down my face and out from under the blindfold. I had to stop the pain somehow, so I raised my arm and indicated in sign language that I wanted a piss. The guard took me to the toilet and I was allowed to urinate blindfolded. Though brief, it gave me the respite I needed, and when I returned to the room I was back onto fingertips again.

After about eight hours I was questioned again, and this time the interrogator took a different approach. He tried to ascertain which regiment I was from. Someone had noted that my boot laces were made of parachute cord, so he sang the praises of paratroopers to see whether my face would betray any signs of pride. I remained deadpan until he mentioned the Royal Green Jackets, then gave a little smile, stopping it almost immediately. He took the bait and spent the next ten minutes pushing the Green Jackets.

I estimated that my next period of questioning started after about twelve hours. This was a tough one. Two policemen in full uniform accused me of breaking into a house and stealing the scissors. For a second or two they really had me going. Their questions were justified to some extent, although I had actually stolen the scissors from a shed. Now I was getting tired, and had to force myself to calm down and think carefully. They could see that they had hit a nerve and started to ask their questions faster and faster. I clammed up, trying to think clearly. I was confused, and couldn't work out whether this was real or a part of the exercise.

'Who's in charge here?' asked one of the policemen. That was it: the one question too many. To gain access to this establishment these guys must have known who was in charge, so now it was clear to me that they were part of the 'game'. 'I can't answer that question,' I said, and they realised they had missed their chance.

The stress positions became agonising and it was getting increasingly hard to take my mind off the pain by counting, so now I started to recite nursery rhymes under my breath. I estimated how many it probably took to get through five minutes and said them over and over again. My right shoulder felt like it was falling off. I had started grunting in pain every time the guards touched it; I also let it hang down and rubbed it whenever I had to change position. I began to pray that someone out there in the dark would notice that I was in pain.

My memory of the rest of the questioning sessions is not so good. I recall being naked and bent over while all and sundry laughed at me. I also remember being offered food and drink, but I had to say I wanted it in order to get it. I was tired: I had had no sleep for two days and I was allowed no respite. When I went into the next session I estimated I'd done eighteen hours. I was almost asleep on my feet.

This time the man behind the desk was sitting in shadow, and the light was turned down. He left me standing and, in a soft Canadian accent, enquired after my health. I gave the standard replies, but I knew that my speech was slow and slurred. After about ten minutes I was swaying on my feet. The questioner told the guard to get a chair and I sat down. 'What is your name? What is your rank? What is your number? What is your date of birth?' In his soft, repetitive, toneless voice he repeated the same four questions, over and over again. He kept this up for a long, long time. My head sank lower and lower onto my chest. I was almost snoring, but the questions kept on coming and I kept on answering. His voice became deeper and deeper and the questions came more and more slowly. 'You're feeling tired, aren't you?' he whispered.

My head shot up straight. '24303195 Private Horsfall. I CAN'T ANSWER THAT QUESTION.' He gave up. He had tried to hypnotise me and he had failed. Six hours to go, I thought as they took me out. Only five minutes later I was taken for questioning again, only this time my blindfold was taken off in the corridor.

Neil, the SAS instructor, was waiting with the training-wing major. 'OK, Horsfall,' the major said, 'the exercise is over. You know who I am and you know Neil. If you look, you will see we are wearing white armbands. The exercise is over. Do you understand?' 'I can't answer that question,' I replied. They smiled and walked me into the exercise area to convince me that it was over. I was paranoid by now. I had only a few hours to go: the bastards weren't going to catch me out. I looked at Neil's watch and then at the OC's watch: 1600 hours. It was true. I had underestimated my time and the twenty-four hours was already up.

I GOT MY debrief straight away. I was criticised for splitting up with Andy, but the important point was that I had passed. All the tiredness of the past two days was swept away in a wave of euphoria. I had passed combat survival.

Kevin had failed interrogation. His ego would not allow him to be insulted by anyone; he had lost his temper and argued. One of the Ruperts also failed: he was found with a sleeping bag and rations that were being delivered daily by someone in a car. So now we were left with Chris, Tony, Leslie, Andy, Ray, Paul, the one remaining officer, and me: seven out of fifty-seven, and one Rupert.

CHAPTER 12

Colditz

TWO WEEKS LATER I reported to B Squadron Sergeant-Major (SSM), who asked what troop I would like to be in. There were four choices: Mountain, Air, Mobility or Boat. Given my love of wild places, I didn't hesitate: it was Mountain troop for me.

There was no ceremony to mark the fact that I had passed selection. I was told to go to the stores and hand in my number-two dress so that wings could be sewn onto the sleeve, and to pick up an SAS beret. That was it – no fuss, no big deal.

Now that I was truly in B Squadron, I paid some attention to the red spot on my leg, which had been there since the end of jungle training and had now grown to the size of a two-pence piece and was ulcerating in the centre. When I showed it to the Medical Officer (MO), he sent me to the local hospital for tests, which revealed that I had a tropical disease called leishmaniasis. The infection is carried by the sand-fly, a tiny insect that is small enough to penetrate the mesh of a mosquito net. The disease itself is caused by a microscopic, two-celled organism that eats away at the flesh until a big hole appears. It was very rare at the time – only a handful of people from the UK had ever caught it. There were two types of infection: the first would eventually clear up on its own; the second would apparently clear up, but would then return years later and break down all the mucous membranes in the body, leaving the nose, mouth, eyes, anus and penis in bits. It turned out that I had the second type: not a nice prospect at all.

I wasn't the only one to have been bitten: Keith had the same symptoms, but on his hand. We were sent to the Cambridge Military Hospital in Aldershot for treatment, which involved having an intravenous injection of Pentostam, or antimony, a heavy metal drug, every day. Antimony cured the disease, but it was also very poisonous to the body, especially to the heart muscle, so I had to have my heart checked on an ECG monitor every other day. I wasn't allowed to go anywhere; bed rest was the order of the day. Thank heavens I had Keith to talk to, or I would have gone completely barmy.

As we were both new in the Regiment, we signed ourselves into hospital as troopers, the lowest SAS rank. To the rest of the Army, who had, at that stage, never heard of the SAS, we were privates, and were treated as such. I later discovered that we should have given ourselves the rank of sergeant in order to be treated with some respect. Too late: every lance-corporal nurse and her pet hamster started to boss us around. After the relaxed discipline of Hereford, this was unbearable: it was turning into a prison-camp farce, so I complained to the Colonel Matron about my treatment. This shocked the ward rigid: privates did not simply knock on the colonel's door and complain. But as far as I was concerned, SAS soldiers did – and after that, I was allowed to take walks into town, provided I rested after the injection and got in at the correct times. Life became just bearable.

After a month in Colditz, I was returned to Hereford, but with a downgraded status, as I was still non-operational. I was sent to learn my personal skill: as an SAS paramedic.

THE SAS MEDICAL course was intensive: four weeks of classroom work, with every evening and weekend spent studying for the end-of-course exam. After this, the successful student would spend four more weeks working in the casualty department of a busy city hospital. Fail, and you could be on your way home, RTU'd. Crammed into these eight weeks were classes on anatomy and physiology, trauma medicine, tropical medicine, midwifery, dentistry, paediatrics and psychology – none of them in any great depth, but enough to be able to help someone in a crisis. I enjoyed the course; I had always enjoyed first-aid – and not just because it got me into football matches for free – and this took it to levels I had never dreamed of. I came top of the course with a 97 per cent pass mark.

I was sent to Frenchay Hospital in Bristol with Ron, a trooper from A Squadron. I had hoped that he would show me the ropes and that we would go for a beer together in the evenings, but it turned out that he wanted very little to do with me; his one desire was to cruise through the four weeks and go home. I, on the other hand, was ambitious: I wanted to put people back together, to learn more. I wanted to be the very best medic in the SAS. However, the hospital staff had different ideas. We stood around for hours waiting for something to happen; occasionally we would be allowed to stitch someone's skin back together. I became bored and started to complain, asking to be more involved, although in all fairness to the hospital authorities I was undeniably an unskilled amateur. I began trailing round different departments, looking for things to do. I eventually found a haven in the plaster room, where I could help mould plaster casts onto people's injured limbs.

On one occasion a serious motorcycle casualty was being examined by the thoracic registrar. He had just decided to send his patient down to the ward for the night when I reminded him that the X-rays of the patient's chest had been taken while he was flat on his back. The registrar, who was a very senior man, looked at me with something akin to anger, then, realising that now I had brought the matter up he couldn't ignore it, ordered more X-rays, this time with the poor victim sitting up. These revealed a large quantity of blood filling one of the patient's lungs, which had not shown up on the earlier pictures. A chest drain had to be put in immediately: it probably saved his life.

Instead of receiving a pat on the back, I was treated with contempt: the doctor was embarrassed by his error and hated me for being right. His reaction reminded me of the bomb incident in Northern Ireland a year or two earlier. However, he would have been a lot more embarrassed if the poor man had died in the night.

The leishmaniasis came back and I was returned to hospital for further treatment. This time the scar was weeping smelly pus and the dressing had to be changed at regular intervals. I went back on the injections. With the benefit of my medical course, I realised that the regular dressing changes were being forgotten, so I started going into the dressing room alone, cleaning and dressing the wound five or six times a day. It now healed very rapidly and once again I returned to Hereford.

Major Jerry from training-wing was waiting to see me. He had my hospital report, which was appalling. It stated that I had shown no interest in the subject at all and that I had made no effort to work with the staff. I told my side of the story, and he said he would look into the matter. I hoped that Ron, my partner on the secondment, would back me up and put them right, but what I had failed to realise was that my behaviour had not been in the best traditions of the Diplomatic Corps. Tact, good manners and diplomacy had been removed from my behavioural armoury by the Parachute Regiment. The SAS had not yet had time to settle me down and mould me into a more responsible adult.

Working in a hospital with professional men and women required the maturity to know when to shut up and smile. Although I thought I had been on my best behaviour, and technically I had done nothing wrong, I had pissed enough people off for them to lie about me in the report. What they should have said, in all honesty, was something to the effect of: 'This rude, abrupt and direct young man annoyed everyone from the time he arrived until the time he left. We didn't like him so we didn't pay much attention to his work. Don't send him back.' I had needed a guide and mentor. Unfortunately Ron hadn't thought this was a job for him – or perhaps I just wouldn't listen.

In spite of the doctor's orders, I started training hard. In a very short time I was running a good distance every day. I should have been downgraded for six months, but with only three months gone I asked the MO to get me upgraded. He talked to the doctors in Aldershot and they agreed.

On 20 December 1979 I reported to the second-in-command that I was fit again. He asked whether I was keen to get back to B Squadron in Northern Ireland. I, of course, said yes, thinking that I would be going in a few days, once Christmas was over. No such luck. I was on the plane to Ireland the following day.

I WAS MET at Belfast Airport by Mac, who took me to a plain white van inside the airport perimeter. Once I had thrown all my gear in the back, Mac opened a small zip-up bag on the front seat and handed me a clip-on holster and a 9mm Browning automatic pistol. I loaded the thirteen-round magazine into the pistol and fed a round into the chamber. The weapon was now cocked. I had only to release the safety and pull the trigger to fire it.

Also inside the bag was an Ingram 9mm machine-pistol. This very small submachine-gun could empty its thirty-round magazine in less than three seconds. Lying next to the Ingram were some spare magazines and two hand-grenades. 'If we drive into a PIRA roadblock, empty the Ingram through the windscreen at the nearest terrorist and throw the grenades,' Mac said. 'If you're still alive after that and the vehicle isn't moving, get out and follow me.' These were my only orders for the move to Portadown.

As we sped down the motorway, I realised that, in spite of my previous tours, this was the very first time I had driven around the country for any distance in a civilian vehicle. The freedom was quite bewildering. I had to come to terms with the knowledge that Northern Ireland was not all a war zone; it was an integral part of the United Kingdom and most people were perfectly ordinary, just trying to get on with their everyday lives. My previous visits had been to bad trouble spots, right in the centre of enemy territory. This was the real Ireland: rolling green hills, slow, meandering rivers that ran into huge lakes, pubs full of people having a beer, and familiar shops.

Mac stopped the van in Portadown and we walked up to the entrance of Woolworths. At the door, two RUC officers stopped us. We flashed our ID cards and stood still while they searched us both. They ignored the pistols hidden under our jackets. By searching us, they helped prevent us from being identified as different from the rest of the people waiting to enter the shop.

It was a strange feeling walking the streets in plain clothes with a gun on my hip. I didn't feel powerful, I felt vulnerable. Once again I was joining a tour late, and I hadn't done any build-up training. I was frightened of making a mistake.

When we got to the camp in Portadown, it was nothing like anywhere I had stayed before. We had two men to a room, our own bar, and recreation facilities: there were squash courts and a gym to train in. There were two troops here in Portadown: Mobility and Mountain; Boat and Air were in Londonderry.

It was almost Christmas Eve, so it wasn't really a time for action. There were no operations taking place, so a good proportion of the squadron were spending all their time in the bar – only half the men were supposed to drink on any particular day, but the rule was apparently being ignored for the festive season. While I was being briefed by Tom, one of my corporals, the whole of 8 Troop seemed to be intent on their mission of getting blind drunk until New Year. For the next week I did nothing except watch people stagger around pissed. Some would drink from one day right through to the next; the only sleep they had was propped up against the bar.

I sat listening and watching what was going on. I didn't get drunk – I was too scared of getting into trouble. I didn't like violent drunks, and there were one or two here looking for an excuse: as the new boy, I would be an easy target. I noticed that the conversation seemed to revolve almost exclusively around people who weren't present, and very little of what was being said about them was complimentary. None of the names meant anything to me, but if my ears were to be believed, the Regiment I had fought so hard to get into was full of incompetents who couldn't do their jobs – at least according to this barful of inebriated tough guys. Tom, the corporal who had taken me under his wing, was a prime candidate for discussion – until he walked into the room. When he did, someone else became the whipping-boy.

As the week passed, I grew bored. I had never been one to enjoy being drunk just for the sake of it: too much booze made me feel sick, and there was nothing fun about vomiting, although this didn't stop a lot of the squadron from partaking of the pleasure.

Once Christmas and New Year were truly over, I settled down to some real work. In 9 Troop I was taught pistol work: draw-and-shoot, rolls, turns, car drills, anti-ambush drills, and so on. Life took on a new purpose and I began to enjoy myself. But I couldn't help picking up on the animosity between the troops: all I ever heard now was people from 8 Troop running down individuals in 9 Troop – and one of the people doing the talking was actually from 9 Troop himself. I hadn't yet made any close friends, and I was on six months' probation, so I kept quiet. The loyalty to one another that I had hoped to find within the SAS didn't appear to exist. Indeed, I was soon to discover that the Regiment has no esprit de corps: instead, it's just a group of insecure individuals drawn from many different organisations in the Armed Forces. There's no bonding process to hold them together after selection, no infantry-style buddy-buddy system that could unite friends and enemies into a brotherhood such as the one that I had experienced in the Paras.

MY FIRST OPERATION with 9 Troop was to carry out a close target reconnaissance (CTR) on the house of an IRA member. We were taken out and dropped from the side door of a moving vehicle onto the grass verge. Leading us was a full corporal named Peter. We moved stealthily across the fields and hedgerows until we came in sight of the house, an isolated farm building in the middle of nowhere.

As we climbed gates we held them still so that they didn't rattle. All orders were given with hand signals. Each of us knew our tasks, so by the time we were finally ten yards from the front door, hidden in some bushes, not a word had been spoken. We hadn't made a sound – even the farmyard dogs hadn't noticed us.

It was our job to record any activity during the hours of darkness, and to make a plan of the farm. Intelligence sources had told us that a wanted terrorist might visit the property, and if he did, we were to 'arrest' him. The four of us lay still all night, watching the house. An hour before dawn, with nothing to report, we moved out and trekked back to our pick-up point (PUP) to return to camp. The job had gone well. Peter, who was a former Para, had led the patrol with a high degree of professionalism. The next night we would have to do it again – but maybe this time we'd have more luck.

There were two main types of operation in Northern Ireland: those that relied on good, hard information, and those that were speculative. If we were working on hard intelligence, then PIRA members were going to get caught or killed. This information usually came directly from sources inside the organisation: most IRA deaths have occurred as a result of their own people giving away their friends to save their own skins. Other ops, based on intelligence reports, were carried out on a speculative basis. These formed the greater part of our work, and were undertaken in the hope that we might get lucky.

The next day Peter was called away, so the patrol was taken out by a sergeant from 8 Troop. This man was a legend within the SAS, renowned worldwide for his bravery, and I felt privileged to be following him. That night we dismounted from the moving vehicle and moved in towards the target. When we were about three hundred yards from the farm, our leader told us to stay where we were while he went to take a look. I waited to be impressed as he walked straight up the road to the farm. When he got to the front gate two or three dogs began to bark furiously. The lights came on and a man emerged from the door and looked around a bit before going back inside. Our glorious leader, who had simply lain down where he was and waited, got up and walked back down the road to where we were. 'Well, there's nothing going on up there,' he said. 'We might as well go back.' He arranged for an early pick-up on the grounds that the patrol had been compromised by the enemy. I was astounded. Why had he done this?

I spoke to Tom about it the following day. 'Perhaps he didn't like getting the job because Peter was supposed to do it,' was his only guess. 'Keep your mouth shut, though,' he advised. 'It does no good to say anything about the Storm Vets.'

The Storm Vets were veterans of Oman, and many of them believed that if a man hadn't been there with them, he wasn't worth talking to. They looked after each other, even when their friends were in the wrong. This I understood. What I couldn't understand was why other soldiers like me, who had been shot at on the streets of Ireland, counted for so little. Perhaps IRA bullets weren't as dangerous as the Storm bullets.

When you work in small groups, fire-power is vital – lots of it. I learned a great deal about all the different weapons available to me and how to use them proficiently.

If we ran into the enemy, our first option was, of course, to get away. The second was to fire as much ammunition as possible in the minimum amount of time, to make the enemy get his head down and give us a better opportunity to make our escape.

I trained with my Browning 9mm every day, sometimes firing as many as four hundred rounds in one session. I had calluses on my right thumb from pulling the safety catch on and off hundreds of times. I liked to wear the Browning in a shoulder holster, as it made the pistol more accessible when I was sitting in a car.

The Ingram was a close-range weapon, great for shock effect. It fired so fast that at close range a man could get the full thirty rounds in his face. The size made it ideal for a car bag, hidden on the floor by the feet.

The M-16 Armalite was a popular rifle; easy to carry, with a thirty-round magazine, it extended effective fire-power up to three hundred yards. We used these on green ops, where uniform was worn and distance was an important factor: in ambushes and observation posts, for example.

Hand-grenades and smoke were always useful in close-quarter battle. If the enemy couldn't see you, he had less chance of hitting you.

Our cars were normal saloons and the only special thing about them was the communications – but that was pretty special because we could talk constantly to headquarters and other unit cars without a sound being heard outside the vehicle.

I learned how to follow suspect vehicles, passing the tail over at prearranged points to other cars and then picking it up later. This often involved some very hairy driving skills, which I did not have. I would sit in the passenger seat gripping the sides as the driver took bends at phenomenal speeds.

In March 1980 the whole squadron returned home. Our next task was to take over as the counter-terrorist team for six months.

CHAPTER 13

Pagoda

THERE WAS NO leave when we got home. We were going to spend most of our time in Hereford from now on and go home every night, so who needed leave?

Team training started almost immediately, run by the squadron handing over to us, G Squadron. This was always the case because counter-terrorist equipment was constantly being improved and even if men had done the job before, it was likely that drills and equipment had changed dramatically in the short time between tours.

The squadron was broken into two teams: 6 and 7 Troops were the red team, 8 and 9 Troops the blue team, and each team was further divided into two, assault and sniper. Although everyone was trained as an assault team member, only half were trained as snipers as well.

I had always loved shooting at long range and offered myself as a sniper. I talked up my time on team competitions and all the shoots I had done at Bisley, the Army small-arms ranges near Pirbright. After a considerable amount of waffle, I got the job and the nickname Bisley Bob, later shortened to just plain Bisley.

The next four weeks were spent practising assaults on buildings, buses, ships and aircraft. I spent long days and nights firing my three sniper rifles at stationary and moving targets. My L49 was the standard British Army sniper rifle, accurate up to a thousand yards in the right hands. The other two were Tikka Finlander hunting rifles, one with a day-scope and the other with a night-scope. These were good only up to three hundred yards. The L49 fired a 7.62mm NATO ball-round, which was standard-issue ammunition. It had great range and could penetrate thick glass, wood and brick. The Tikka fired 5.56mm hollow-point. Hollow-point was the best anti-terrorist ammo: when a round hit a man's head, it flattened itself, releasing all its energy into the point of impact. This created a massive entry wound but no exit wound – the bullet never came out. Fired at the skull, it had almost a hundred per cent kill rate, and the zero penetration of the hollow-point prevented rounds going through terrorists and hitting hostages behind. It also stopped a wounded man from pulling the trigger as he died (with his head turned inside out, a terrorist hit with a hollow-point died, full stop).

IN APRIL WE officially took over from G Squadron and became the Pagoda team, the code word for the counter-terrorist team. We settled into a weekly routine in the killing house, a series of indoor ranges with ricochet-proof walls. Here we would practise with our MP-5 Heckler and Koch submachine-guns (SMGs) and our 9mm Browning pistols. Four hundred rounds per man per day was not unusual.

The MP-5 is the best SMG in the world. It fires from a locked-bolt position, using a delayed blow-back action, which reduces the recoil and weight transfer as the weapon fires. Loaded with a thirty-round magazine, it weighs only 6.5 pounds. With training, a man can fire a three-round burst into a four-inch circle at five yards without aiming through the sights.

One drill was to burst into a room where a live hostage was sitting in a chair. He would be surrounded by targets, each with a four-inch circle on its face. As we entered the room, we would fire a short burst at each target and rescue the hostage. The team leader would not be happy unless all the fired rounds were inside the circles.

The sniper team spent full days on the ranges, using all our sniper weapons. When we arrived, we would fire one round from each combat-ready weapon. If we had to shoot someone for real the following day, the first shot was the only one that would count. We would then spend the day firing at different ranges and at targets moving at different speeds. With practise, we could group our shots into a one-inch-diameter circle at one hundred yards and hit a man in the head at two hundred yards when he was running. If he was standing still, we could hit him somewhere in the body at six hundred yards. Hitting a target is not just a case of pointing a weapon and pulling the trigger, no matter what it looks like in the movies: the skills involved take endless hours of practise, and you're only ever as good as your last day's training.

At least once a week we would attack different types of target using live hostages, CS gas and blank ammunition. We each took our turn at being a hostage, which wasn't any joke. CS gas in confined spaces is a real body blow; it's no fun coughing, weeping and choking for ten or twenty minutes after being gassed.

MANY OF OUR weekends were devoted to training with the police. An exercise would begin with the team members at home. We all wore bleepers, so we could be alerted by a series of numbers indicating an exercise call-out. Having arrived in camp, we would prepare the six white Range Rovers and six Transit vans that carried all our primary equipment, and then drive as quickly as we could to the exercise area, which could be anywhere in the UK. We drove in convoy, the lead vehicle in constant contact with all the vehicles behind. When the opposite carriageway was traffic-free, the message on the radio would be 'Road clear', then all the following vehicles would overtake any intervening traffic. When a car appeared coming towards the lead vehicle, the message would be 'Traffic' and the followers would all pull over to the correct side of the road and wait for the clear signal again. Even with blue lights flashing and sirens blaring, it scared the hell out of ordinary drivers when they were overtaken by six Range Rovers round a blind bend.

Once at the incident site, the squadron commander would liaise with the police. When the situation was deemed to have broken down, we would attack the target and rescue the hostages. We got to try out various different methods of entering and assaulting buildings, and different targets.

We would sleep with all our equipment, standing by day and night for any emergency. On Sunday we would go back to camp and clean and prepare everything for a call-out. Monday we would start all over again. All this became just routine.

Being in Hereford for a long period of time gave me a chance to develop my relationship with Heather. She was the best thing that had ever happened to me. She cared about everyone, and saw right through my tough-guy exterior. If I was putting someone down for being weak or inadequate, she would remind me of my own weaknesses, and then build me back up by telling me that not everyone could be like me – thank God for that small mercy. She never lied about anything important: her sense of honesty was profound. She wasn't timid, though: if she thought I was wrong, she told me so, and more often than not, especially where my behaviour was concerned, she was right.

Heather gave me everything she had, emotionally; she was soft, warm and caring, and for the first time in my life I felt that someone loved me unquestioningly, and in return, I began to feel secure about myself. I relaxed, and stopped viewing every other male on the planet as an aggressor. I became less aggressive myself to the world at large. If I went into a pub, I didn't glare at men who got too close to me, or insist on standing with my back to the wall. Being single had been a lonely experience that had involved going from one place to another and from one girlfriend to another. All that now changed: for the first time in six years I had a home to go to and a beautiful woman there waiting for me.

We had nothing. I was still on private's pay; she was on income support. There was a three-piece suite, two beds, a cooker, and a table and three chairs. It took us two months to save up for curtains. 'The SAS comes first,' I told her. 'We'll never get married.' 'Yes,' she would say, 'but if we ever did . . .'

ON WEDNESDAY, 30 April 1980, the Pagoda team was waiting to go to Scotland to take part in another exercise with the police. The vehicles were ready, and we were sitting around drinking tea in the blue team's waiting area. It was going to be a long drive to Edinburgh, and we wouldn't be back until Friday.

At 1120 hours, on BBC Radio, Margaret Thatcher, the British Prime Minister, was heard to say, 'I almost lay awake at night thinking, what would I do if we had fifty [hostages] taken at our embassy?' She was referring to the continuing problems encountered by United States President Jimmy Carter in Tehran: all the American embassy staff had been taken hostage by members of an Islamic fundamentalist organisation, supported by the new revolutionary government of Iran. A rescue mission had been mounted by the USA and had failed, resulting in the deaths of many American soldiers and the severe embarrassment of the US government.

As she spoke, just two miles away from BBC Broadcasting House three Arab terrorists were walking from their temporary headquarters at Lexham Gardens, Earl's Court, to the Iranian Embassy at 16 Princes Gate, one of London's most fashionable terraces. Police Constable Trevor Lock, a tall, well-built man aged forty-one, was midway through his shift guarding the front door of the embassy. He was a long-serving member of the Diplomatic Protection Group (DPG), and was armed with a .38 Smith and Wesson police revolver that contained only six rounds of ammunition. Inside were Sim Harris, a long-haired, bespectacled BBC sound recordist, and Chris Cramer, a BBC TV news field producer, who were chasing up delayed visas for a future visit to Iran.

As DJ Jimmy Young played the 'The Other Side Of Me' for the Prime Minister, the three young Arabs raced from a red car and fired several shots through the glass-fronted doors of the embassy building. Splinters of glass exploded into Trevor Lock's face, and before he could react he was forced, bloody-faced and shocked, through the doors and into the building, an Uzi submachine-gun thrust into his chest. In the entrance hall, the original three Arabs were joined by three more, who had apparently been waiting on some pretext inside.

PC Lock and the BBC men were placed in a small upstairs room with embassy chauffeur Ron Morris. With their hands held above their heads, they watched and listened to the increasing commotion in the building. The gunmen were shouting for Ali Afrooz, who was Ayatollah Khomeini's chargé d'affaires in London. They finally found him and threw him in with the British hostages. He had a nasty gash on his face and a black eye. The gunmen apologised constantly to the British prisoners, saying again and again that their problem was not with any non-Iranians.

Back in Hereford, as we were waiting to leave for Scotland, word of the takeover at the embassy came through. Big Bob smiled coldly. 'My Tikka is ready,' he said, closing one eye and squeezing an imaginary trigger. At about midday, Major Jerry called us into the tearoom for a briefing. The exercise was off.

Now I saw Major Jerry at his best, with something to get his teeth into. He breathed confidence and enthusiasm into the rest of us. By the time he had finished talking, I knew why he was in command of a squadron. We were to wait in Hereford to see how things developed. In the meantime we could go home and grab anything we might need for a prolonged period away, like extra shaving kit or money.

I went back to Heather's flat and gathered some bits and pieces. She would be expecting me back in a couple of days, so I needed to let her know something about what was happening. Because she wasn't my wife, if anything went wrong the Army wouldn't contact her. I left a note on the mantelpiece telling her that I would be away for longer than I thought. If she needed any more information she should watch the TV.

Back in camp, information started to come in via the television and radio. In cases like this, the media, with all their resources, can often find things out faster than the intelligence services. We double-checked all our equipment and waited, all of us secretly hoping beyond hope that this would really be it and that we would be called in. Such an incident had never happened before in the UK; the only previous comparable situation was London's Balcombe Street siege, and in that case, the IRA terrorists surrendered when they were told that the SAS were on the job. The Regiment had also assisted and advised at Mogadishu, in Ethiopia, when a Lufthansa jet had been hijacked, but our team had not actually been used in the operation.

By 1215 hours all traffic through Princes Gate had been diverted, a whole area, covering one square mile, had been cordoned off, and a growing army of press photographers and sightseers had begun to gather.

Deputy Assistant Commissioner John Dellow took charge of the police operation, backed up by Commander Peter Duffy, head of the Metropolitan Police Anti-Terrorist Unit. By 1700 hours, Deputy Assistant Commissioner Peter Neivens was telling reporters that he believed that there were as many as twenty people in the embassy, with perhaps three gunmen. In fact there were twenty-five hostages and six gunmen.

Information was coming in every minute, with constant updates on the TV. The terrorists were anti-Khomeini, and more information about Trevor Lock and the other British hostages was coming to light. The gunmen were now demanding the release of political prisoners in Tehran.

We saw the British hostages as a bonus – they increased our chances of being sent in; if all the hostages had been Iranians on Iranian sovereign territory, the possibility of our involvement would have been remote.

By 1800 hours the military had still not received a request to become involved, but the head-shed (senior officers in HQ) decided that we should move the unit nearer to London.

We drove out of Hereford in dribs and drabs, leaving town by different routes, with orders to get together in the cookhouse at Beaconsfield when we arrived. Tom, Mac, Nick and I loaded ourselves into our white Transit and set off via Gloucester to the M40. We arrived at about 2300 hours, and made our way to the rendezvous.

At about midnight we moved on to Regent's Park Barracks and got our heads down for the night. By now the siege was well under way. The terrorists were led by 'Salim', a slight man, about five foot six tall, with a goatee beard. He wore blue jeans and a green anorak. He was the only one of the six who could speak fluent English. The other terrorists went by the names of Faisal, Abbas, Shai, Makki and Ali. All were heavily armed, with automatic weapons, hand-guns and grenades. They said they were members of the Arabistan People's Political Organisation. Their initial demands were for the release of ninety-one political prisoners, members of their movement. They also wanted to highlight the plight of the four and a half million Arabs who were suffering under the régime of Ayatollah Khomeini.

At the embassy, Ali Afrooz and an Arab journalist named Mustapha were given a two-and-a-half-page statement that the terrorists wanted broadcast to the world. They were told to telephone several media groups to make the announcement, but the calls were interrupted by the police and they had to hang up.

Since the hostages had been taken, one, a pregnant woman, had become ill. She was vomiting and complaining of stomach pains. Salim was asked to provide her with a doctor. The police refused to allow any other hostages to be taken, so Salim allowed the woman to be released.

By Thursday morning the situation was developing rapidly. The Home Secretary, William Whitelaw, had given authority for the SAS to deploy closer to the target. The police, meanwhile, had established phone contact with the terrorists, and negotiations for the release of the hostages were underway.

By 1015 hours, Chris Cramer was writhing on the floor in agony, holding his stomach and sweating profusely. He had become very ill during the night and was apparently getting worse. Sim Harris spoke to the police negotiators on the telephone and asked for a doctor. The police offered drugs, claiming, 'To get a doctor to enter the building would require permission from a higher authority.' Cramer was carried to the ground floor and laid on an old mattress by the police telephone. 'Get me a doctor, I can't stand the pain,' he cried down the line. The police told him they could not find a doctor who was prepared to enter the building, so Harris persuaded Salim to release the sick man. He agreed, reluctantly, and this was a great success for the authorities. They had established that the terrorists were prepared to negotiate the release of some of their hostages, if the situation was appropriate. Every individual released was a step towards a successful conclusion.

Salim, feeling that he was losing ground, now upped the stakes. He demanded a plane to fly to the Middle East by midday. He warned that the building was booby-trapped and claimed that he could blow it up at a moment's notice. The police negotiators told him that the midday deadline could not be met, so it was extended for two hours. The terrorists, apparently undecided as to what to do next, allowed the two o'clock deadline to pass without further demands.

At 2000 hours, Trevor Lock appeared at a window on the second floor. He told the negotiator that the terrorists were going to kill people if their demands were not met. Unbeknown to anyone, Lock was still in possession of his .38 pistol, which was in its holster under his overcoat.

At 0100 hours the whole squadron moved into the Royal College of Surgeons, two doors away from the embassy. We parked a large pantechnicon truck at the end of the block and passed all our equipment over the wall. This took a considerable amount of time. The gear was then taken around the back of the building and in through the rear doors. The police had already begun to use the second floor as an incident control centre. We took over the remaining available space, reorganised our kit and prepared for the Immediate Action (IA). This was the first assault plan, drawn up quickly as soon as the team was on the ground and ready to go. It allotted everyone a point of entry and an area of responsibility. If the terrorists started shooting, at least there was a plan, albeit a worst-case scenario – obviously, the more time we had to prepare, the better. My role would be to pump gas in through the windows as the assault team went in and then be prepared to follow them in as support. If the assault went well I would then be responsible for handling the prisoners.

I got out of my blue jeans and sweatshirt and started to kit up. First I put my gas suit on over my underwear and T-shirt, then, on top of this, I wore a set of plain black overalls. Over the overalls I wore my body armour, which had a ceramic insert in the front to stop high-velocity bullets. The next layer was a black suede utility vest, with pouches for stun-grenades and a knife attached by a quick-release fastening for cutting myself free of entanglements. Around my waist I wore a thick leather belt with a leather pouch divided into three narrow compartments, each containing a thirty-round magazine for my MP-5. Strapped to my right thigh was a quick-release holster containing my 9mm Browning pistol with an extended twenty-round magazine.

I picked up my MP-5 and placed the sling attached to it across my back. The sling was clipped at the front and held the weapon tightly across my chest. In this way I could move through restricted entry points and, with one thrust of my left hand, release the clip and bring the weapon into the firing position to engage the enemy.

All this equipment weighed more than thirty pounds. I was carrying one hundred and forty rounds of ammunition and two stun-grenades. As a small comfort, a shell dressing for treating gunshot wounds was strapped to my right shoulder.

Despite what was claimed in the otherwise generally accurate media coverage, we didn't wear balaclavas; our faces were covered by standard NATO issue SR-6 gas masks, with the hoods of our dark green gas suits pulled over our heads and sealed tightly to prevent gas penetrating to our skin.

Our team's intelligence section was led by 'Belt Kit Joe'. While we were preparing ourselves, he was setting up an intelligence centre on the second floor. The police hadn't been able to get their act together in this department, probably because there were so many different units involved: each different police group had its own rank structures; senior officers had no central authority and didn't know how to deal with a situation of this magnitude. Because Joe was military, it set him apart from these internal politics, and all the police units began to bring their information directly to him. By the time of the first briefing, he had already put together a very good plan of the embassy.

The Iranian embassy contained fifty-four rooms. Many of the internal doors were security doors, and some of the windows were made of armoured glass. At that moment Joe didn't know what was where, but the caretaker had been located and more information would be available soon. Media photographs had been enlarged and placed on a large board in the operations centre. We spent a lot of time studying them in order to be able to separate the bad from the good if we went in. Clothing was as important as faces in terms of recognition. One mistake and I could find myself shooting a hostage, or get shot myself as a result of hesitating.

We quickly settled into the routine that we had practised over and over again on exercises. Red team stood by in their kit while blue team rested in their overalls. After eight hours we would swap over. We had brought in camp-beds, but Captain Justin had found himself a comfortable bed upstairs. A cartoon soon appeared on the wall depicting him with a crown on his head, ordering more steak and champagne for breakfast.

All we could do now was wait – the hardest part of all. To relieve the boredom, practical jokes and adolescent gags became the order of the day. *Wacky Races*, the popular children's cartoon of the time, had a squad of gangsters, the Ant Hill Mob, constantly trying to rescue Penelope, the damsel in distress. Each of our teams began referring to the other as the Ant Hill Mob, or the Ants for short, and there were frequent cries of 'We'll save you, Penelope'. Our language was full of security-speak that was unintelligible to anyone else: 'I'll meet you at the obvious, with you know who at the obvious time.' The police were bewildered by our behaviour, and found it difficult to converse sensibly with any of us.

By the end of the day the caretaker had been exhaustively questioned and blueprints of the building had arrived. When it was discovered how many of the doors and windows were reinforced, it became clear that if an assault had gone in early, several of us would have been killed.

EARLY FRIDAY MORNING, workers began digging up the road close to Princes Gate. The noise provided camouflage for the Secret Intelligence Service, who were hand-drilling holes in the walls of the building to insert a number of listening devices to help gather information.

At 0900 hours, Trevor Lock and two other hostages, Mustapha Karkouti and Dr Ezati, the Iranian press attaché, appeared at that same second-floor window. A gun was being held to the back of Ezati's head by Salim, who shouted that he intended to kill a hostage if his demands were not met. Ezati collapsed, foaming at the mouth.

At 1100 hours, one of the women hostages told Salim that she had heard noises in the wall. Salim became very agitated, and asked for reassurances from the police that nothing untoward was happening. The police assured him that while there were hostages in the building they would not risk their welfare by doing anything stupid.

Meanwhile, a mock-up of the layout of all five floors of the embassy had been erected at Regent's Park Barracks. It was constructed from hessian and timber, and was extremely fragile. We were taken, half the team at a time, to view the mock-up, so that we could familiarise ourselves with the layout of the building. Unfortunately, at this stage we did not know what our specific tasks would be in the event of an assault, which meant that we had to try to familiarise ourselves with the whole building, an almost impossible challenge. I returned to the Royal College of Surgeons none the wiser.

Our plans were being updated regularly. The IA was now becoming a full-scale assault plan, with several different options. The terrorists had earlier asked for an aircraft, so we had to make various plans in case they were allowed to leave the building and travel to an airport. Obviously, at any point the situation might change and we could be called to take action. We had to be prepared for every possible contingency: the one thing we didn't want to have to do was to improvise a rescue mission for which we had not planned or rehearsed. Proper planning prevents piss poor performance...

The deteriorating situation in the embassy caused us to stand to, ready for immediate action, several times. If Salim or one of the other terrorists decided that enough was enough and started killing the hostages, we would be ready to go in at a moment's notice. It was a credit to the negotiator that he always managed to keep the situation calm.

Meanwhile, in the college, we continued to apply our own methods of dealing with the tension: cornflakes in sleeping bags, salt in tea, and water pistol ambushes at high noon. This did nothing to instil confidence in our police colleagues; in fact, they were beginning to view many of us as complete buffoons who took nothing seriously. We would take it seriously all right when the time came, but we were not going to sit around all day sharpening knifes and glaring angrily at each other, like something out of a Rambo movie. We spent most of our time watching the world snooker championships on TV.

Before we could launch any attack, the police would have to officially hand over control to the military. In a sudden emergency this could be done by the senior police officer on the ground, but if we were

A soldier loses weight in the jungle! Some of the candidates for SAS selection lost more than a stone in weight during their jungle training.

BELOW On patrol in Belize, 1983. You could spend a cheerful hour or so in the morning getting rid of ticks in your skin, some as big as pennies.

The assault team on the roof of the Iranian Embassy in 1980, preparing to abseil into battle.

BELOW The SAS soldier burning on his rope during the Embassy assault.

Going in on the top floor…

BELOW …and on the first floor. Only seven years earlier I had been a frightened young man, bullied and scared. Now I was walking forward into a fire-fight, the fear under control, my commitment to the task complete in the knowledge that I was ready, that I was the best man for the job.

In 1982 the SAS deployed to Oman for a major exercise. There were a few veterans who had been there before during the war against Communist rebels in the early 1970s.

BELOW Mortar fire control, Oman, 1982, during Exercise 'Sandy Wanderer'.

9 Troop drove south across a desert of shifting dunes called the Wahiba Sands, about halfway down the Omani eastern seaboard. Then we divided up into patrols and carried out a programme of medical assistance.

BELOW Baluchi soldiers in the service of the Sultan of Oman, Salalah 1983.

Debts mounting and children to feed, I tried to get work on the oil rigs in 1990 but ended up accepting an offer to serve as a mercenary in Mozambique. I became a major in FRELIMO, the government armed forces, then engaged in a war with RENAMO guerrillas, funded by the Apartheid regime in South Africa. This is the unforgettable landscape: sheer rock kopjes rising above the plains of northern Mozambique.

RIGHT The 'Christmas Baby'. He had next to nothing, but he raised his little fist and offered me the rest of his food. If ever a man was taught the lesson of Christmas, I was, there among some of the poorest people on Earth.

Anyone for a second-hand T-54? One of our tanks at Coromanna, Mozambique after the RENAMO attack.

BELOW Bad driving could cost more casualties than enemy action: rolling this vehicle took the lives of forty men.

Laying anti-personnel mines along the perimeter at Coromanna in 1990.

BELOW Mozambican soldiers were as brave as any in the world. They would follow their leaders, staying by them until they died.

carrying out a planned assault, permission would be requested by the Police Commissioner from the Home Secretary, William Whitelaw, who would, in turn, refer the request to the Prime Minister.

The siege was now two and a half days old, and the terrorists had failed to achieve any of their aims. They wanted a platform from which to tell their story to the world, and their failure to acquire that platform was increasing the tension. They were becoming tired as the days wore on. They were also becoming familiar with the hostages, which would make it harder to execute them without provocation. Something had to give.

They now asked for three Arab ambassadors as negotiators and reiterated their demand for a plane to the Middle East for themselves and the hostages. They promised to leave the non-Iranians at the airport. The negotiators stalled for more time. The longer they could delay any decision, the more chance there was of a surrender. As the third day came to an end, a female hostage again reported noises from the wall. Sim Harris asked Mr Naghizadeh, the second secretary, to order the women to keep quiet about the noises, but they took no notice and continued to try to ingratiate themselves with their captors.

The mood was changing, and we could sense it. We were now forbidden to leave the building. As it became dark, we stood to, ready once more to go in. Inside the embassy an argument was taking place between two terrorists. My heart pounded in anticipation. I stood by the back door, ready to go, but the storm subsided and we could breathe easily again.

AT 1147 HOURS on the Saturday, Ali Afrooz pleaded with the police to take the terrorists' threats to kill someone seriously. Trevor Lock then read out a prepared statement, in which he stated that the police's delaying tactics were causing great tension.

At 1530 hours, BBC boss Tony Crabb spoke with Sim Harris about broadcasting the terrorists' statement to the world. Harris was visibly frightened, and impatient with the lack of co-operation from the authorities. Didn't they realise his life was in danger? Salim, who was holding a gun on Harris, became visibly angry, so Tony Crabb agreed to make a broadcast as soon as possible. Salim relaxed, so Crabb asked whether he was prepared to make a goodwill gesture by releasing some hostages. Salim said he would.

By 1900 hours there was still nothing broadcast on the radio, so Salim sent Trevor Lock and Mustapha to the window to ask why. The police said that they would only allow the transmission to go ahead once two hostages had been released, and not before. On hearing this Salim lost his temper and declared that he was going to kill a hostage, but Mustapha managed to calm him down and persuaded him to release one of the captives, pointing out that if this got him his broadcast then that would be a considerable achievement. Mrs Haydeh Kanji, another pregnant hostage, was released.

Subsequently it became clear that Salim was truly at the end of his tether, and not in the mood for further compromise. 'Either there is a broadcast or a hostage will be shot,' he proclaimed. He added, however, that he was still prepared to release another hostage if the broadcast was made. The police confirmed that the broadcast would be made at 2100 hours.

At the appointed time a statement was read out word for word on the BBC World Service, and Salim, true to his word, released another hostage. For the moment the tension had eased.

Inside the college, however, tension was increasing. Soldiers who had never worn their ceramic plates during training started to insert them in their flak jackets. Some of these jackets had flaps that covered the lower waist. These had always been unpopular, as they were heavy, but now they were becoming as hard to find as rocking-horse shit.

As night fell, the whole squadron was assembled in the ops room for orders. Major Jerry briefed us on a full-scale assault on the building. As there were so many rooms in the embassy, the whole squadron would act as one assault team. Support would come from extra troops brought in from Hereford. As many access points as possible would be breached simultaneously, every floor would be hit at the same time. Entry points would be blown with special explosive charges, designed to remove windows and doors without killing anyone standing behind them. One team would move across the roof and lower a set of charges down into a chimney-like hollow in the centre of the building. At a given signal they would explode the charges, descend a small stairway from the roof and take out the top floor. Another team would abseil from the roof to the second floor, blow in the windows at the rear and take out this area. At the front of the building, a third team would jump across from the neighbouring first-floor balcony and enter the main hostage holding area. Team four was to blow the double doors at the rear on the ground floor and hold the stairs. (I was in team four.) Team five would take out the basement after also entering through the back door. Two men were to remain outside to control prisoners. This was the reception party. The extra dozen or so troops that had come up from Hereford would take the sniper rifles and offer cover from the surrounding buildings.

ON SUNDAY, AS we sat watching the Benson and Hedges snooker championships on TV, the police negotiations seemed to be going well. Aside from the broadcast, no concessions had been made to the terrorists, while hostages had been recovered and information had been gathered that would make any assault more likely to succeed.

Inside the embassy, however, nerves were beginning to fray to breaking point. Salim began writing anti-Khomeini slogans all over the walls. He knew that he was losing the psychological battle with the police and if he was going to make a stand, it would have to be soon. The alternative was to lose face in front of the world. He was torn between two options: to surrender, or to kill a hostage. First he would scream and threaten, then he would calm down. He asked Sim Harris whether he thought he had gone about things in the right way. Harris told him that although most of the Western world sympathised with his cause, they would not tolerate the murder of hostages. If he killed someone, he could not hope to win.

Afrooz and one of the embassy workers, Lavasani, took great offence at Salim's insults to their highest religious leader. Lavasani lunged at one of the gunmen and was promptly wrestled to the ground. A weapon was cocked and held to his head. For a moment it looked like the man was going to die, but Trevor Lock intervened and bawled Lavasani out in front of everyone.

We were aware of the noise and confusion, and once again we stood ready to go. Our tasks hadn't changed, but in the event of an IA we in team four would now go in without using explosives, which were all deployed elsewhere. Sledgehammers would have to do the job instead. I knew that before we could go in there would be a hiatus while we took official control. I also knew that until someone was actually killed, it was unlikely that the attack would be authorised. I stood calmly at my position by the rear door of the college. My gas mask was pulled back and I was drinking a cup of tea.

Now the police had no idea what to make of us: we had been buffoons before; but here we were, waiting to go into the building, calmly drinking tea and talking about missing the snooker on TV. I suppose they thought we were strange, but as far as I was concerned, all this had been going on for some time now and there was no point in getting excited until something was actually about to happen.

In the embassy things began to calm down again, but Lavasani had now become isolated from the group as someone the gunmen could hold a grudge against. It appeared as if he actually wanted to be a martyr: he had told Harris that he was single, with no responsibilities, and perhaps he had deliberately set himself up as the victim should Salim decide to kill someone. Before the incident with Lavasani, the negotiators had believed they were winning; now the chances of the situation breaking down had increased, so, with this in mind, top military lawyers were brought in to brief us on the legal situation in the event of an assault taking place. We were still subject to the full weight of the British legal system: any action we took had to be justifiable in the eyes of the law. It was very similar to the situation in Northern Ireland. We couldn't just kill the terrorists: we had to take them prisoner unless we believed that our lives, or other people's lives, were in immediate danger. The law stated that we should rescue the hostages and, if necessary, kill the terrorists; in our hearts, we wanted to kill the terrorists and then save the hostages. What was important was that we knew what to say if something went wrong.

It is rarely what a man does, but what he says which convicts him of an offence. We were being protected from the possibility of someone, from the safety of his easy chair, later judging us for our behaviour in the face of an enemy who had been trying to kill us. We knew that if we attacked, we would win. We were committed to our task and we outnumbered the enemy ten to one. Who would die was the only question remaining. I just hoped it wasn't going to be me.

AT 1110 HOURS on Monday, 5 May, Trevor Lock told the police that Salim would kill a hostage at 1140 if his demands were not met. Ten minutes later he asked for the negotiators. He wanted them quickly.

The 1140 deadline passed without incident. At 1215 Lock told the negotiators over the phone that Lavasani was being tied up. Salim picked up the phone and calmly told the police that they had had enough time.

Within seconds three shots rang out. Salim came back on the phone and said, 'I will kill one now and another in forty-five minutes. The next time the telephone rings it should be to tell me that the ambassadors are coming. I do not want any more messages.'

At 1315 Trevor Lock informed the police that the gunmen had shot one hostage and that they would shoot another in thirty minutes. There was still some doubt as to whether someone had actually been shot or not. Was it a bluff? No one knew. Once again the deadline passed. It was down to a face-off. Either Salim shot someone or he surrendered. Salim knew that they were calling his bluff.

Police Commissioner David McNee sent a letter to Salim. It said:

I THINK THAT it is right that I should explain to you clearly and in writing the way in which my police officers are dealing with the taking of hostages in the Iranian Embassy. I and my officers deeply wish to work to a peaceful solution of what has occurred. We fully understand how both the hostages and those that hold them feel, threatened and frightened. You are cut off from your families and friends. But, you need not feel threatened or frightened by the police. It is not our way in Britain to resort to violence against those who are peaceful. You have nothing to fear from my officers provided you do not harm those in your care. I firmly hope that we can now bring this incident to a close peacefully and calmly.

SALIM WAS NOT impressed.

We made our final preparations for the assault. Abseil ropes were fixed to the roof, explosives were prepared and moved close to the forming-up points, gas filters were checked, laces were tightened. Now it looked as though something might be happening, the police officers fell silent. They had done their best; now it was our turn.

As the siege approached its climax, we watched another battle reach its grand finale: Cliff Thorburn and Hurricane Higgins were slogging out the last few frames of the snooker final on TV. We were ready. There was nothing left to do but wait calmly for the order to go or to stand down.

In the Cabinet Office briefing room, the Prime Minister, the Home Secretary, the Police Commissioner and SAS Colonel Mike Rose were trying to come to a final decision as to whether to hand over control to the military and stage an assault on the embassy. Margaret Thatcher said that if the terrorists killed another hostage, the assault should go ahead. Shots had been fired; all we needed now was a body.

At 1913 hours four shots exploded from the interior of the embassy and a few seconds later Lavasani's body was thrown onto the front steps, in full view of the world's media. Five minutes later Lavasani was confirmed dead, and Margaret Thatcher gave the order to hand over control to the military. The assault was on.

I CREPT QUIETLY out of the back door of the college and across the concrete patio towards the rear of the embassy. I looked ahead of me at Robert as he began to insert detonators into the explosives and place them on the back door, then I looked up. Above me, four men began to descend slowly from the roof on their abseil ropes. Behind me Big Bob was wielding an eight-pound sledgehammer as a back-up should it be needed to get through the door.

I gripped my MP-5 in both hands and thumbed the safety catch, assuring myself once again that it was off. The only sounds I could hear were the static hissing in my earpiece and the sound of my heart pounding in my ears. My greatest fear now was of making a mistake that might endanger a life – especially mine. My mind raced. Watch the windows, Robin. What do I do if someone looks out now? Don't rush. Is my pistol still in my holster? Where is my partner?

The police dogs, which were being held back just inside the doors of the college, began to feel the tension in their handlers and started barking and howling. Why don't you shut the bastard dogs up, I thought. The fear that had for so long been my greatest enemy welled up inside me like a balloon, waiting to escape from my throat. Hello, I thought, I'm glad you're here. Without you I wouldn't be functioning at my best. I need to be scared to be alert.

The smallest sounds were magnified and time seemed to slow down. Around me team members moved into position calmly and without undue haste. Only seven years earlier I had been a frightened young man on the brink of adventure, bullied and scared. Now I was walking forward into a fire-fight, the fear under control, my commitment to the task complete in the knowledge that I was ready, that I was the best man for the job.

Knowledge and training had dispelled my fear. I was in control.

The sound of breaking glass made me look up. One of the descending abseilers had put his foot through the window. Ahead of me Robert struggled to finish preparing the explosives that would remove the door from its hinges. Major Jerry had to make a decision, and fast. Had we been compromised early?

Salim was on the phone, talking to the negotiators, as the glass broke. 'I heard something, something is happening!' he shouted.

'Don't worry, it's OK,' he was told by the man at the other end of the line. 'There's no problem, nothing to worry about.'

'Yes there is, there is a noise!' Salim shouted.

Major Jerry could hear the conversation as it took place. He took the microphone from the hands of his signaller and said, 'GO, GO, GO!'

Now we had to improvise – only half the men were in their start positions. Boom! The explosives in the central chimney exploded. The team ran down the stairs and into the top floor as glass, debris and smoke shrouded them in a cloak of invisibility. The abseilers, already down on the rear balcony, broke the windows and threw stun-grenades into the room before following them in. At the front, two men leapt over the balcony and placed their own charge. Before they could move back it was fired, removing the window. In they went, just in time to see one of the terrorists raising his gun to a hostage's head. Two bursts and the gunman was dead.

In front of me Robert was trying to get the wires into the firing device to remove the back doors. 'Never mind that,' shouted Big Bob. He ran forward with the sledgehammer and mashed the door to pulp. His partner launched two stun-grenades and in they went.

I looked up as three bullet holes appeared in the window above my head. Dangling on his rope about twelve feet above the balcony and twenty feet from the ground was one of the assault team. He was stuck, his rope jammed in the figure-of-eight abseil device attached to his harness. The curtains beneath him had been set on fire by the grenades that had exploded when the first group had entered. The flames were climbing higher and higher and were now lapping against his legs. His screams of pain sounded over the radio.

I saw two of the team on the roof attempting to cut him down, but it was a difficult task as he was now kicking himself away from the wall to get free of the fire. The rope would have to be cut so that it parted on the in-swing and he fell onto the balcony and not onto the solid concrete steps further down. I watched him dangle in the flames and considered what, if anything, I could do to save him. I felt helpless, but, realising that I was not going to be able to do anything useful, I took my place by the rear door and got on with my job.

I was a reserve, ready to respond in any area where help was needed. My partner, 'Ginge' from 8 Troop, was standing opposite me, staring into the gas- and smoke-filled room. As the sound of gunfire swelled into an almost continuous crescendo, I saw a man stumbling around at the bottom of the stairs. He was wearing a large black overcoat. His fair hair identified him to me immediately. 'Over here, Trevor!' I shouted. He turned and stumbled towards me, and I took his arm and led him to one of the reception party on the back door. PC Trevor Lock had been our priority. He was one of us, one of the team. He had to come out alive, and the guys upstairs had indeed got him out first.

As I returned to my position just inside the door I could hear Major Jerry shouting down the radio for information, but everyone was too busy to respond. In front of me a chain was beginning to form on the stairs: everything appeared to be going to plan. 'Reserves go in now!' Major Jerry shouted on the radio. Ginge launched himself forward into the building, with me following behind. As we entered the front reception area by the stairs, hostages started to tumble down, thrown from man to man until they reached me. Ginge and I became an integral part of the chain and proceeded to launch hostage after hostage towards the door and the waiting reception party.

'Watch out, he's a terrorist!' shouted one of the men on the stairs. I looked across to where the shout had come from. One of the assault team hit the man with the butt of his weapon and launched him down to where the stairs cornered sharply to the right. He stumbled around the corner and down the last few steps. It was Faisal, and he held a grenade in his right hand. Without hesitation I fired one short burst of four rounds at his chest. All four of the team in the foyer also opened fire.

Faisal slumped to the floor with twenty-seven holes in him. He didn't spasm or spurt blood everywhere. He simply crumpled up like a bundle of rags and died.

More hostages were on their way down now, arriving thick and fast. The gunfire had subsided. One of the officers from the team upstairs came down shouting at all and sundry, 'Get out, get out, the building's on fire.' He sounded a bit worked up, so I grabbed him by the arm and shouted, 'You get fucking out, I've got to make sure everyone else in front of me is out first.' He looked at me for a second and then, realising the sense in what I'd said, went out the back door.

Now I saw the soldier who had messed up his abseiling come down. His eyes were glazed and one of his legs was terribly burned. He must have been in great pain, but he refused to let anyone help him. At least he was down safe – he had the two men on the roof to thank for that.

As the flames crackled around us, the different sections of the team started to report in. Their areas were clear and their soldiers were out. Ginge and I pulled back and went to help with the prisoners.

Outside on the lawn, the hostages were laid face down with their wrists handcuffed behind their backs. They would not be released until they were all identified and calm. Sim Harris was twisting to one side and looking at one of the handcuffed men. 'He's a terrorist!' he shouted. Big Tony, one of the reception party, pulled the man in question to his feet and began to walk him away from the group. At first I thought he was going to lay him down a short distance away, but he continued walking, towards the rear door of the flaming building. I ran over with Ivan, a new member of 9 Troop, and made sure that Big Tony laid the man down on the ground where the police could see him. We never knew for sure what Big Tony had in mind, but I had my suspicions.

While the police and their dogs surrounded the prisoners and began to take over, we were ordered over the radio to return to the Royal College of Surgeons. As I walked through the back door I was assaulted once again, only this time by policemen. Their huge hands slammed down on my back and words of admiration flowed freely. 'Well done, lads, brilliant.' I was bowled forward into Stevie from 7 Troop. He stopped and turned to the worshipping throng. Pausing theatrically, he pulled up his gas mask, exposing his swarthy features, and smiled. The policemen fell silent, waiting for the heroic pearls of wisdom about to issue from this conqueror's lips. 'Who won the snooker?' he asked.

OUR JOB WAS done. All we had to do now was go home to Hereford. We had suffered only two casualties: the man on the rope, who had severe burns to his legs, and Gwyn, who had shot the end of his own left index finger off. He had been using a shortened version of the MP-5, the MP-5 Kurtz, and in the excitement he allowed his finger to wander over the front of the barrel as he fired.

As we reorganised, we had to hand over any weapons that had been fired to the police so they could be checked by forensics and then matched to our stories at the inquest. As we handed them in, we had to state how many rounds we had fired. 'Twelve rounds,' said the man in front of me. 'Four rounds,' I said. The next two men in the line were old veterans of many campaigns, the élite. 'Three magazines each,' they informed the policeman. I looked back, astounded. How on earth could they justify firing that much ammunition? They had been tasked to clear the basement area; there had been no terrorists in that zone. I hadn't been there, but all my training had taught me to fire only when I was presented with a clear target. These two men had apparently been room-clearing as though in a war zone. Thank heavens they hadn't been upstairs.

William Whitelaw arrived and we were all called into the lobby of the college to hear what he had to say. He had tears of emotion in his eyes as he spoke. 'I always knew that you would do a good job,' he said, 'but I never knew it would be this good.' He wanted us all to go out front, to be paraded in front of the world's press – to be famous for a day and have our pictures taken. Major Jerry soon put a stop to that idea, and we packed ourselves into the back of police vans and the pan-technicon and disappeared back to Regent's Park Barracks, where our own vehicles were parked.

Shortly after we arrived, Margaret Thatcher turned up to see her 'boys', as she called us. We lined up and were introduced to the PM one at a time. As my turn approached I was truly excited at the prospect of meeting her. She extended her hand, which was immediately crushed in my over-enthusiastic grip. Demonstrating years of practise, she allowed her hand to go limp in my grasp. She was small, much smaller than I had imagined, and her make-up looked like it was cracking from her skin in layers. Perhaps it was that way for the cameras she had been facing outside Downing Street. The older guys weren't fazed by her at all. 'When are we going to get a pay rise?' some of them asked.

The news came on, and we moved over to a TV in the corner of the room which had been brought in specially. There was no other furniture, so we sat down on the floor to watch the assault. Maggie Thatcher sat down with us and joined in the cheering as we watched ourselves in action.

IT HAD BEEN quite a day, but now it really was over and all we wanted to do was get home. Without much thought, we bundled everything into the back of our Transit van and, with Tom driving, left London, heading out towards the M4. As we passed through Chiswick, one of the back wheels of the van clipped the kerb and we ended up at Heston services to repair a puncture. We managed to get the spare wheel ready, but then realised that the tools were hidden beneath all the unused weapons still in our possession. If we took them out, the weapons and ammunition would be in full public view, even though it was dark. As we were trying to work out what to do, I saw an AA van parked about fifty yards away. 'I know, I'll get the AA to change it,' I said. Before anyone could protest I strolled over and asked the AA driver if he had heard about what had happened in London that day. He said that he had, becoming quite animated about events. 'Well, I'm one of the blokes who did it,' I told him, 'and I have a problem.'

I explained our predicament to him and, not sure whether to believe me or not, he drove over to take a look, probably as much out of curiosity as anything else. Confronted by four tired-looking heavies, and with the signal from a police radio bleeping in the front of the vehicle, he was convinced, and changed the wheel for us. The AA can take some credit for their involvement that day – and we weren't even members.

It took another three hours to get to Hereford, with a stop at Greasy Joe's café in Cirencester en route. Without the weapons that the police had confiscated, the team was effectively out of commission for a couple of days, so we unloaded what we could and cleaned up. By the time we had finished it was about three in the morning; we were told to report in after lunch the following day. I went home and climbed into bed with Heather.

The following morning Heather and I were sitting with Derek from 8 Troop and his wife in The Golden Egg Café. The siege was on everyone's lips. Behind us a group of people were saying how they would love to meet the men who had carried out the mission. Derek and I smiled, while our partners almost hugged themselves, basking in their secret knowledge.

True to tradition, a piss-up was organised almost immediately. No wives or girlfriends was the order of the day – not a decision I was really enamoured of, but some men's wives are better company than others,

I suppose. Gifts flowed in from all over the country: cases of whisky from breweries, Cup Final tickets from football clubs, Derby day tickets, and so on – the list was endless. The squadron itself got to see a few bottles of champagne at the piss-up; the rest disappeared to destinations unknown.

But I felt somewhat withdrawn at the party: drink alone wasn't enough to get me in the mood. Trevor Lock was there with his wife, and it was a pleasure to meet him properly and to know that I had played a part in saving his life. But what really caused me to leave early were the recriminations that were already beginning to circulate.

The two men who had saved the life of the burned abseiler were criticised for not leaving him and completing their mission. Ivan was criticised for preventing Big Tony from topping the last terrorist. I defended the people in question, and of course made no friends in the process. Then I realised that because I was also involved in saving the last terrorist, I too would be a subject of criticism behind my back. It depressed me that such a great occasion should be demeaned by such petty-minded behaviour.

The medals were the final icing on the cake. Instead of making awards for individual acts of bravery, or awarding the squadron a unit citation, the Army simply made an allowance of five Queen's Gallantry Medals. The Regiment had to decide who was to receive them. The colonel was awarded one, even though he had spent the whole mission with the PM at Downing Street. The squadron commander, Major Jerry, got nothing, and he had planned and led the whole operation. The remainder were virtually pulled out of a hat. Big Bob put the whole medal fiasco in a nutshell when he said, 'Medals are like haemorrhoids – eventually every arsehole gets one.' I couldn't agree more.

BEFORE THE SIEGE very few people had heard of the SAS. Now the whole world wanted to know us. Instead of getting straight back to training, as we should have, we were turned into a performing circus, demonstrating our techniques to any interested member of the royal family and their corgis. Our standards dropped appallingly until the next squadron took over; then we could rest on our laurels no longer.

Prince Charles and Princess Diana were amongst the royals who attended the demonstrations. Subsequently they were asked whether they would like to participate in an assault by driving the Range Rovers up to the practice building, which was custom-made for assault training. The drill was for the drivers to stop their vehicles close enough to the building for the ladders fixed on top to be slammed against the wall, enabling the troops to enter quickly on the first floor.

Two pairs of flame-resistant overalls were provided for the royal couple, and they prepared to drive towards the building. Princess Diana's door was firmly shut, but no one had noticed that her window was wound down about two inches. I was mounted on the rear of the vehicle, while Ginge was seated next to Diana on the passenger side. Everything went smoothly at the start. The princess drove the heavily laden vehicle up to the edge of the building, just beneath a window. The ladders on the roof banged forward against the wall and the assault began. Stun-grenades were launched through the windows and were followed by the men.

Ginge and I were standing close to the right-hand side of the Range Rover, giving cover to the assault team, when a stun-grenade bounced back from the wall and exploded at our feet. When they went off, the practise-grenades would send out quantities of explosives to create secondary detonations. One of these secondaries took place in the gap at the top of the driver's window, right next to Diana's head. Ginge was closest, and reacted like lightning. He pulled the door open and dragged Diana from the vehicle by her right arm. Her hair was smouldering where sparks were coming into contact with the lacquer in her hair. I closed in and helped douse the sparks while Ginge held her still. Thanks to his quick reactions, her skin was not burned, although her hair was rather singed.

That lunchtime Princess Di had her hair remodelled into a short, swept-back style. The newspapers raved about it for days.

CHAPTER 14

Sandy Wanderer

ONCE B SQUADRON had finished with counter-terrorism, we were given time for training. Most of the men were sent on team jobs, doing special training tasks for foreign governments. The team would go to the country in question and teach whatever techniques the country was paying to learn. These jobs were very lucrative for the British government, and not too bad for the instructors as well. I was still in disgrace because of my behaviour on the medical course, so I was packed off to F Troop in Belize, which wasn't considered a particularly attractive post, but I liked the jungle, so I thought I could make the best of it. This time when I arrived in the country, I was pleasantly surprised: I was given a two-man room in the sergeants' mess, and all the amenities were open to me. This meant better food, good facilities for drinking and relaxing, and no interference from other ranks. There were only sixteen of us to patrol the whole central border of Belize; that meant one patrol in the north, one in the south, one in Airport Camp and one off-duty.

As soon as I was in-country, I was back in the jungle, only this time I wasn't being tested. Our job now was to fly by helicopter to a certain map reference, then abseil into the trees from two hundred feet, build a makeshift camp and send up a marker balloon showing aircraft where to drop their bombs. The idea was to test the effect of various bombs on jungle camps. We carried out our task and were then winched up, one at a time, back into the Puma helicopter. Going down into the trees on a rope was a bit dicey, but getting winched up was far worse. As I climbed higher I started to spin, and there was nothing I could do to control it. When I was finally inside the chopper I was so dizzy I lay on the floor for fear of staggering back out.

After a short time the Harrier jump-jets flew in and dropped cluster-bombs into the camp. When we went back in to see the effects, we were surprised to discover that hardly any of the structures we had built, and none of the man-sized targets we had put in place, had any holes in them whatsoever. Conclusion: cluster-bombs are ineffective against infantry in trees. The second time I abseiled down to check the results, the helicopter moved sideways slightly and bounced me over the edge of a slope while I was trying to get out of my harness. The string that was holding my rifle across my shoulder fell across my throat and I became entangled in my equipment. The helicopter crew could not see me through the trees, assumed that I was OK and began to ascend. Sam, who had descended just before me, reacted instantly and pulled the quick release on my harness, slipped the string from under my chin and spun me upside down. As I hit the ground I watched the abseil rope and harness fly up through the trees and out of sight. Two more seconds and I would have been hanged on the thin piece of string, and probably been decapitated into the bargain. Sam's quick reactions had saved my life.

The aircraft came back the next day and dropped thousand-pound bombs. This time we found devastation of unbelievable proportions. Conclusion: don't get anywhere near an angry thousand-pound bomb in the jungle.

Then it was back into the trees for two or three weeks to patrol the border. The terrain in the Mayan Mountains was totally unexplored, so every day was a new adventure. High waterfalls, huge vines and new sights and sounds filled my senses; with enough food and medicine, I could have stayed there for the whole twelve weeks of the tour. I loved the freedom of being allowed to soldier for long periods of time without having some senior chasing around behind me.The longer I spent in the jungle, the more adjusted to the environment I became. The mosquitoes didn't seem to bite me any more. My hands became so calloused that thorns wouldn't penetrate deep enough to cause bleeding. I had no soap; often I simply plunged in to one of the fast-flowing rivers, fully clothed, and let the water wash through the clothes while I wore them. As time passed I found that I could move so quietly and sit so still that I could be invisible to comrades only a few feet away from me. Once I was sitting in an ambush site, silent and motionless, when a small green humming-bird came and hovered only inches from my eyes. I kept very still and watched this wonderful creature defy gravity, until it occurred to me that it might think my eye was a flower and attempt to dip its beak into it, so I blinked – in a flash of colour it was gone.

I settled down to working hard in the jungle and enjoying my time off on the Caribbean quays. A former sergeant had built a small hotel, The Pirate's Lantern, on an island called Ambergris Quay. We would visit him there and spend our time off in paradise. Tinned food and alcohol were expensive on the islands, and a crate of whisky and a ten-man ration pack could pay for all my food and accommodation for a week: my first venture into private business was smuggling. Belize is a poor country, and in comparison to the locals, we were rich. We could eat lobster and drink beer all day and every day that we were off-duty. Belize City itself was a primitive location, with open sewers and barefoot children running in the streets; at night packs of roaming stray dogs would follow me down the road until I reached my hotel or transport. I wondered what they would have done if I had been drunk and collapsed in the gutter. The only other city was Belmopan, the seat of government. Most of the Negroid population lived in the cities; the Amerindians worked the countryside, growing crops and living on subsistence farming. Halfway through the tour, my patrol set up a training camp to teach jungle survival to the local infantry and air force. We built a comfortable site for ourselves and then flew them in twenty at a time. I revelled in this – we were passing on to them most of the things I had learned on selection only eighteen months before. I would hunt game with a shotgun and demonstrate how to kill and prepare food. I would follow my students through the trees, always remaining within earshot but out of sight, listening to their opinions and silently laughing at their mistakes. This was the life: I truly loved being a soldier, and when I was teaching what I loved, I was as happy as a pig in a barrel of truffles.

I returned home to England, and Heather, just after Christmas – my second away from home. I had made the best of Belize and had enjoyed myself tremendously; now I was instructed to sit the medical course again. In spite of not officially being a medic, I had carried out all the duties of a medic in the jungle, so, for the next four weeks, I frustrated my instructors by endlessly staring out of the window while they were teaching, then, when they asked me a question I would answer it correctly. I continued to study the subject, but almost at my leisure. At the end of the course I achieved ninety-nine per cent in the exam. When I asked what I had got wrong, I was told, 'Nobody gets a hundred per cent, Bob.' This time I went to Birmingham for my hospital experience, with a man from my own squadron. We got on well, and I had learned a few things about working with civilians by now, so I came back with an excellent report. Major Jerry was happy and awarded me my Special Forces pay. It came through in April and was backdated for a whole year.

We didn't sit around for long – we never did. Now we were off to Oman to carry out desert warfare training, in an operation code named Sandy Wanderer. Many of the SAS who had served there in the 1960s and 70s had subsequently joined the Sultan's special forces and were now officers in his army, earning very good money. Some of the veterans were looking forward to seeing their old mates. The squadron was billeted in barracks just outside Muscat and allotted different troop tasks: 9 Troop was to drive from north to south across a desert of shifting dunes called the Wahiba Sands, about halfway down the country's eastern seaboard, on the coastal plain opposite the island of Masira, then divide up into patrols and carry out a medical programme.

Crossing sand dunes in Land Rovers fitted with standard tyres is no easy business. Keeping the vehicle moving forward was important: once traction was lost we would have to place steel plates called sand tracks under the wheels to get the vehicles moving again. Not being able to stop and check our route, we sometimes found ourselves plunging over the edge of sand dunes into empty space, and falling ten or twenty feet into the soft sand below.The desert was a joy, provided there was enough water. The huge sand dunes, sometimes several hundred feet high, would make us feel hemmed in, but as we moved onto the open plains the flat, distant horizon would disappear in the heat haze, the reds and yellows changing their hue as the sun moved across the sky. Then I would feel lost in the great emptiness.

The sun was the enemy in the daytime, and the cold was the enemy at night. The dry wind that blew into my face gave no relief from the heat, and my skin and lips began to dry and crack as the dust drew the moisture from them. I soon discovered why the desert Arabs cover their faces and heads with a shamagh. This large piece of cloth, when wrapped around the head, kept the heat off your neck and the sand out of your hair. When the hanging piece at the back was drawn across the nose, it kept the sun off your face and the sand out of your mouth. I never wore anything else on my head for the remainder of the trip.

It took us four days to cross the sands. Our guide always managed to find the wells, where we would camp at night. I would set up a camp-bed and snuggle into my sleeping bag and look up at the clearest night sky I had ever seen. All the constellations were visible: there was no cloud and no light pollution. I knew 8 Troop would be having a great time practising astronavigation.

When we reached our destination and split up, my patrol consisted of the Regimental Medical Officer, Richard, plus Sam and Gwyn from 9 Troop, Tiny from 7 Troop, and Neil as the patrol commander. Also attached to us was an Omani major, our guide and liaison officer.We set up base in a small village called Hai, which had been built around a well in the middle of nowhere. There were a dozen trees close to the water source, and about fifty camels. The headman, the Wallait, had a concrete house surrounded by barbed wire. The rest of the village, a total population of about two hundred, lived in traditional Arab tents. There was even a small shop that sold pitta bread and tinned tuna.

On the edge of the village was a medical centre located in a

Portakabin forty feet long by ten feet wide. A British nurse was providing limited medical aid to the community from here. Richard moved into a spare room in the Portakabin and the rest of us erected two tents outside for our own accommodation. We moved most of the medical supplies into the building, and Neil established the routine for the next few weeks. Gwyn was to take Sam as linguist and me as medic to patrol the whole area within a two-hundred-mile radius and offer medical treatment to the Bedou, the desert nomads who lived in tents. We set off the following day to explore. Every time we found a small group of people, Sam would make all the traditional greetings in Arabic, and we would then be invited to sit and drink coffee with our hosts. Most of the people we encountered were healthy and content. Some families had sons working in the cities earning good money. Some owned Toyota Land Cruisers, which were far better at crossing the desert than our Land Rovers.

Arab tradition has it that a bad pain can be cured by an even worse pain somewhere else on the body; I discovered many people with burn scars from this kind of healing. Because an injection can be painful, many of the people I attended would demand just that – an injection. I carried iron injections that were intended for anaemic women, although they could also be a help with impotence in old men. These proved to be popular, and as soon as I appeared in the vicinity the call went out: *'Tabeeb, Ibra min fudluck.'* Translated, that's 'Doctor, injection please.' In general it was an enjoyable training exercise. I practised my medicine, Sam his Arabic, and all of us practised our desert navigation. After a couple of days out we would return to Hai to resupply and to relax.

Richard had hired a local man to sleep under the Portakabin and guard the drugs. One day I saw him passing medicine out of the back window to one of his friends. I walked up to him carrying my rifle and, as I was unable to speak his language, gave him a glare that told him I was not pleased. He immediately ran off and told the Wallait that I had threatened to shoot him. To resolve the situation I apologised for threatening to shoot him and the guard kept his job. The theft was never mentioned. To this man's mind the drugs were the Sultan's and he was entitled to them.

Halfway through the trip I came across a village where several young children had died recently. The elders allowed me to see the children who were sick. They all had very high temperatures, but no other symptoms that I could associate with the problem. I gave the parents a two-day supply of junior Disprin to bring down their temperatures, then I took blood and returned to base to report my findings to the MO. We tested the blood for malaria, but with negative results, so the next day I returned to the village with Richard. When we arrived, the elders would not let us see the sick children until I had given them each an injection. They wanted *Ibra*. Their attitude to the children was, 'If God wills it, they will live or die; we can always make new babies, but Allah cannot give us an injection.' Their intransigent and uncaring attitude was strange to me and I became angry. OK, I thought, if you want *Ibra* you shall have it. I drew up two millilitres of sterile water and injected it as quickly as I could into the buttocks of the first elder. The speed of the injection left his buttock muscle in agony. That should cure all your problems, I thought, as he writhed across the floor.

My 'treatment' had the desired effect: the rest of the elders changed their minds about the injections and let the doctor see the children, who, he discovered, were dying of a once-common childhood disease: measles. We returned to Hai and signalled to headquarters in Muscat that we had a measles problem and wanted to inoculate the local population, and within twenty-four hours the Omani Minister of Health had sent a team of nurses and medics to the area to give injections. In Oman, measles is not a disease that occurs in every generation, so there is no genetic immunity. Between us we probably prevented the deaths of hundreds of people.

Major Jerry turned up a few days later to see how things were going. 'What do you think of the desert, Horsfall?' he asked.

'Great, sir, fucking great, I love it here,' I answered swiftly: I had learned my lesson – even if I had hated it, he would have got the same reply. In fact, that was the only opinion he ever got from me about anything from then on. The SAS, the parched desert, the insects in the jungle, the scorpions in my boots – they were all fucking great, sir!

We were nearing the end of the trip, but before we left, we had to carry out an exercise with Omani Hunter jets. It was our task to guide them onto targets of our choosing. No ammunition was used – it was a dry exercise. The night before the exercise we had visitors from the Omani Southern Defence Regiment, a British major and some friends. On their vehicles they had some beer; by chance we also had some booze that had been flown in from Masira the same day. We billeted our friends in our tents and had a party. Neil consumed rather more than his share, and the following day we couldn't rouse him to take part in the aircraft fire control exercise, so we left him asleep in the tent.

The jets came in and we selected different targets for them. If a soldier on the ground sees a surface-to-air missile fired at a jet that he is guiding onto a target, he shouts 'SAM, SAM, SAM!' down the radio. The pilot should then carry out evasive manoeuvres and fire his afterburners to accelerate away from the danger.

Tiny thought it would be a good idea to use Neil's tent as a final target, so I guided the jet in on its attacking run and, just as it was over the tent, I shouted, 'SAM, SAM, SAM!' The noise was deafening from where we stood. God knows how it sounded inside the shaking tent – the Hunter had been only about fifty feet from the ground. As the aircraft flew over the horizon, we all watched the tent for movement. The spitting image of a shaggy, sandy-haired, red-eyed Honey Monster slowly poked its head through the tent door.

'What's up with you lot?' asked Neil, as we fell about laughing.

'Best alarm clock you'll ever get,' said Tiny.

Neil was in his late thirties, with an old, worn-looking face. He was carrying a bit of weight around his middle, which might have fooled some younger men into doubting his fitness. They would have been sadly wrong. Only a few days earlier, our vehicle had broken down forty miles from base and our radio wouldn't work, so Neil picked up one water bottle, his rifle and a compass and ran all the way back to camp across the desert to get help. It took him about eight hours on one litre of water.

Before we returned to the UK, we had a party at the Beach Club in Muscat and the usual vast quantities of booze were consumed. The troops insulted all the local dignitaries and officers who came along to say thanks, so they left early. Three months in the desert is a good excuse to let off steam, I suppose. I was happy: I had impressed my superiors with my medical work, and I felt comfortable enough about my future. Then I spotted Mal, the troop sergeant and my secret enemy, asleep in a chair by the water's edge. He had arrived from 9 Troop (Mountain troop) with a terrific reputation and I had been looking forward to working with him. However, a mate of mine had overheard him in the NAAFI saying that he wanted to get rid of me and Tom. And this was before he'd even met me! Anyway, the opportunity was too good to miss. Chalky and I picked up the chair and deposited him in the surf. He came out of the water raging like a mad bull and threatening to kill whoever had done such a terrible thing. He had the reputation of being a very hard man, and many people were frightened of him. I kept my head down until the following day. When we got back to the UK, he was still threatening to kill the person who had dunked him. The troops were warning me to keep out of his way. I did just that, until he walked straight up to me and asked me whether I had carried out the terrible deed. 'Yes, I did,' I replied. He walked away and never mentioned it again. Despite his reputation, I would have fought him no matter what. If I had denied what someone had obviously told him, I would have shown my fear. I didn't.

His reputation took another pounding later on, when a member of 8 Troop dropped him with one hit. The guy had been a karate student, and the power of his punch aroused my interest. I also realised for the first time that such reputations are built on past events – as time goes by, the foundations of such reputations can begin to crumble. The Regiment taught us everything about fighting with weapons, but nothing about unarmed combat, which was disappointing, as I still got intimidated by aggressive individuals who were mouthing off.

So once back home, I joined the local karate club under a second-dan black belt called Tom, and spent the first year lining up with seven-year-old kids, learning how to stand on one leg and kick. The art gripped me by the balls and I became addicted; every Wednesday and Friday would find me at karate class, training for two hours. On my trips abroad

I practised everything I had been taught, and then returned home to learn more.

As I progressed up karate's grading system of coloured belts, I began to gain more and more confidence. My aggression continued to subside; I felt less and less inadequate in comparison to my colleagues. With Heather showing me a great deal of love and loyalty, I actually began to feel content with my life.

Christmas 1980 was spent at home in Hereford because B Squadron was back on the counter-terrorist team. When the holidays were over, Heather told me that she was pregnant.

'Oh well, I suppose we had better get married, then,' I said, unromantically.

'Not on your life,' she answered. 'If you think I'm going to marry you just because I'm pregnant, you can think again.' We agreed to wait until the baby was born and think about it. But Heather had another problem with marrying me. Since we had been together she had told me every day that she loved me. I had never said the words.

DELTA IS THE USA's counter-terrorist team, based in North Carolina. When the unit was formed in 1977, they based their selection methods on our own British SAS techniques. In the spring of 1981, B Squadron travelled to Fort Bragg to train with them. Their compound of windowless buildings was hidden inside high walls in what used to be the camp prison. The Americans, as usual, had everything that money could buy – except a sense of humour.

The Delta team guys all appeared to be living out a fantasy of what they really were anyway: they were tough, so they had to behave tough; steely-eyed stares and huge, bulging muscles were the order of the day. Conversations were short and about work only – they took themselves incredibly seriously. B Squadron found this attitude amusing. As far as we were concerned, if a man was truly tough, why would he need to spend his time proving it when it wasn't necessary? When we had finished the job at the Iranian embassy, the Delta team commander had sent us a plaque, on which was written: 'To the brave British Commandos who assaulted the Iranian Embassy on May 5, 1980. Well done.

It just goes to show, you can't make chicken salad out of chicken shit.'
It appeared that there was a sense of humour lurking somewhere, so
the comedians of the squadron set out to find it.

I was amazed by their armoury. Their armourer would custom-
design each sniper's rifle to the individual's finger- and arm-length and
hand-size. The ammunition was carefully manufactured on-site, to the
highest specifications. Each grain of cordite powder was weighed exactly
before being placed in the cartridge. Many of the high-velocity rifles
were silenced effectively. When I used these weapons adjusted to me
personally, my accuracy improved enormously. In a country where
guns are part of the culture, these guys really were the experts. What
they could do with weapons technology left us in the Stone Age.

We flew up to Chicago to train on wide-bodied passenger aircraft.
Delta assaulted the planes first, and we played the terrorists and hostages.
When we assaulted them, we attacked with water pistols. They were
more dumbfounded than amused by our antics; there wasn't a smile
anywhere.

When we socialised, they had troops in plain clothes following us
everywhere. The Yanks were totally paranoid. Perhaps they thought
we'd been tasked with eliminating the odd NORAID (Irish Northern
Aid) fund raiser while we were in town! We soon figured out what was
going on and confronted the followers. They apologised, and insisted
that they were only following orders. After that we would invite them
over for a drink. The farce continued until one day when Major Jerry
was preparing to brief us. Paul from 7 Troop walked in wearing a pink
foam Stetson hat and a pair of blue-and-yellow glasses with battery-
operated windscreen wipers, carrying a Thompson submachine-gun
water pistol with a half-gallon magazine. It was the first time I ever saw
Major Jerry lost for words, and the first time I saw members of Delta
team actually crack a smile.

Of course, now we had proved ourselves complete idiots, it was
time to go to work. We set up a joint exercise with Delta playing the
enemy and the hostages; we had to rescue the hostages. After five days
the enemy had made it almost impossible to mount a rescue, and were
now demanding a bus to make their getaway. We provided one. As

they drove past us at about twenty miles per hour, we stormed it and rescued all the hostages in seven seconds flat. Delta team were as amazed as the Metropolitan Police had been the year before. How could these idiots be so good at their jobs?

I GOT BACK to Hereford to find Heather in a bad way: she had miscarried our baby. The Army had not felt obliged to inform me, or to bring me home, as we were not married. She was grieving terribly. We had nicknamed the baby Mitch, and what she was going through was just the same as if the baby had been born and then died.

Seeing Heather suffer so much, and caring for her as well as I could, made me realise at last just how important she was to me. After a few weeks I made my mind up and took her to a fancy restaurant called the Pilgrim. I told Heather – for the first time – that I truly loved her, and then I proposed. This time she accepted me, and we agreed to get married in September, before my tour on the counter-terrorist team came to an end.

As the day of the wedding approached I constantly asked myself whether I was doing the right thing. Was I going into this because I wanted to, or because I felt morally obliged? Each time I came back to the same conclusion: I wanted to get married. The Wednesday before the wedding I finished my karate training, then went on to my stag night. When I walked into the pub with my instructor, the bar was empty. Oh boy, it was going to be one of *those* stag nights. No one had turned up. I had just ordered a drink when the door flew open and the whole troop paraded in wearing blue T-shirts with different slogans emblazoned across them: *Who is Bisley?*, *Is Bisley Bruce Lee?*, *Bisley Bores Me*, *I Bore Bisley*, and so on. And I was presented with my own shirt, which read, *I AM BISLEY*.

The usual stag night routine followed, with me getting as drunk as I have ever been in my life. My friends and colleagues took me to the SAS club, where I crawled around the dance floor trying to bite women's ankles, and then ended up decorating the furniture with my previously digested dinner. When I was eventually unconscious, they took an arm and leg each and carried me face-down to a taxi, scraping my nose along the floor. My neighbour and friend, Alan, took me home and carried me over his shoulder in a fireman's hoist to the front door. As I lay over his shoulder the pressure on my bladder was too much and I pissed all over his chest. Well, a friend in need . . .

I was so ill I didn't get back to work until the Friday; on the day of the wedding, I was still unable to look at any form of alcohol. The marriage ceremony was like a fairytale, though, and everything went like clockwork. Heather was the picture of beauty as her father walked her towards me. The white peacocks embroidered into the lace of her wedding dress shone as they caught the sunlight through the church windows. She was so perfect that I knew I was the luckiest man on earth to be marrying her.

We made our promises and, as we signed the register, the choir sang 'Ave Maria' from the balcony. I asked Heather to walk slowly with me to the exit: we had to savour this moment for the rest of our lives. We did, and it was a wonderful feeling to hold her on my arm and show the whole world that she was married to me.

We went to South Wales for our honeymoon. It had to be close to Hereford, as I was still on the counter-terrorist team and I had to check in twice a day to see whether I was needed. After only three days, the squadron was called to Ireland. They told me to stay where I was and have a good time, which I did. By the time I got home, Heather was pregnant again.

CHAPTER 15

Operation Mikado

ON FRIDAY, 2 April 1982, General Leopoldo Galtieri, leader of the Argentine military junta, launched a surprise attack on the Falkland Islands. The islands, situated only two hundred miles east of the Argentine mainland, had been a bone of contention between the United Kingdom and Argentina for almost one hundred and fifty years. They had belonged to Britain since Britannia had ruled the waves; the population were British by descent and spoke English. The islands were of no strategic value, and most diplomats believed that at some point in the approaching decade they would come under Argentine control for trade and economic reasons.

Unfortunately, the political and economic situation in Argentina was deteriorating fast. There was a rising public outcry against the fascist policies of the government. Political activists and dissenters were vanishing in the night in their thousands. The cost of living for most Argentines was rising at an impossible rate. Galtieri needed a diversion to deflect public opinion. Invading the Falkland Islands was an ideal opportunity to whip the country into a patriotic fever and avoid confronting his other problems.

Facing the Argentine invasion fleet and six hundred Argentine regular soldiers were just fifty-two British Royal Marine Commandos stationed on the islands. The following day, 3 April, after a brave but futile resistance, and in the face of overwhelming odds, the Falkland Islands and the island of South Georgia were surrendered to Argentina. Back at home, the Regiment prepared for action.

G and D Squadrons were ready to move within hours. B Squadron, much to our disappointment, was placed on stand-by. A Squadron was the current counter-terrorist team, so they were seriously pissed off too.

Some time in the second week of April, Margaret Thatcher made it abundantly clear that Britain was not going to take the invasion lying down. A task force was being prepared to take back the lost territory. G and D Squadrons had already departed; at the time we didn't know exactly what their destination was, but Ascension Island in the mid-Atlantic was a good bet. We began getting everything we had into tip-top condition. The weather in the South Atlantic was wet and cold and heading towards winter – anything that could deal with Antarctic winds and temperatures would be a bonus. Special socks and sleeping-bags, along with Gore-Tex jackets, were issued or specially purchased from mountaineering stores.

Major Jerry was coming to the end of his tour as squadron commander and was soon to be replaced by Jack. In spite of this, he thrust himself headlong into the preparations for Operation Mikado, the designated title of B Squadron's task for the war. We were eventually called in for an operational briefing on the same day that several new men from selection joined the squadron. Imagine how they must have felt when, on their very first day, Operation Mikado was laid out before them and the rest of the troops.

B Squadron was to prepare to fly to Ascension Island by VC-10, and from there we would transfer to two C-130 Hercules transport aircraft to fly on to Argentina, refuelling in midair. We were to land on one of three military airbases that held the Argentine Air Force's top weapon, the Super Etendard fighter-bomber, the jet that carried the Exocet air-to-ship missile. The Exocet was capable of sinking a major warship from a range of thirty miles. We were to land both our transports on the main runway and drive out of the rear doors in Land Rovers mounted with machine-guns. Our mission was to destroy the jets while they were still on the ground; once we'd done that, the survivors were then to make a hundred-mile dash to the Argentina/Chile border, where we would contact friendly forces and be evacuated to safe territory. Two RAF Special Forces crews were tasked to fly the mission. Once on the ground, they would have to make their way home with the rest of us. Preparation training was to begin immediately.

We could get three long-wheel-base Land Rovers into each plane. The wheels had to be chained to the floor with quick-release straps, and the rear cargo door was fitted with special ramps that dropped down when the door was lowered to allow the vehicles to negotiate the eighteen-inch drop to the ground without damaging the suspension. The Land Rovers had 7.62mm General Purpose Machine-Guns (GPMGs) mounted on front and rear, with boxes containing four hundred rounds of ammunition bolted alongside each gun. Smoke canisters were fitted to the bodywork to give cover from fire when discharged. Anti-tank weapons and explosives, plus the personal equipment of the four-man crew, filled the remaining space in the rear. Each aircraft was to carry thirty men: twelve on the three Land Rovers, the remainder on foot.

Night after night we spent hours on end flying at low level, avoiding radar and landing one behind the other on some distant airfield in the middle of nowhere. As we flew over the sea, the waves appeared sometimes to touch the wingtips – we were barely a hundred feet above the water. On one occasion, immediately after landing, the rear C-130 had to make an emergency take-off over the top of the leader, as there wasn't enough space left for him to stop behind us. I always felt very vulnerable in the hands of a pilot: I had no control, and there was nothing I could do to improve my own chances of survival except hope.

As time went by, it became clear that some of the operational planning had not been undertaken in any depth. With sixty intelligent and experienced soldiers taking part, it wasn't long before questions began to be asked. Sixty men landing on an airfield would be pretty insignificant: six Land Rovers and another thirty-six foot-soldiers wouldn't be able to cover the territory required very quickly. The Argentine Army had barracks close to all their airfields, and Air Force defence units in place, some of which included Surface-to-Air Missiles (SAMs). We were at war, and these aircraft were of great importance to the enemy: they would certainly be well protected.

Question How are we going to land without the Argentines being alerted?

Answer By speaking Spanish to them over the radio.

Question What about the SAMs?

Answer By the time we land it will be too late to fire them.

Question Why do we have to land on the runway? Why can't we land away from the target and walk in quietly?

Answer This is the way Brigadier de la Billière wants it!

Morale began to take a plunge. Jack had now taken over the squadron, and something needed to be done to restore confidence. Unfortunately, Jack wasn't any keener on the job as it stood than the rest of us.

WHILE ALL THIS was going on back at home, the task force had sailed south to confront the enemy. The Paras, the Royal Marines and the Guards comprised the main infantry force. On 22 April, D Squadron deployed on South Georgia but had to be pulled out because of the extreme cold. Two helicopters were lost in the bad weather, but without casualties. On 3 May, G Squadron deployed on West Falkland and set up observation posts (OPs) to pass information back to the task force.

On 4 May, HMS *Sheffield* was sunk by an Exocet missile south-east of East Falkland. Our mission was given the go-ahead by Downing Street: we were to depart on 11 May. A reconnaissance team was deployed immediately and within twenty-four hours they had landed on Ascension Island and flown on to the Falklands. They parachuted into the sea wearing wet suits and were picked up by HMS *Hermes*. A helicopter then flew them into Argentina.

Now I had only a few days to come to terms with going to war for real. The task force had arrived, and we were taking casualties. Our mission was, to be frank, a suicide job, but if the loss of one SAS squadron could prevent the destruction of an aircraft carrier, it could mean the difference between winning and losing the whole campaign.

Heather was now eight months pregnant – we'd been told it was a boy – and I had started to wonder whether I would ever see my son born. I had told her nothing about the task we were to undertake; she obviously watched the news, but the full truth of what I was setting out to try to achieve would only have frightened her even more. But now I had to go, and we both had to face the possibility that I might not return. That last night, while she was out working, I sat alone and replayed the video of our wedding. I watched as we made our vows and kissed. I tried to hold as many images as I could inside my head to take with me into battle. Later, I lay by her side, wide awake, looking down at her. I felt torn between my obligations to her and my obligations to the Army. In principle I could have refused to go, but I knew I couldn't do that. I was a Para and an SAS soldier and if the last ten years were not to be proved a lie, I would have to face my fear and go forward.

In the end it wasn't the Army, or Queen and country, or even my mates that I went for – it was for me, once again, to prove that I was every bit as good as the rest of them.

I FELT THE tears welling in my eyes as I left Heather on the doorstep that morning. This might well be the last time I ever saw her, this woman who had given me a sense of homecoming, of emotional strength and self-worth. I held her in my arms, wishing I didn't have to go. She eventually sent me on my way with a smile on her face and tears in her large deep-brown eyes. Once my back was turned, I hardened my heart and tried to put the image of her to the back of my mind so I could deal with the task in hand.

We loaded all our equipment into the four-ton trucks and settled ourselves down in the green Army bus, ready to drive to RAF Lyneham. We were waiting for the squadron commander to arrive when word came through that he and the 6 Troop staff-sergeant had been relieved of their duties, for failing to take a positive attitude towards the task. Some of my colleagues thought that they were voicing the opinions of many who saw the job as suicide; others called them cowards. I didn't regard them as cowards – it must have taken a great deal of courage to stand up and say that they thought the operation was a non-starter. However, a soldier's primary duty is to do as he is told, especially a Special Forces soldier, and any indication to the contrary – 'We value your opinions' – is just bollocks. One of the 9 Troop sergeants stood up and asked whether we were going to back the two relieved soldiers. Nobody replied, and he sat down again quietly, possibly contemplating what might well have turned into an attempted mutiny.

The Regiment's second-in-command, Ian, was given control. He was a popular man and well known to us all, and he immediately put a positive spin on the mission, saying that to have any chance of success we had to approach it in the right frame of mind. We all knew he was right. It had to be done.

THE DRIVE DOWN to RAF Lyneham was jovial enough, many of us playing cards with what money we had in our pockets, since it wasn't going to be of much use to us where we were going – or so we thought.

The Land Rovers had already gone ahead with the C-130s. The cargo holds of the VC-10 were filled to the brim with our equipment, so we had to stack all our weapons in the fuselage aisle. A lot of our gear had been supplied by the United States: satellite communications that gave us a direct link to Hereford, multi-barrelled rocket-launchers and our own Milan anti-tank missiles. It would take ten hours to reach Ascension, and we would have to refuel in Ghana in order to cover the four thousand miles. As soon as we landed we would be given our final target, depending on the information received from the recce group and on which airfield, according to the aerial photography, the Super Etendards were based. We were to take off immediately to launch the mission.

But when we landed, plans began to change rapidly. There was to be a short delay before we left – no reason was given. We were taken to a small military base called Two Boats in the centre of the island. As we drove the short distance to the base, the ground sloped away from the road, allowing us to look down over the landscape. To the west I could see a barren volcanic desert, apparently completely devoid of plant life, while to the east, the ground rose up to the tip of an ancient volcano that had been formed from the mid-Atlantic Trench. Its eastern side was covered with forest and lush vegetation. The weather was hot and humid, but a fresh wind blew in from the sea, relieving the heat.

The island was dominated by one other feature: the airfield. Victor refuelling aircraft, Canberra bombers, VC-10s and C-130 Hercules were taking off and landing almost continually, day and night. The airfield was run by the United States Air Force, which had a radar tracking station and base on the south of the island. We took the opportunity created by the delay to go to the Cable and Wireless office in George-town and phone home. There wasn't much to say other than that I was still alive and didn't know whether I would be able to call again.

It turned out that the recce group had failed in their allotted task: when their helicopter had landed, a distress rocket had been discharged. The patrol commander believed that the landing had been compro-mised and ordered the pilot to fly the whole group to the Chilean border. The satellite photographs showed that the Argentines were moving their aircraft from base to base, never leaving them long in one place – a sensible move under the circumstances. In brief, we lacked enough information about where the enemy aircraft were to mount the mis-sion with any reasonable chance of success.

WE SIMPLY HAD to wait. Time is seldom wasted where the well-trained SAS soldier is concerned. Our rations were not exactly good at Two Boats, so we set off to invade the USAF canteen, known as the Volcano Club, where steaks, burgers, fries and ice cream were avail-able twenty-four hours a day. We were going to war, so who cared about the calories? Beer, fresh meat and fish appeared from hidden sources, and in no time at all barbecues and piss-ups became the order of the day.

We prepared to go in again a few days later. It was just a matter of getting on the Hercs and going, and once more I steeled myself for the job ahead: to attack the enemy on his home ground and then to be hunted down like an animal as I ran for safety. And yet again the mis-sion was cancelled. US President Ronald Reagan brought pressure to bear to prevent the war escalating onto the mainland of Argentina. Given all the aid we were receiving, it was only sensible for the British government to accede to his request. The war was going in our favour, so why push it?

This new delay didn't help me at all. It was bad enough preparing for a kamikaze mission, but to then have to stand down yet again was almost mind-numbing. The booze began to flow copiously amongst the troops, until the squadron sergeant-major put a stop to it and began giving us useful work to do. We set up small training exercises on the Ascension airfield, test-firing our weapons and training in satellite communications.

We also trained and worked as infantry sections for the first time since I had joined the Regiment. I was surprised to discover that many of the senior ranks had never operated as infantry in their lives; the majority of the troopers were more qualified in this than the senior ranks. Most of my own sergeants didn't have a clue about infantry battle-drills. They couldn't give section or platoon orders and, consequently, would be dangerous to have around in a fire-fight. I for one wouldn't have followed some of my own sergeants to the shithouse in a platoon or section attack.

One of our sergeants had quite a reputation as a mortar man, and gave a lesson on mortar fire control to the troop: this skill enables troops to call for mortars to be fired on enemy positions and to direct the fire accurately onto the target. As a mortar man myself, I tried to point out that he had missed out one small but highly pertinent point when giving the lesson: the command known as 'direction'. Without this command, the bombs were as likely to land on your own head as the enemy's. I was told by my troop commander, David, a new captain from the Gordon Highlanders, that I had a bad attitude. So much for trying to be helpful.

My frustration increased when we were given a choice of weapons to take with us: either our 7.62mm SLRs (self-loading rifles) or the .223mm AR-15 Armalites. The former has an effective fire range of six hundred yards, the latter three hundred yards. The Argentines had Belgian 7.62mm FNs with an effective fire range of six hundred yards. The SLR weighed more, and so did the ammo, but it was the obvious weapon to use in a situation where there were no trees or cover and the enemy could engage us at six hundred yards. Every former infantryman was carrying an SLR and twenty magazines of ammo; almost every former corps man was carrying an Armalite. No one in authority had the experience to order them to take the correct weapon for the terrain.

War was bringing out the worst as well as the best in the SAS.

We continued to update our plan and offer new ideas to Hereford for approval. We suggested a number of other ways we could knock out the aircraft. Every suggestion was met with a No. Back at home, DLB – Brigadier Peter de la Billière – insisted that the raiders had to land on the airfield. We didn't like this guy: there was no talking sense to him. He clearly wanted his Entebbe-style raid; it was his plan and his baby and he wasn't going to change it for anyone. We were prepared to do it, as we had already proved by getting on the aircraft, but we weren't too happy about wasting everything by being shot out of the air and killed before we even landed on Argentinian soil.

One tragedy had already occurred, on 12 May, when a Sea King helicopter with twenty-three men onboard suffered an engine failure while cross-decking. Fourteen members of G Squadron lost their lives in the subsequent crash – almost a whole troop, a quarter of the squadron. When the OC read out their names a terrible silence descended. We all had friends amongst them. In some ways it seemed unreal – that we could lose more men in an accident than we had ever lost in any campaign since the Second World War.

Back in Hereford the Regiment wives were asked to come into camp for a briefing from the families officer. Heather was now in her last month of pregnancy: the baby could arrive at any time now. No one had any idea why they were being called in, so when the families officer began his talk by announcing that fourteen men had lost their lives the previous day, every woman instantly leapt to the quite justified conclusion that it was her own husband who was dead. Some burst into tears, while others clung to one another in horror. Some minutes later, when the major got around to announcing that next of kin had already been informed, the women realised that it was other peoples' husbands who had been killed; other wives who had received the bad news.

The families officer then went on to bring the women up to date with the war. He warned them about security and the press, and finished by telling them that if the next operation planned came off, there would be 'a bloodbath'. Whatever his intentions were, he sent the wives into a state of shock. When Heather left, the only thing she could remember was that many had already died and that there was going to be a 'bloodbath'. Confidence was being instilled at home as well as abroad . . .

TIME DRAGGED ON Ascension Island. Every time we thought we were going in, the mission was cancelled. Time and time again we prepared, and time and time again we were stood down. At one point it became clear to someone that 9 Troop was being led by less than adequate senior ranks; the troop was consequently left out of the mission plan. I should have been relieved, but common sense and war make strange bedfellows and instead, I was appalled that I would be left out, so I went to the OC and pointed out that as I was one of only four Milan missile controllers in the squadron, I was invaluable to the mission. I was duly put back on the job, and spent the next few days asking myself why on earth I had done such a thing.

Between 21 and 25 May, three warships, the *Ardent*, the *Antelope* and the *Coventry*, and a huge cargo ship, the *Atlantic Conveyor*, were sunk by the Argentine Air Force. The *Atlantic Conveyor* had been carrying many of the Sea Harriers and Chinook transport helicopters and this great loss put our success in jeopardy. The southern winter was closing in, ships were being sunk, and the transport aircraft had almost all been lost: the main infantry troops would have to go everywhere by foot. If any further large losses were incurred, the outcome of the war would be highly unfavourable for us. Yet again Operation Mikado raised its battered head, and we prepared once more to go into the breach. There was no change to the original plan. We unhappily surrendered to the inevitable and got back on with the waiting. By now, though, the incursions of the Paras and Marines, who had succeeded in covering enormous distances on foot, had forced the enemy to retreat to the north. There was no longer any good reason to attack the mainland.

The squadron still had an ardent desire to be involved though, so the OC put together a last-minute plan to fly south and parachute into the sea. Once there, we would prepare to launch an assault on Port Stanley airfield and snatch our moment of glory. As we were to be picked up by ship, we wouldn't need to make the drop with all our kit attached to us, so it was decided to place it in one-ton containers attached to parachutes and follow these down into the sea. This would make the drop safer from our point of view – we would have less weight to pull us under the water if our personal equipment failed to float. We were to wear warm clothing covered by a dry diving suit, which had seals around the neck and wrists to keep water out. The sea temperature would be around one degree Centigrade: if the water got into his suit, a man would die of hypothermia in less than five minutes. We were used to preparing all our own heavy-drop equipment, but the RAF insisted that they prepare the one-ton boxes. All our operational kit, including our bergens, was in those boxes – we were dropping completely clean.

ON 10 JUNE we took off in our two Hercs from Ascension Island. After eight hours we were refuelled by a Victor tanker. Our aircraft refuelled successfully, but the second plane damaged its fuel receiver and had to return to base. We were left to go on alone.

Fourteen hours later, our Herc was circling over the drop zone and preparing to release our containers when, suddenly, the OC went rushing up to the cockpit. The pilot was apparently running into his spare fuel and wanted to abort the mission. Rumour has it that a violent argument ended with the OC drawing his pistol and the pilot agreeing to make the drop.

The tailgate of the Hercules slowly opened and the cold air rushed into the fuselage, chilling my cheeks. I was busy putting masking tape around one of the wrists of my friend Derek's dry-suit – the all-important seal had torn as he put it on. The RAF dispatchers sent the parachutes out the back and I watched as the chutes opened and pulled out their one-ton loads. I expected to see the containers floating down into the sea, but, to my surprise, I saw nothing except what appeared to be parachute canopies floating in the wind, alone. The aircraft circled once while we clipped our static lines onto the wires that ran down either side of the fuselage and checked one another's parachutes. When the red light came on, I marched forward to wait behind the first two men, who were already standing on the edge of the tailgate. I was filled with excitement: this would be my first operational jump into action. Green on, and we leaped out into space at eight hundred feet. I glanced down and saw two warships waiting below. The sea looked green and cold, but there were no breaking waves and the water appeared safe enough.

About twenty feet up, I pulled the quick-release strap on one side of my harness and dropped the remaining distance into the sea. This action prevented the canopy from inflating with water and pulling me under, while the remaining link with the parachute gave the Navy something with which to pull me on board their little motorboats. I snapped a glow-stick and the fluorescent chemicals lit up and glowed green. I held it up to signal my position as I dropped into the troughs of the waves. The large swell continually caused me to lose sight of the pick-up boats, and the cold water on the back of my neck was giving me a headache. I hoped the masking tape on Derek's wrist was holding out.

After what felt like an age, I was pulled into one of the boats and taken aboard the HMS *Andromeda*. Alongside was HMS *Glamorgan* with a hole in her rear port side, where a missile had found its target. The Navy acted glad to see us, and took us all to the petty officers' mess for hot drinks and food.

When the OC arrived, we discovered why I hadn't seen our containers float down to the sea on their parachutes: all the containers – with all our equipment – had become detached from their parachutes and plummeted into the sea. Many had burst open on impact, and an awful lot of our gear had been destroyed. It appeared that the RAF had failed to take into account the fact that the one-ton containers did not actually have a payload weighing one ton. Being light, they had swung heavily and released themselves from their fittings, which, given that the boxes were underweight, should have been closed.

We had come all this way, only half of us had actually managed to arrive at our destination, and now much of our fighting gear was at the bottom of the sea: what a complete fuck-up.

One of the falling containers had spun across the bows of *Andromeda*, just missing the ship. As one of the POs (petty officers) commented, it would have set things off nicely if we had sunk a frigate into the bargain!

I couldn't see any way that we could now be of practical use as a unit, but the OC came up with the idea of rescuing one of the G Squadron sergeants, Roy, who had been captured when his OP was discovered. The officer he was with was killed in the fire-fight that ensued; he himself escaped serious interrogation because he was black and managed to convince the class-conscious Argentines that he was just the officer's batman – it never occurred to them that he could actually be an SAS sergeant. He was being held on West Falkland, in Port Howard. Now we were going to rescue him.

ONCE AGAIN THE fates were against us. As we steamed west, the signal came over the ship's radio that a white flag was flying over Port Stanley: the Argentine Army had surrendered. My immediate response was to shout for joy – I was going to live, I was going home to see my son born – but around me I could see only disappointment on my colleagues' faces. We had missed the show. These were the same men who, just a few days before, had been complaining bitterly about our mission – there's just no pleasing some people.

I was happy. I had done my best and had been prepared, as were all the others, to carry out any mission presented to me, no matter how ill-conceived it might have been. The fates had simply conspired – for, or against us, depending on one's point of view. I had nothing personally to be ashamed of, but I had made a significant discovery: I had found out just how expendable we all were in a war. I had also discovered many disconcerting weaknesses in my own unit, which left me with a great feeling of dissatisfaction.

ON 18 JUNE I returned from Port Stanley to the *Lancelot* to discover that I was the father of Alexander, who had weighed in at eight pounds, eight ounces, and that both he and Heather were doing fine. I cracked a few celebratory beers with the lads, but it was all too far away to seem real. However, the war was over, and the OC got me on the first available flight back to the UK, on 26 June, some twelve hours before the others followed.

When I got home I had to change into civilian clothes at camp and then cadge a ride from the duty driver. It was 2.30 in the morning, but Heather was awake and waiting. I was home, the war hero in her eyes. As far as I was concerned, I was nothing of the sort: just a lucky sod who in the end had done bugger all. Our son, Alexander, was asleep, so I didn't disturb him until he began murmuring. When he did, I picked him up in my arms and he opened his eyes and looked at me. At that moment my heart almost burst with love. It was as if someone had tied a string that could never be broken, joining my heart to his. Never in my life had I felt such an intensity of pure, uninhibited emotion.

Whatever adversity you come up against in life, the cure for it is love, and the more people love you, the more you're capable of loving other people. There's nothing quite so inspiring as the love that a child gives to an adult. It's totally without question and without reason. When somebody loves you just for who you are, it's magical; it makes you see yourself in a different light. That day tears ran down my cheeks, and I knew that nothing would ever be the same again.

AT THE END of every operation, the SAS indulges in a debrief. The idea is to go over all the actions undertaken and see if there are any lessons to be learned from them. We sat in the new Pal-udr-inn Club. The vast space, so white, open and boring it had apparently been designed by a mortuary attendant, was filled to capacity with all the members of the Regiment. First, the colonel, Mike Rose, got up to speak. He congratulated the men on their performance and told us all how wonderful we were, but there was no mention of the many mistakes that had been made: how troops in OPs had not been covered by their comrades in the rest area; how the Johnson boat engines whose unreliability the troops had complained about for years had almost cost us the lives of several men when they failed. Nor was there mention of the catalogue of disasters that left B Squadron out of the whole campaign. Time after time we were told how great we had been. Many of us had hoped for a more productive debrief, so that we could actually learn from the mistakes that had been made.

At the end of the colonel's speech, Brigadier Peter de la Billière stood up to make his contribution. This was to be his valedictory address: he was to hand over to the new brigadier that same day. De la Billière had never been highly thought of by the enlisted men of the SAS. No one doubted his courage, or his ability as an officer, but the general consensus was that he was a ruthless, arrogant glory-seeker who didn't give a damn about anyone but himself. Hitherto I hadn't had an opinion one way or the other, but now that the Falklands campaign was over, I felt I had good reason to share this assessment.

The RSM told us to sit up as DLB mounted the rostrum and began to go over the good points of the campaign. He threw in the odd joke, but nobody laughed, not even the officers. At last he got around to B Squadron: and he roundly denounced us, as unwilling to do the job he had asked us to do. The hatred in the room was tangible. How dare he say such a thing? I wanted to stand up and tell him to piss off: we had been willing to go from day one – hadn't we boarded the plane? We had tried to improve a ridiculous plan and had been denied by an arrogance that had bordered on stupidity.

He finally patronised us with a story about an SAS major serving in France in the Second World War, who was driving towards a position to meet up with his men when he was stopped by locals and warned that there was an ambush ahead. Ignoring their advice, he went boldly on to join up with his group, in spite of the danger.

We sat waiting for the story to end with an account of how this great hero had saved his men from certain death and achieved the objective of his mission. DLB concluded the story, 'The major carried on and drove into the ambush and was killed.' The room erupted in loud, spontaneous laughter. Here was this man, trying to convince us that we too should have been that stupid. We continued laughing, in spite of the RSM's orders to stop, until the focus of our anger removed himself from the stage in favour of his replacement. As soon as the new commander stood up, the room was filled with respectful silence. We had had our moment: the SAS had laughed DLB out of the door.

CHAPTER 16

The Final Curtain

THERE WAS TO be no rest for the wicked. Within a week of getting back I was told to go to Lympstone in Devon to attend the Royal Marines Sniper Instructors' course. This was the only sniper course in the British Armed Forces that had run continuously since the Second World War. What made it so special was that only soldiers who had attended and passed with the top grade of Marksman could go on to become instructors, thus maintaining the standards in perpetuity.

Being a military sniper is not just about being a good shot. First, you have to get within range of your enemy, then you have to identify him, kill him and escape, all without being seen. All this naturally requires the infantry soldier to develop his fieldcraft to extremely high levels.

The course lasted for six weeks, five days a week. The subjects taught included observation, judging distance, camouflage and concealment, stalking, shooting, map-reading and aerial photography. To pass the course as a qualified Sniper, a student had to score sixty-five per cent on all the subjects in the final week; to pass as a Marksman he had to score eighty per cent in all subjects. There was no leeway: fail one subject and you failed them all.

I had never worked with the Royal Marines: they had always been the Parachute Regiment's greatest rivals, and the Falkland Islands campaign had done nothing to change that. Still, to my mind they were bloody good soldiers.

I was sent to Lympstone as a corporal, accompanied by an Operation Storm veteran. Simon was a rare creature for one of his generation, being both a light drinker and very good company.

It didn't take long to settle into the regimental system of the Royal Marines. The snipers were operating fairly independently of the rest of the camp, so there were no real bullshit problems to overcome. The men were very much like Paras, but with a less extrovert and more mature attitude towards one another – whether that was because they had all just returned from a war I couldn't say, but I liked them a great deal and respected their standards of soldiering and fitness.

There were only twelve men on the course: two SAS, two SBS (Special Boat Service) and eight Marines, and it began with demonstrations of the standards we were expected to achieve. We were taken out onto Westbury Common, given binoculars and told to search for a sniper who, we were informed, was within two hundred yards of us. None of us could see him. Suddenly a shot rang out, giving us an indication of his whereabouts, but there was no smoke to give him away. An instructor walked out and stood within ten feet of the sniper, and again a shot rang out. Still we saw nothing. The instructor finally stood next to the hidden man and touched his head. Even then we could see absolutely nothing until, almost as if to convince us that he was really there, the sniper stood up.

To an SAS soldier, the map-reading was almost a non-event. If by now I couldn't place myself to within ten yards' accuracy using a British Ordnance Survey map and the assistance of an aerial photograph, then I was in serious trouble. Even so, the importance of map-reading in terms of the course was not just to get to the right place, but also to be able to visualise the relief of the land. If there was a rise or a forest between you and the enemy, then why crawl? However, if there was nothing behind you, you could be silhouetted from miles away.

Judging distance *was* a skill that I needed to practise. I had to be accurate to within ten per cent, eight out of ten times to pass as Marksman, or seven to pass as Sniper. There are many aids to judging distance. One technique is to judge that an object is no more than so many yards away, then no less than so many, and then take an average. Judging accurate distance is important to a sniper because if you get to within range of the enemy and then miss because you have set the sights on your rifle to the wrong distance, it is all wasted effort.

Camouflage and concealment exercises consisted of giving a man with no camouflage five minutes to run out to the front and become invisible, before going through the 'two shots and hand on the head' procedure previously described.

Observation was my weakest skill. Twelve items of military equipment, some of it Russian, were placed in an open area up to one hundred and fifty yards in front of us. To score, it wasn't just good enough to see an item and to describe it as, for example, a magazine. You had to be able to say that it was a 9mm British Sterling submachine-gun magazine to get a whole point. Anything less might score half. To top this, only a small portion of the object would be visible. You had to score nine out of twelve to pass as Marksman, eight to pass as Sniper.

Shooting, again, was not just a case of hitting a target. At six hundred yards with an L42 sniper rifle, NATO-issue 7.62mm ball ammo and a three-times magnification scope, all sorts of other factors came into the equation. The wind direction, the light and the slope all had an effect on the fall of the shot. Shooting started at two hundred yards and gradually moved out to six hundred. In the final shoot, ten rounds had to be fired within one minute from maximum range. The target was man-sized, and was divided into a central area that scored five points and an outer area that scored four. A miss scored zero.

The final exercise was the stalk, which combined all the aforementioned skills. We would be issued with a map and aerial photo and be given two hours to get to a target marked on the map. The target was three trained observers with binoculars, who knew that we were coming. We were to be followed by the training staff, who were in radio contact with the observers. If we were seen, we would be withdrawn and failed. We had to get to within 250 yards of the target and then fire one blank round and reload. If the observer could not see us, then we would fire another shot, with a walker standing within ten feet of us.

After the second shot, the walker would point to where we were. He would then place his hand on the end of the rifle barrel or on our heads. If we were still unseen, he would ask us what our target was doing with his hands. This ensured that we could actually see the man in our sights. The observer would scratch his nose or wave. The instructor would then check our sights for wind and elevation. If these were correct he would look to see whether there were obstructions that might deflect a bullet to the front and check that there was a viable escape route to the rear. If these factors were also in order, only then would we pass the stalk test.

I had to withdraw from the course for a week to look after my son, Alexander, because Heather had gone into hospital with appendicitis. This cost me valuable time and practise, but in spite of this I entered the final week confident about everything except the observation test.

Everyone gets two tries at the tests in the final week. I passed everything to Marksman standard on the first try except the observation: I scored eight, one point short. If I didn't get nine on the second try I would pass as Sniper but not as Marksman. The second test came around, and I desperately searched the foreground with my binoculars, trying to identify each blade of grass. I broke the area in front of me down into foreground and middle ground. I knew the objects were less than three hundred yards away, so I didn't need the distant ground. I swept the ground, using first my naked eyes and then the binoculars, going backwards and forwards across the scene, trying to spot breaks in the natural order. I needed one more point, one tiny extra item to make the difference between good and excellent. When the result came through I scored exactly nine points. I was ecstatic. I had attended the hardest infantry course in the world in terms of individual soldiering skills and I had achieved a top pass.

Two of us achieved Marksman and four passed as Sniper; the remainder failed. We went out into Lympstone that night, and for the first time in my life I performed a Zulu Warrior: I stripped naked and danced in the pub in full view of the general public while my coursemates threw beer all over me. A good time was had by all – except for the young lady who tried a little too hard to see the proceedings and was wrestled away by her boyfriend.

I RETURNED TO Hereford full of hope for my future. I discussed my aspirations with a friend of mine, Peter, who rapidly disillusioned me by letting me into a little secret. 'Bob, they sent you on that course because they knew it was hard. Certain individuals hoped that you would fail it, so that you could be RTU'd.' This was confirmed later when, after a promotion conference, Stuart was promoted and I was held back. Individuals on the conference had described my perform-ance as coursemanship, whatever that is supposed to mean. I inter-preted it as 'We don't like him'.

Later I was told by Mal, now the troop staff sergeant, that I was to be sent to Chamonix in France on an Alpine Mountain Guides course. I responded enthusiastically, and within two days found myself removed from the list.

It appeared that there was a conspiracy against me; certain people wanted me out. I believed that all I had to do to get around the problem was to achieve higher and higher professional standards. I made great efforts not to offend people and to avoid arguments. I was growing up: my karate training was calming me down, and I was no longer the insecure young Para who had arrived three years before. But the grouse-beaters had formed their opinion of me long before, and carried on airing their views over the copious rounds of beer that they continued to absorb.

It began to be apparent that the Regiment's official opinion was formed on the basis of what people had heard, and not what they actu-ally knew.

A REPLACEMENT SQUADRON commander arrived just in time for us to take over the counter-terrorist team again. A new technique for landing quickly on target had just been developed, known as fast roping.

Fast roping had been in use by the Royal Marines for some time to get onto the decks of ships from a helicopter when the sea was run-ning high. The helicopter would hover about thirty feet above the ship and suspend a fifty-foot-long, two-inch-thick rope over the pitching deck. The Marines, wearing leather abseil gloves, would grab hold with both hands and slide down the rope to the ship. It was quick and easy.

When we did it, however, it was taken to extremes. Four two-hundred-foot-long ropes were mounted on the tailgate of a Chinook helicopter hovering at 190 feet. Four ranks of ten men were lined up behind them in full assault kit with body armour. We followed one another down the rope from this tremendous height with only our bandaged hands and abseil gloves between the ropes and certain death. The idea was that at night we could descend quickly to the ground in complete darkness and have ample spare rope to compensate for a slope, but the way we were doing it was unprecedented. It eased up a little only when one man broke both his legs.

It was after one such training session that Mal came up to me and told me that the new squadron commander wanted to see me. He hinted that there might be some problems regarding my future in the SAS. He was sympathetic, but unable to look me in the eye. It surprised me that an SAS staff sergeant with his reputation didn't have the balls to tell me straight out that he didn't like me and wanted me out.

I went to the new OC's office fully aware of the situation. Being new, the OC had very little to go on, except the word of Roy, the squadron sergeant-major with whom I'd had a number of run-ins, and Mal. He sat me down and explained that it was his duty to tell me that at the end of my second tour my contract would be terminated. His reasons were that the men in my troop didn't like me and didn't want to work with me. With nothing to lose, I asked him where this information had come from. He declined to answer.

'Well, sir,' I said, 'if this is true, then I will be only too happy to leave, but as you are new, perhaps you would at least be decent enough to ask all the individual members of my troop, with the exception of Mal and Gwyn, whether this is in fact the case.'

The OC agreed to my request, and I left the office to tell my troop members the score.

Robert, the corporal in my troop, went directly to the OC on my behalf to counter the allegations. The other troop members were discreetly interviewed over the next two weeks. Finally, I was called into the OC's office again. He said that it appeared that a mistake had been made. Roy was sitting behind him; I didn't need to look far to find the source of the mistake.

The OC went on, 'We are going to promote you and send you to training-wing after the next promotion conference.' I left the office thinking that my faith in justice had been rewarded, and that now I could get on with my career. I couldn't have been more wrong.

ONCE WE HAD taken over CT duties again, our first task was another trip to the Delta team in the USA. This time we were to carry out a full counter-terrorist exercise, with all the wealth of the US Special Forces at our disposal. Our mission was to go into an exercise area in Georgia and rescue forty hostages held by a terrorist group, in a situation similar to the US embassy crisis in Iran in 1980. I was picked as one of the six-man reconnaissance team to go in and send back information on the target. The team consisted of David, my troop commander, Tom, Henry, two Delta troopers, and myself. We had rations for six days and clothing equipment that bleeped if we were shot by the enemy.

The exercise was a set-up. During the course of it, it was alleged, amongst other things, that I had 'lost my weapon', an insinuation that preceded me back to the UK. On our return, the whole patrol – David, Tom, Henry and I – was placed on Colonel's Orders. I knew what the score was so I went to headquarters and put in my application to purchase my discharge from the Army immediately. Since joining the SAS I had always believed that I would serve my twenty-two years and collect my pension. Now, at the age of twenty-seven, I was beginning the process of buying myself out. The Sergeant-Major and Staff-Sergeant had had it in for me and a couple of other guys for ages; they were prepared to go to any lengths to get rid of us and the officers just couldn't see it. That's the trouble: at that time the officers only served a couple of years in the SAS so the real power lay with the senior NCOs (non-commissioned officers), some of whom had been there since the Ark. If the SNCOs told the officers you were trouble, there wasn't a lot you could do.

Curiously enough, I have only recently found out just what a set-up that exercise was. I'm learning to fly at the moment and my instructor is ex-SAS himself. He had volunteered for this same exercise because he fancied a trip to America but was warned off. 'You don't want to go on this exercise', he'd been told repeatedly until he took the hint.

So there I stood outside the CO's office, waiting for my hearing. None of us had been officially charged with any crime – rightly, given the fact that we hadn't committed one, not even a breach of military discipline. This was a kangaroo court that could send me back to the Paras, reduce my pay by eight thousand pounds a year and destroy my family life – and it had no right under military law to do so.

Tom had gone in ahead of me. When he came out he looked as though his whole life had been taken away. He had given up everything to serve with the SAS, and in spite of the Regiment's failings, he loved every part of it. He had been sent back to the Paras. He looked totally broken and forlorn. How could they do this to him? He had given himself to them body, mind and soul for eight years.

I wasn't prepared to let anybody treat me like that. I knew the final curtain was about to fall, and I was going to have the parting word. I marched in, head held high, and looked straight into the colonel's eyes. The OC stood to my left.

The colonel was a little man. I had been told his family were landed gentry who owned large areas of Scotland; born with the proverbial silver spoon in his mouth, he knew nothing about ordinary people. He glared up at me. 'Your senior NCOs have stated that you have been walking on a razor blade for a long time and I have decided that you will return to the Parachute Regiment with immediate effect.'

I almost smiled. Well, I thought, fuck you all if you haven't got the brains to see what you are doing. 'That's OK,' I said, 'because I've already put in my papers to buy myself out.'

'Oh,' said the colonel, 'I would think carefully about that. The wind blows cold on the outside.'

Patronising prick, I thought. I said, 'Well, it doesn't blow too fucking warm in here, does it?'

The colonel's face turned purple. 'Get out!' he screamed. 'Get out!'

I saluted smartly, turned to the left and marched out. I must have given a completely different impression to the one Tom had as he left the room.

The OC came out a few minutes later and told me that the colonel had approved my discharge and, in the light of that, had revoked the RTU. I would be out within two weeks and would not be expected to perform any duties in the interim period.

Regardless of the problems that I and many other young NCOs had encountered during this time, the operational effectiveness of the Regiment was not unduly effected. The selection process was still choosing the very best replacements. These replacements would always be able to fill the gaps until the older generation had finally moved on.

IT TOOK ME two days to hand in all my equipment and say goodbye to twelve years of commitment. Many of my comrades came and offered their sympathies. In all truth, though, I felt as if a great weight had been lifted from my back. I had told the Establishment to go to hell; I could manage without them and I would prove it. This wasn't the end, this was a new beginning. From my shattered dream, I was waking up to a whole new civilian world.

CHAPTER 17

Crisis Management

NOWADAYS THERE ARE any number of companies selling ex-SAS soldiers for various roles around the world: bodyguards, security managers, mercenaries and military advisers are in great demand. In November 1984 there were not as many, and the money was not as good.

There is, however, an unofficial organisation which makes sure that former SAS soldiers are gainfully employed. After all, it would be extremely unfortunate if a man were to use those highly specialised skills taught to him by the Regiment to rob a bank, for example – not, I might add, a difficult task for a well-trained and organised professional. I was sent to Joe, a former Regiment soldier who'd broken his back in action who now made his living by introducing soldiers to contracts. Within two weeks of leaving the Army, I was attending an interview at 60 Park Lane, the prestigious London address of a man I had not then heard of: Mohamed Al Fayed.

The interview was conducted by two men. One, Brian, was tall, bald, aged about forty-five and very rough in his manner. His heavy-boned face and flat features made him look like an old skinhead. I reported on my history and mentioned my karate training, which I thought might improve my chances – by then I was a senior brown belt, just one step away from black belt, the top ranking in karate.

The second man, Mick, was shorter, with wide shoulders and narrow hips. He had a full head of sandy hair and an open, smiling face. He was a former Parachute Regiment physical training instructor, and it suddenly dawned on me that he was the man who had walked backwards across the tranasium bars to help me when I was fifteen. His manner was friendly. At one point he asked, 'This karate, does it mean that you can tear men's hearts out and kill with a single blow?'

He was serious, so I gave him a serious answer: 'No, it just means that I am fitter and faster than I would be without it.'

The interview ended, and I was sent home with my train fare and fifty pounds for my time. By the end of the week I had the job: I was bodyguard to the Al Fayed family. The pay was more than I had received in the Army and I would work one week on and one week off. I was ecstatic; my immediate money problems were solved and I had a job.

But my wonderful job was not quite what I thought it would be. I worked a twelve-hour shift, either standing on the roof guarding the site of Al Fayed's new penthouse, then under construction, or sitting at a desk beside the front door checking in visitors and monitoring the closed-circuit TV screens. The money might have been OK, but the job was mind-numbingly boring. Any actual bodyguarding was done by Brian and Mick, who guarded their job as strenuously as they guarded their client.

There were only eight on the team at first, including Mick and Brian. Of the remaining six, three would work one week and three the next, and only at night. Every morning I would run around Hyde Park and Kensington Gardens, a distance of about five miles, then I would go to bed just as the sun rose. It was like being a bat: we woke up and came out in the dark and went to sleep before the dawn. In winter we rarely saw the light of day.

As time went on, the demands on the team began to increase. Mo was generous with pay and tips, but I was often asked to work overtime, which sometimes meant three weeks without a break. Not only was this bad for my health, it was bad for my marriage. Brian had his favourites, and when Mo went off on his yacht other team members were chosen to go with him, live the high life and then get tipped a substantial amount at the end. I wasn't chosen until one Sunday, when another member of the team couldn't make it.

Of course I jumped at the chance to go, but an hour later I was told I wasn't needed after all because the original team member had turned up. An hour after that, just as I was about to leave for home, I was told to get ready to go on the trip again. I went home. It had taken me almost six months of civilian life to learn the word 'no'. I didn't have to do as I was told any more, and I wasn't going to be taken advantage of. Needless to say, I was never asked again, but I didn't intend to be a bodyguard for Mohamed Al Fayed for the rest of my life anyway. After twelve years of mindless obedience to the Army, suppressing my individuality, I wasn't going to be messed around again by anyone.

Mo's eldest son, Dodi, was twenty-eight at the time. He had been the executive producer of the Oscar-winning film *Chariots of Fire*, and was considered to be one of the most eligible bachelors in London, regularly dating Koo Stark and other famous beauties. His car was an Aston Martin Lagonda, and even though he always wore a baseball cap and jeans, he loved the nightclub scene – Annabel's, Tramps and Harry's Bar in Mayfair were his favourite haunts. He spent most of his time in the USA, but when he was in the UK, I became his regular companion and driver on late-night trips. He didn't really need a bodyguard – he never walked, and never left the sanctuary of his West End hangouts.

Dodi rarely entered into conversation with me; although he was always polite, there was no friendship or intimacy that might have made the job more palatable. I would spend hours waiting for him to decide where and when he was going out, only to have him change his mind at midnight. Bodyguarding the rich and famous certainly wasn't the exciting business that I had imagined: for all my skills and training, I was used – and treated – as little more than a highly paid chauffeur and minder. Mind you, that never stopped Dodi telling all his female acquaintances that the man sitting across the room, sipping Perrier water, was his personal bodyguard. Some of these women would approach me for dates and leave their numbers, but I never followed them up.

Like many wealthy people, Dodi loved the image of the tough guy.

He had a gym in his apartment, with towels draped around to give the impression that it was in constant use. He once asked me to teach him karate, but then never got as far as the first lesson. He liked the idea of fitness and strength, but not the work that had to go into achieving them. It was enough to rub shoulders with the rugged brutes from the SAS and hope that some of it stuck.

Still, the tedium of the job had its compensations. First it allowed me to be at home for the birth of my first daughter, Charlotte. With no pressure from work, this time I was able to assist at the birth of my perfectly formed tiny little girl, so tiny, in fact, that when I held her my fingers met together around her waist. I had time to care for both Heather and Charlotte before finally returning to work: no wars, no operations, no Army politics and no problems.

I ESTABLISHED a routine of karate training to lead to my black belt. By the summer of 1985, I was training six days a week. When I was at work I would go to the roof at night, change into a sweatsuit and work out for at least an hour at a time. At home, I would attend three three-hour lessons a week, as well as courses at weekends. I put two inches on my chest and felt ready for anything.

I'd established speed of thought through counter-terrorist training; it combined well with the karate. If I had found qualifying for the SAS hard, I discovered that winning my black belt was a far harder mental process: it needed continuous self-discipline, of a similar standard, but over a longer period of time.

Originally karate had appealed to me because I thought it would help me to handle myself in a violent situation, rather than my usual reaction of simply exploding, lashing out with punches and kicks and hoping that it would work. Early on, my karate teacher told me that I was very different to his other students. 'With them,' he said, 'I have to try to put the aggression in; with you I have to take it out, and that's unusual.'

After a year's training, someone told me, 'You're a much calmer guy, much happier; you're not so aggressive, so nasty.' I found that the stronger and the calmer I became, the fewer potentially violent situations

I got into. People didn't find me so intimidating any more, so the frequency of these incidents diminished without my ever having to use what I was learning.

And when situations did arise, I was able to use the mental discipline instilled by karate to cope better, not because I was capable of punching someone harder, but because I was now capable of thinking more clearly, analysing situations more calmly. With karate the physical aggression is there to be used if you have no choice, but you know when to stop. The discipline stops you crossing the boundary into animal violence.

Karate is a bit like chess: your opponent is thinking seven moves ahead, but if you're firing on all cylinders, you're thinking eight moves ahead. It's a question of planning. Your opponent sees what you're going to do and counters, so you counter his counter. When two equally matched, experienced opponents meet, you'll see them moving around each other and no actual fighting takes place because all the manoeuvres and counter-manouevres are in their minds. It's a mental game, with each opponent neutralising each move before it happens.

KMS, FORMED BY former SAS major David Walker, derived its name from a joke: someone had called the major's operation Keenie Meanie Services (SAS soldiers often being described as 'keen and mean') and it had stuck. KMS had taken over the task of protecting the Sultan of Oman and organising his armed forces when the secret war involving the SAS had ended there in 1976. The money earned had allowed the company to diversify into other areas of 'crisis management'; when I approached them for a job, their main theatre of involvement was Sri Lanka.

India gained independence in 1947, and Sri Lanka, against the wishes of most of the population, was also given its own government. The country was populated by two ethnic groups: the Hindu Tamils and the mainly Buddhist Sinhalese. The Tamils had always been in the minority, but they held education in higher regard than did their Sinhalese compatriots; hence they had controlled all the administrative services under the British, and were also more successful as businessmen. Their success had created envy amongst the poorer Sinhalese. When the Raj ended and democracy took its place, discrimination against the Tamils gradually forced them back into the north-west corner of the country, to an area known as the Jaffna Peninsula.

By 1986 the Tamils were demanding a homeland of their own: a portion of the country where they would not be ruled by the intensely bigoted Sri Lankan government. A group of radical Tamils, with support from Tamil Nadu, the south-eastern corner of India, began to use terrorist tactics to bring about their political aims.

With very little experience of counter-terrorist operations, the Sri Lankan government was fighting a losing battle, until KMS offered to supply experienced British instructors to teach and train their armed forces and police. I made an appointment with David, the human resources manager, a former SAS captain and Welsh Guardsman. It didn't take long to get the job. KMS already knew all they needed to know about me.

I was given two weeks to prepare to leave and invited back for an operational briefing in a week's time. The pay wasn't much better than what I was already getting, but it was time to move on. The worst part of the new job was that I would spend five months abroad before I could come home for four weeks' leave.

The briefing was attended by other former members of the Regiment, some of whom I knew. Billy was a short, broad Scotsman and former Para, and a fellow rugby player from A Squadron. He had a flat nose and a no-nonsense attitude. He also had a wonderful sense of humour and a liking for whisky. We would be going together to the east of the country, to an area called Marduroia, two hundred miles inland from Colombo and eighty miles from the port of Trincomalee. Our task was to set up a new officer training school and teach counter-insurgency and internal security tactics. Under no circumstances were we to venture north or take part in active operations against the enemy. The job was controlled by Colonel Brown, my old training major, since promoted and retired.

We arrived at our 'new' officer training school to discover that the only thing that was new was the instructor team. The camp had belonged to a Canadian construction company which had built an irrigation system with foreign aid then when the job was complete, had arranged to take all their plant home. The Sri Lankan government refused them export licences, obviously hoping either for larger bribes, or that the plant would be left behind, offering some minister or other the opportunity to sell it and line his own pockets. In their frustration the Canadians had finally removed various essential items of equipment and left the place to rot.

We were two hundred miles from civilisation. The previous week a bus had been halted by insurgents and the passengers separated into Hindu and Buddhist; the Buddhists were machine-gunned to death on the spot.

My room was a dank green cube with a wooden wardrobe and a single bulb hanging from the ceiling. I hung my mosquito net over the bed and sprayed the room with insecticide. As the spray descended behind the wardrobe, a loud clattering sound like a castanet made me leap backwards. I crept closer to investigate the noise, and three cockroaches the size of serving spoons scuttled out in disgust. Indiana Jones, eat your heart out – these were the biggest cockroaches in the world, the size of battle tanks. I didn't know whether to stamp on them or lay mines.

Another of the instructors, Henry, had a similar welcome in the toilet. When we investigated a loud shout from Henry's quarters, we found him standing on the toilet with a cobra disappearing quickly down the drain behind him.

In spite of the discomfort, we were a good team, all ex-regular SAS, including my old friend from 9 Troop, Peter; we paired up and worked well together. Training consisted of physical training before breakfast, followed by various technical and practical lessons to teach young officer cadets how to conduct effective operations. I was allotted the task of teaching unarmed combat to the troops. The biggest problem we had was their caste system: when it came to fighting, great loss of face would be suffered by a senior-caste member if he were defeated by a lower-caste member. I overcame this to some degree by constantly impressing on them that they were all dependent on one another in war. I kept the troops away from their officers and, with the help of the team programme, began to mould them into a unit that was not divided by prejudice.

The Sri Lankan enlisted man was a joy to behold and an experience to work with. He never told the truth; rather, he always told you what he thought you wanted to hear. (My own children have been known to do the same thing. Have you tidied your room? Yes, Dad.) Nothing could be left to chance; everything had to be double-checked by the instructors themselves. The Sri Lankan manner of tilting the head to one side and then the other to indicate the affirmative could easily be confused with the negative, creating even more problems. But, as we would with children, we put up with mistakes in good humour; there was very little point in inflicting punishment.

One night we returned from an ambush operation at two in the morning to find that our truck and driver were no longer waiting for us. We force-marched the fifteen miles back to camp, arriving in time for breakfast. When the driver was asked why he'd returned without us, he said he had been frightened of the dark and had come home.

I relished the job. The teaching and soldiering combined made me remember why I had loved the Army so much. We worked hard: fourteen hours a day in temperatures that exceeded forty degrees Centigrade; even with my sleeves rolled down and a hat on, I still got sunburned on the back of my hands and my throat.

I was also the senior medical authority in the area. One day a soldier fell from a helicopter skid and dislocated his knee-cap. When I got to him, the young man was grey with shock and pain. I wrapped a figure-of-eight bandage around his knee and asked about a doctor. The nearest one was in Batticaloa, an hour-long drive in a Land Rover over roads that would have bounced him to hell and back. I laid him back and slipped my fingers under the knee-cap, which was to the side of his leg. I had never done this before, but I had read about it. I straightened his knee slightly and lifted the knee-cap upwards, and, to my surprise and intense relief, it popped right back into place. The grey man by my side suddenly turned black again as his pain subsided and a weak smile spread across his face.

A short time later, a young officer came in wounded: he had a grenade fragment lodged in his throat. Because he was an officer, a helicopter was summoned from Trincomalee, but it would take four hours to get to us. I had to keep this man alive until the chopper arrived and we could fly him to Colombo – maybe six hours in total. He was already in shock when he arrived, and he was coughing up blood, which indicated the possibility of blood leaking into his windpipe. I put him on an intravenous drip and tried to examine the wound to locate the source of the bleeding, but as I did so he lost consciousness. I thought he was about to die.

I was the only thing between him and God, and I had to do something. I rolled him on his side and opened the IV up so that the fluid flooded into his veins, increasing his circulation. He continued to breathe and gradually regained consciousness. The grenade fragment was embedded deep and couldn't be safely removed, but I located the source of the bleeding and clamped it off. With airway management, he remained stable until he arrived safely at hospital six hours later. He recovered from his wounds. I got a helicopter ride to town and a long weekend away for my trouble. It was a wonderful feeling to be able to use my hard-won skills in this way, and even better to see the instant benefit that another human being could derive from my training.

There were, of course, Sri Lankan officers in the camp, and we had to defer to them in terms of administrative authority. They were typical Third World officers: very rank- and class-conscious, they regarded the camp transport as a private perk, and saw each day as a new opportunity to use their power to pilfer as much as possible. They often boasted openly about how they had tortured Tamil prisoners and then burned them alive. Many of my comrades had witnessed such incidents, but had been unable to interfere. On one occasion a mine exploded just outside a village on the Jaffna Peninsula and the television news reported that thirty Tamil Tigers had been killed in hand-to-hand fighting with government forces. One of the contracted helicopter pilots told me what had really happened: the government troops had gone into the nearest village and wiped out every man, woman, child and animal. Sri Lanka is full of mass graves. I don't know whether the animals counted as terrorists in the final head count. My friend had been flying the area commander over the operation at the time; he left shortly afterwards in disgust.

In spite of all its hard work, the team was denied the right to travel to Colombo for rest and recreation when there was no work at weekends, mostly because the Sri Lankan officers took all the transport. Morale started to drop and we finally took to paying for our own vehicle to make the bone-shaking six-hour journey to the coast for two nights of drunken debauchery in the Yacht Club and the city hotels.

One Sunday night we were on the way home when our local driver saw a wild elephant cow walking towards us in the headlights. In his panic he stamped on the brakes, making them screech, and the elephant charged. It's no fun sitting in a minibus that is moving backwards at four miles an hour with a seriously upset three-ton monster chasing you in the headlights. Fortunately, she gave up after a hundred yards and stomped off into the trees. I discovered afterwards that I was clutching my little 9mm Chinese pistol in my hand – it would have been probably about as effective as a fart in an artillery battle.

AFTER THREE MONTHS, I came to the conclusion that I was working for the wrong side. The information that continually flooded in to me from the other Britons working in the country painted a picture of a bigoted government, suppressing a minority in a similar way to how the Nazis treated the Jews before World War II. They controlled all the media and most foreign correspondents. The Tamils had my sympathy, and I no longer wished to stay. I spent another long weekend in Colombo with Billy, then we both quit on the Monday morning.

The day before we flew home, an Air Lanka TriStar was blown up on the runway at Colombo international airport. The bomb killed a large number of people, removing the tail from the jet in the process. We could see the remains as we took off on our return journey to England.

CHAPTER 18

FRELIMO

ON 5 JANUARY 1990, my second son, Oliver, was born: a beautiful child, with a full head of black hair, square shoulders and his mother's big brown eyes. I, meanwhile, had decided to go after a job as a paramedic on an oil rig. I sent off endless letters with my CV, but to no avail; I had to start claiming unemployment benefit, and things got tough. The debts mounted up, until at last I felt obliged to accept an offer to go to Mozambique as a contract soldier: I was about to become a mercenary. I signed on the dotted line and accepted an advance payment. I was going to be a major in FRELIMO, the legitimate armed forces of Mozambique.

The enemy were a guerrilla force called RENAMO, who had operated against the African National Congress (ANC) in South Africa with the support of the South African government, until Pretoria cut off supplies and money in 1998. Drawn mainly from former Portuguese residents, RENAMO had been a thorn in the side of the Mozambican government for a long time. In their own country they were considered criminals, and in South Africa they were now a major embarrassment, so they had nowhere to go. Left with little choice, they carried on raiding the communication lines, living off the land and the local villages.

My job, along with several others, was to train the FRELIMO forces to defeat them. I didn't really relish the idea of leaving home again, but

I felt I had little choice. Two days before I left, a letter arrived from Occidental Petroleum, offering me the job I had wanted, but it was too late. I had signed up and given my word. I caught the plane to Johannesburg in March 1990, just before my thirty-third birthday.

IT WAS ONLY a short hop from Johannesburg to Maputo, the capital of Mozambique. In spite of its cash-starved, run-down appearance, Maputo still displayed signs of its historical legacy in the wide, tree-lined boulevards and gorgeous Portuguese architecture. There was little sign of war, but many signs of the lack of resources that war had created. The country was once Africa's most popular and beautiful holiday resort, but when the Portuguese moved out, they took absolutely everything with them, leaving nothing behind.

As I sat in my hotel waiting to be briefed, I was reminded why I was there. Russian Hind D gunships and Hip transport helicopters passed over the shipping lanes to the west, flying low on their way back from some mission or other. The Russians had departed only a few months before: the crumbling economy in the Soviet Union, combined with Gorbachev's Glasnost policies, did not warrant further spending in Africa, but the hardy Russian weapons remained and continued to be used.

My briefing was given by a former Parachute Regiment captain, Dave, a young, dynamic and intelligent soldier who was frustrated by working in an administrative role when he wanted to be up-country, where he was sending me. The camp I was bound for was called Coromanna, and was just inside the Mozambican border with South Africa. A dam-building project was taking place there using foreign aid, and a military base had been built close by. My job was to offer basic infantry training to raw troops.

The next day I flew up-country in a single-engine five-seater aeroplane. As the vast bushland of Mozambique passed beneath me, I expected to see some animal life, but the country was bare. Even at low altitude there was nothing apart from the people outside the village *shambas* (huts). War had destroyed everything. A hungry man with a machine-gun will kill anything to fill his empty belly. Now there was nothing left to kill except one another.

The landing strip appeared out of the bush, and I could see the surrounding country: a green, cultivated area surrounded by *shambas*. A narrow, slow-moving river wandered down from a large white concrete dam that retained a reservoir, and meandered easily away to the south. Large green military tents stood in rows, leading away from a few white single-storey buildings with flat roofs, while dusty roads led out to all points of the compass. Away to the west, and close to the dam, the land rose by a few hundred feet. Here there was a gathering of longhouses, Portakabins and permanent-looking warehouses. To the north end of the dam was a construction site with heavy plant dotted about, apparently standing idle. The impression of peace and tranquillity was deceptive.

I was happy to find several old friends on-site, including Billy from my Sri Lankan days. The rest of the team – Terry, Scott, Paddy and Faz – were all ex-SAS too. We were barracked on the hill, each of us in a small individual quarter of a Portakabin with its own shower. We were the fortunate ones, living amongst the Italian, Finnish and Swedish engineers who formed the construction consortium building the dam. Those less fortunate, the Mozambican FRELIMO officers, lived in the barren stone buildings below us on the plain, while the troops lived in tents. When the wind blew, dust swirled around these makeshift homes, and when it rained the tents leaked and the ground became a soggy morass of liquid mud.

Initially we had to take the troops only for weapons training, drill and fitness. This was simplicity itself. The Russian assault rifle, the AK-47, was the most straightforward and efficient weapon in the world: hard to break, easy to strip, clean and assemble, and almost idiot-proof. There was little need for an interpreter, as a simple 'copy me' system sufficed.

Fitness training was great fun. Many of the troops ran barefoot, because boots hurt their feet. I taught them the filthiest British military running songs I knew, which they didn't understand, and they taught me their own versions. I swear they could run and smile all day. Distance, however, was a problem. The peace and tranquillity I had observed were sustained by a ten-mile perimeter boundary fence;

outside that was a continuous five-yard-wide minefield. Inside these defences were heavy machine-guns, positioned so that their fields of fire interlocked, and woe betide any wanderer who set off a mine at night.

RENAMO were not the sort of men to be put off by mines, and in my second week we were woken in the early hours of the morning by gunfire from the perimeter. Mortar-shells began to land amongst the tents, and enemy troops poured through the minefield and into the camp. We were aware of this only because of the reports that were coming in over the radio, and the lines of green tracer that flew from right to left in the darkness below us. Contrary to popular belief, high-explosive mortar-rounds don't make a big flash at night, but they do kill lots of people. Our established task in the event of an attack was to defend the Europeans and evacuate them from the north of the camp. This attack, though, appeared to be deliberately avoiding our compound.

We gathered our charges together in one of the houses and prepared to move out. I had only two things to carry: ammunition and water. For the immediate future, anything else was surplus to requirements. By the time we moved out, the firing had died down and the mortars had ceased completely. It occurred to me that there had been very little return fire from our own troops in the last ten minutes. Crouching down so as not to silhouette ourselves on the skyline, we moved up the hill. I was not frightened – none of the firing had come close, so I'd been given very little cause for alarm. Fear was reserved for those times when something serious was actually happening. Suddenly my ears were filled with the whoosh of Katushya rockets flying down into our compound. Less than two hundred yards away, the main storage building exploded into a thousand pieces as rocket after rocket hit home. As debris began to shower down, we crawled under the front porches and covered our heads with our hands. Now I *was* scared, shit-scared, that those rockets were going to creep this way. More rockets could be heard, but they started to sound as if they were exploding further away.

As I crept from under the building, I couldn't help laughing as I looked into faces with eyes as wide as saucers. No one said anything; we just set off again up the hill. Crouching didn't seem so sensible any more, so we ran, dragging our charges through the gate and into the bush. We walked and stumbled for about ten minutes and then, in the middle of nowhere, we settled down for the night, placing the engineers and one of the wives in the centre to try to get some sleep while we formed an outward-facing circle and waited for the battle to end.

I sat facing south. The glow of burning buildings showed over the edge of my near horizon, and an occasional burst of fire burped into the night. Eventually all became still. A cold wind blew down from the mountains to the west, and I began to shiver. Although it had felt like an age, all the firing had ceased within an hour. We discussed whether or not to return. In spite of the cold, it was decided that we would go back at dawn, when there was less chance of being shot by our own troops.

We returned to absolute carnage. The medical facility was full of wounded troops, some of the injuries inflicted by gunfire, but most by mortar fragments. I offered to help, but my lack of Portuguese was such a hindrance that eventually I left the orderlies to their task and went back to mine. Outside the medical facility, a line of dead bodies lay in the warmth of the early morning, with flies already climbing in and out of any orifice or wound that offered them an opening. Out by the tents, an old Russian T-54 tank that had been part of the defences was now a burned-out shell. Troops and officers sat around in stunned disarray, not knowing what to do first.

It was important to get a grip as quickly as we could. All the dead, sick and wounded had already been moved, so we set about rebuilding the tents, relaying mines and feeding the troops. We were told that food and some young women had been taken from the *shambas*, but few had actually been killed.

At first it was difficult to determine what had really happened in the camp as no one appeared willing to talk. Subsequent subtle enquiries uncovered some of the hideous truth: neither the machine-guns nor the tank had been manned – by anyone at all. The officers had run away, leaving the troops with no option but to follow suit. There had been no defence to speak of whatsoever.

Scott, surmising that RENAMO did not have Katushya rocket-launchers, suggested that he and I take a walk up to our own launch sites to see what the rockets were aimed at. We reported our intention to visit the sites to the FRELIMO colonel, but not our reasons for wanting to do so. He advised against it, saying that the sites were surrounded by mines, but we went anyway. As we approached the launch sites, it became clear that it would be impossible to bury mines in the solid rock kopje we were climbing. At the top our suspicions were confirmed: we had been fired on by our own troops on the night of the attack.

When we returned, the colonel had already heard of our expedition and wanted to arrest us as spies. We refused to be arrested and held onto our weapons. The FRELIMO captain who had come to ask us politely to go with him was sent away with a flea in his ear. Africa was no place to be arrested or disarmed by some local tinpot colonel who wanted to cover his arse. Before things got out of hand, Scott wrote a report stating that we had visited the Katushya site on a routine inspection and found nothing out of the ordinary. With this to hand, the colonel allowed the matter to rest.

As our relationship with the troops developed, so did my respect for them. They were simple men who expected to live short lives. They had grown up with war and violence: death was a normality to them. Disease from malaria, bilhartzia and malnutrition took more of them than any war ever could. Many were illiterate, and some could speak only their tribal language. It took very little to make them happy, and they were as tough as old boots. I soon learned to admire them.

As the training programme developed, we began to run courses for NCOs, showing them how to take command and how to teach others. Before lunch one day I gave two soldiers the task of preparing a lesson to be presented that afternoon. After lunch I asked the first soldier if he had prepared the lesson; he answered, 'No.' I was astounded by his brazen insolence, and sent him out from under the cooling shade of the tent to run around the flagpole with his rifle over his head until I told him to stop. Half an hour later he fell down, so I had him stand to attention in the sun until the second soldier finished the lesson.

When it was over I asked the first man, through my interpreter, why he hadn't prepared the lesson. The interpreter laughed and told me that I had got the wrong man – it was somebody else I had given the order to before lunch. 'Right, Cassimo,' I said to my undeserving victim, 'you're excused PT tomorrow morning.' The poor guy actually smiled.

One thing we were rarely short of was alcohol. Umberto was the local supply representative: he made all the food purchases, including booze, and shipped them in from South Africa. He ran his own local bar on the edge of the camp and on the rare occasions the troops actually got paid, fleeced them rotten. He was Italian: small, rotund and loud. He was jealous of his power and cowardly in the extreme when the guns began to fire. We didn't like him much, but we used his bar as frequently as we needed to.

One evening while we were drinking, an argument began between two soldiers. I had my back to the fracas until Paddy exclaimed, 'Jesus, is dat a fucking grenade in his hand?' I looked over my shoulder to see one soldier shouting loudly at another while he held a hand-grenade close to his right ear. His left thumb was through the ring attached to the pin and it was clear that he intended to kill us all if he didn't win his argument. Some Africans can be absolutely serious when they threaten to take their own lives. Only the previous year a demoted RSM had walked out onto the parade ground and killed his replacement, then he blew his own head off with his AK-47.

I jumped over a small dividing wall, ran towards the man and wrapped my left hand around his right, keeping the release mechanism on the grenade closed in case he pulled the pin. I placed my right hand on his larynx and squeezed as I threw his head into the wall. As he couldn't breathe his body began to relax and his thumb came free of the ring. He slipped down to the ground and I took the grenade from his hand. After bending back the pin to prevent it slipping out, I placed it in my pocket and returned to my beer.

The lads seemed impressed, and a few free beers passed my way over the next hour. Shortly before we left, a soldier who I did not recognise came up to me, stood to attention and asked for something. I turned to my interpreter, who explained that the man wanted his grenade back. If he went back to his unit without it, his sergeant would beat him.

WHEN WE HAD finished training our soldiers, we purchased two beers for each of them, a luxury they could ill afford on their month's wages. They sang and partied into the night, and the next day they flew out to join operations in the north. I was surprised by how much I wanted to go with them.

Dave came up from Maputo and took over as commander of the team. I liked him immensely for his direct and enthusiastic approach to problems. Umberto had boldly stated that he didn't need any protection from the English. He had his rifle and his truck and knew exactly what to do if the enemy ever attacked again. He was quite rude to Dave, who told him that he was free to do as he pleased and left it at that.

I was to be moved further north to join another team in Nampula, so our friendship was to be short-lived. A little while before my departure we were attacked again, only this time we had ensured that the defences were manned. A heavy machine-gun opened up on the camp from outside the perimeter and once again a breach was attempted through the minefield, but on this occasion it went wrong. Our Katushyas pinned the enemy down until the only threat was the continuous firing from the machine-gun.

While all this was happening we were sitting on a wall outside our bashas, drinking beer and watching the fireworks. Umberto ran up in a dithering panic, demanding to be told what we intended to do. Dave said, 'We know what we are going to do, Umberto. You, of course, can look after yourself.' Umberto was last seen going round in circles in his truck as team members drifted off to their rooms.

I sat on the wall for a while, watching the green tracer soaring into the air and burning out long before it fell to earth. I decided to take a truck and drive down to the defences to have a closer look. I hadn't had much to drink, but then, it never took much where I was concerned. I parked up by the rear of one of our guns that was returning fire and watched for a while before I decided – without rhyme or reason –

to go out through a gap I knew of in the minefield and sort that fucking machine-gun out.

I walked along the wire, searching for a post with a white marking at the base. It didn't take long, even in the darkness. The wire was fixed in its normal way: six innocuous strands of barbed wire that stood head-high. I had to take only five big steps and I would be through it and into the minefield. I did it in three and slipped through the strands of wire on the far side. It wasn't difficult to keep my bearings – the wire was a good guide. Now, though, I had to be careful not to get shot by my own side, who were happily wasting ammunition, with about as much effect as the enemy.

After a very short time I was crawling towards the sound of the machine-gun. I had a hunting knife, two grenades and my AK-47 with three thirty-round magazines and no support. Dumb was not the word. For some reason I had imagined that there was only a three-man gun team and no other troops. I kept my head down as I crawled closer. About a hundred yards from the gun, I heard voices shouting and realised that there were enemy soldiers everywhere – probably a platoon strength of about thirty of them. Sobriety, fear and common sense suddenly poured into my head, and my heart began to pound over the noise of the machine-gun. I thought of running into the darkness and hoping that I would not be seen. Panic welled up inside me before I realised that fear was killing my ability to think. I lay still, safe in my bush, flat on the floor. I breathed deeply and cursed myself for getting into such a mess. What would Heather say?

I calmed myself and decided to go back the way I had come. As I turned and began to crawl away, I felt as if my whole rear end were lit up, asking for someone to shoot holes in it. My arse felt as big as a barrage balloon, and my nose was ploughing a furrow that a farmer would have been proud of. When I had crawled about fifty yards I began to feel safe. I couldn't hear voices above the roar of the gun any more.

I stood up and turned to look back towards the enemy gun. As I did so, I collided with a man approaching from the opposite direction. We knocked each other backwards, and then regained our balance at about the same moment. He said something to me in Portuguese and came closer to see who I was. He must have assumed that I was one of his own men. The night was pitch-dark, and he couldn't see me any more clearly than I could see him. Just then the gun decided to stop firing, probably to change barrels, or because of a problem with the firing mechanism. Silence descended.

I couldn't shoot him – I would be heard. I couldn't run – he would kill me. I dropped my rifle and stepped forward. The man spoke again, but I wrapped my left hand around his head and dragged him forward onto my hunting knife. I pulled his face into my shoulder to muffle his voice and drove the knife up under his ribs, searching for his heart. He uttered a cry muffled by my clothing and then bit my shoulder. His arms and legs flailed and kicked, and I fell forward on top of him. He struggled, and I mentally begged him to die so that I could get away. You bastard, I thought, why won't you bloody well die? I had tears in my eyes – something inside me didn't want him to die, didn't want to be here doing this. After a brief and frightening struggle the man relaxed and became still. I felt a shudder go through my body, as if his ghost had passed through me.

I lay there quietly for a few moments. I wanted to cry or shout or urinate – I didn't know which. I shuddered again and partly wet my pants. I waited a moment more and then drew the knife out. Slowly I rolled away and found my rifle lying only a few feet away. I had no sense of breathing or thinking, but I remember crawling a good distance more before I stopped next to a tree and vomited until my stomach had no more to give.

I was lost in the dark, and no longer had any idea where the gap in the minefield was. So I sat next to my pool of vomit until the dawn light appeared in the sky to guide me back. It wasn't a problem getting in – the gunners were asleep behind their positions – so I crept back to my truck and drove home.

I felt exhausted and, in a strange way, ashamed of what had happened. Without any good reason I had placed myself in danger, had almost got myself killed and had killed a man with my knife. I wasn't proud and I didn't want to open myself up to ridicule, so I told no one. I wasn't so sure about my prowess as a soldier any more. I had lived the image of the ruthless killer; when I had shot a man, it had been easy. But with a knife, and at close range, it was something far more unpleasant – it was personal.

So now I had done it: I had faced extreme fear voluntarily. I could at last look at myself and see the 'tough guy' of my childish imagination. The image disgusted me – it wasn't and never had been my true vocation. Perhaps that was what my leaders had been able to see in the past.

There is no euphoria in these situations, only utter fear: your eyes bulge and your heart comes up into your throat and you want to empty your bowels and pee yourself. You can't hear anything because of the blood pounding in your head. You don't know whether you're making a noise, whether your opponent's making any noise, and you have to make a decision quickly. I decided instantaneously that I was going to kill this man, because that was my best chance of staying alive. Holding him close as I stuck the knife into him was a peculiar experience. It was like: I want to live, and for me to live you've got to die, and I can feel you dying.

I'd always wanted to experience a situation in which I was truly tested, but now I had, it all seemed so bloody pointless. It wasn't an experience worth having. There was nothing good about it in any shape or form; there was nothing to be proud of.

My clothes were caked in blood, and I burned them so that the laundry girl wouldn't ask questions. The next day I went out to the area where it had all happened, but there was no sign of the body, just a great pile of empty cases where the enemy had been firing the machine-gun.

The following week I moved north.

MOZAMBIQUE IS a huge country, almost three thousand miles long. Nampula lies about fifteen hundred miles north of Maputo, in the middle of the country and about eighty miles in from the east coast. The reason for having a team here was to protect a rail link being rebuilt between Nacala on the coast and Malawi to the north-west. Nampula was situated at about the halfway point. The French rail company,

SNCF, were building the new line from Nampula to Malawi, but they had a major problem: the trains were being ambushed and the line was being destroyed faster than it could be built.

Although the trains were escorted by large numbers of troops, they had no idea how to defend themselves against an ambush, so they would just stay on the trains behind steel plate until the ambush was over. The country was fast running out of steam engines.

There was already a small team at Nampula which had taken over the command and training of the soldiers with some success. Roger was the team commander. Since the British team had been in charge of training, counter-ambush drills had been taught and successful retaliation had been mounted against RENAMO.

Led by British mercenary officers, Mozambican soldiers were as brave as any in the world. They would follow their leaders, staying by them until they died; previously, they'd followed their officers in running away.

Once the success of these retaliatory missions came to light, the local FRELIMO officers became embarrassed and decided to bring both operations and the building of the railway to a halt.

The French had expected to build nearly a mile of new line daily. By the time I arrived, this had been reduced to less than two hundred yards per day. Frustration was growing all around. For the next few months only four or five trains ran the full distance to Malawi, and no new line was built at all.

In comparison to Coromanna, Nampula was a peaceful place. There were no attacks on the town, and we lived amongst the local people, who were wonderful in too many ways to describe. At home I had heard old people talk about the closeness that they felt for one another during the Second World War, how they suffered deprivation and terrible loss and still remained cheerful. That was how these people were: mostly happy with their lot, putting on a brave face, demanding nothing and expecting nothing.

I spent the next few months with them, making friends and tolerating the endless frustrations created by the African system of politics. The EU was threatening to withdraw financial support, the French company wanted French protection, and the railway was standing still.

As Christmas approached, Roger and I decided to spend it at Nacala, on the coast. Our housemaid, Muanasha, asked to come along: her dead husband was buried there, and it was where his parents still lived, and cared for her children. We took her to visit the grave and then her children. The grandparents were former Portuguese colonists who had stayed behind. Their house was run-down but clean, and the children were lovely. For Christmas they had a small plastic toy doll each and nothing else. Roger and I wrapped up bars of milk chocolate for them and took a joint of meat that we had brought along from our cold-box so that the family could have Christmas dinner. The children were happy, but the grandparents were quiet. They had seen too many soldiers not to be wary.

On Christmas Eve we went to church with Muanasha, only to find that people turned away from her because she was with white men. We left her to her worship and went home to prepare for Christmas Day on the beach.

The following day, loaded up in our Land Rover with cold-box, steak, champagne and lots of other goodies, we set off for the sea. We stopped a local fisherman on the way to buy a fresh grouper and then trundled up the sandy beach until we thought we were alone. Roger put up the barbecue and I set up my hammock under the trees. The flat sea was azure-blue, and small waves lapped at the golden sand. I could see fish swimming within five yards of the shore. It was a tropical paradise.

As the smell of our cooking drifted along the coast, our idyllic solitude was gradually invaded by a growing number of local people. At first they sat and talked, but soon they began to ask for water, and then food. As the numbers grew, I found myself looking at our dwindling stock of goodies and feeling quite resentful.

A short distance away a young mother was sitting watching her child playing. He was about eighteen months old and running around naked, kicking a plastic football. His mother unwrapped a piece of paper, inside which was some bread. She tore the bread into pieces and occasionally fed a piece to the child. Meanwhile I had become angry, and refused to give any more of my Christmas dinner to the 'scroungers' who were sitting around our fire. I shouted a few angry words and sat down heavily on the ground, glaring at everybody around me. As I sat there, the small boy toddled towards me with his crust of bread in his hand and took a bite. Then he raised his little fist and offered me the rest of his food.

I hung my head in shame. If ever a man was taught the lesson of Christmas, I was at that moment. Scrooge had been visited.

I was never quite the same again after Mozambique. I felt that I had finally been tested, and I wished heartily that I hadn't. When I left, in January 1991, almost two hundred people came from Nampula to wave goodbye. It was the only country I was ever truly sad to leave. Now, when an African speaks of his homeland and sighs, 'Ah, Africa,' I like to think I understand a small part of what he is feeling.

CHAPTER 19

Another Man's Jungle

BACK HOME HEATHER had had enough and, to be honest, so had I. Mozambique really left its mark on me. I was distant, confused and isolated. I had discovered myself and I didn't like what I had found. Were all men really just frightened little children spending their lives faking toughness, posing as hard guys to hide just how scared they really were? I couldn't put it into words so I retreated into silence. Heather became convinced it was her fault, that she'd done something wrong. But I couldn't get past the terrible gulf between a country where children were starving and life was so cheap. Now I was home in affluent Britain where people complained if Tesco ran out of fresh salmon. It all seemed so pointless. My life seemed empty. My continued absence had put pressure on our marriage; now it was starting to create cracks. Heather promised to divorce me if I went abroad again. So I quit and stayed home.

I opened a small security company in South London and wrote a short book about women's self-defence called *Unleash the Lioness,* but after two years I was so broke that I took a short contract to go to Guyana as paramedic for a gold mine run by a French-Canadian company, Omai Gold Mines. One of their workers had suffered an accident and died because of the lack of medical care. I was to be the man who provided such care when accidents occurred.

The mine was sited on a river in the middle of the South American rainforest. There were six hundred men and women working there, mostly Guyanese labourers and French-Canadian engineering staff. A former British Para officer, Alistair, was camp administrator, and the head of security was one of my old B Squadron pals, Fred. Alistair was a tall, blond, highly intelligent, well-spoken man in his early forties, who had the ability to manage all types of people. His firmness and honesty earned him a great deal of respect. Fred was a huge, muscular Fijian, with a wide face and a broad grin that lit up his handsome, light-brown features whenever he smiled. He was frightened of nothing, living his life from day to day and never worrying about tomorrow. He took every problem in his stride as and when it occurred, and is still probably the most popular man I have ever known.

I thought my task would be simple: I would work under a doctor and deal with accidents as and when they happened. Doctors, however, rarely want to live in the middle of the jungle, and in this case, the camp doctor lived in Georgetown, two hundred miles away and visited the camp by helicopter twice a week. I was to be the senior medical officer on-site, supported by two male nurses, a medical technician and an ambulance driver.

I went looking for the medical centre and discovered a Portakabin behind the canteen, next to the waste pipes and swill bins. Mud surrounded the whole area, and there was no way of entering the room without carrying a pile of filth inside. When I did go inside, I found a mish-mash of equipment and medical stores falling from shelves and lying around on the floor. More than half the building was being used as private accommodation by the former medical officer, a male nurse who had been on-site from the beginning.

I evicted him from the building and set about reorganising the facility into somewhere I could reasonably work. I divided the building into three areas: a reception area and lab where the technician could work with his microscope; an examination room and dirty theatre where dressings and minor wounds could be treated; and, at the end, furthest from the door, a sterile theatre for performing minor surgical procedures. I found a large quantity of unused material, including examination tables, lights, shelves and oxygen cylinders, which had been purchased and stored until such time as a new medical facility could be built. The budget for this new facility was almost a million Canadian dollars – half a million pounds. The ambulance was a fully equipped American paramedic vehicle that would work perfectly on the streets of Miami. Here in the jungle, where there were no roads and lots of mud, it was standing idle.

Alistair advised me to do as much as I could without permission and explain myself later, otherwise nothing would get done. There was an old shack overlooking the river that had been used as a shop, but which was about to close, so I asked whether I could use it as a consulting room and dispensary. With permission for this in hand, I went the whole hog and arranged for the medical cabin to be moved next to the shack, and had a concrete base laid for the ambulance to park on.

Now I had a working medical facility that could service the whole mine, with a waiting room, a dispensary, an examination room, a lab and a sterile surgery. This took just two weeks to achieve, thanks to the French-Canadians, for whom nothing was too much effort – provided they could see the reason for it. Being British and speaking French was also a great help.

I needed to be able to react to emergencies quickly, so I commandeered a four-wheel motorbike and fitted it out with a trauma pack. With this and a radio, I could get to any accident in any weather at any time. Finally, I had uniforms made for all the staff so that we looked like a proper medical team.

My male nurses were Guyanese, and had more clinical knowledge than I could ever have acquired with my military background. I allowed them to take most of the responsibility for everyday examinations and treatments. My technician was there primarily to identify any outbreaks of malaria and dysentery. I became the manager of the whole operation.

I started to rock the boat pretty early on, when I discovered that the drugs that had been purchased were all close to the end of their shelf-life. It turned out that the human resources manager was pocketing the difference in price between new drugs and the ones we actually had. He was related to the President, so nothing had been done about it, and I made an unwanted and influential enemy.

Across the river from the mine were a number of bars with a copious supply of pretty young women, mostly from Brazil. I felt that it would be a good idea, if the men were going to take advantage of the goods on sale, to try to keep the girls as clear of venereal disease as possible. The mine disagreed, and declared the far riverbank off-limits to the workers. This led to drunken French-Canadian miners trying to paddle over the fast-flowing water at night and nearly drowning. One local man was killed when an alligator got him – a few pieces of body were found downstream about a week later.

After this, the miners began to use bribery to get across. The situation was unfortunate, because they went home every two weeks to Canada, some of them with unpleasant presents for their wives.

The Amerindians soon heard about the medical centre and began to bring their children, most of whom were suffering from severe cases of malaria. Although the native population had a very strong resistance to the disease, child mortality rates because of it were still very high. But as we treated those who arrived, more and more followed, until the mine decided to stop us spending their money this way and banned us from treating anyone who wasn't a company employee.

Of course, I got into trouble a few times subsequently for attending to emergency cases, but what the hell . . .

I put together a blood donor programme: mine employees would donate blood to the Georgetown blood bank to help stocks at the hospital. Then I found out that most of the blood disappeared into private practice for invisible sums of money, and I gave up on that idea too.

Meanwhile I had to train all sixty security officers in first-aid, and run training exercises for evacuation in the event of a serious accident. We had a runway for light aircraft and reasonable hospital facilities in Georgetown, but the Canadians knew that if things became really bad, they would need to go elsewhere as soon as possible.

Six weeks in, I was sent on a three-day tour of hospitals in Trinidad and Barbados. I had one day on each island to tour the hospitals and decide where we should transport a serious casualty by air. Trinidad had just built and equipped a new hospital, but they had no staff to operate it. Barbados, on the other hand, had marvellous facilities because of the flourishing tourist trade and the investment by American insurance companies.

By the third night I was back in the jungle. Everyone thought I had had a pleasant holiday, but in fact I was shattered – I'd taken on too many tasks too quickly. One evening, after leaving the medical centre, I found myself lying on the floor of my room with no recollection of how I had got there. I had collapsed with exhaustion. I handed myself over to Alistair, who sent me to town for four days' rest.

Moving around in the jungle without a rifle in my hands was a strange experience. For the first time I felt vulnerable. One day the workers discovered a five-yard-long anaconda in a wet area next to the mine, in the process of swallowing a yard-long alligator. The locals, who had a great fear of snakes, killed it and left it to rot. When I came across it I photographed it and skinned it.

An Amerindian in Belize had taught me that big cats didn't like humans. If you left them alone, they would leave you alone. They didn't recognise men as food and would attack only if threatened, or to protect their cubs. On one occasion I was returning from the sawmill, about a mile from the mine, my four-wheeler bouncing and sliding up the muddy tracks as I raced to the top of the next hill. The noise of the engine must have been muffled by the slope and the trees, because when I crested the hill I came face to face with a full-grown jaguar.

I stopped about eight yards from him and froze. He was crouching as if to pounce. I knew I had surprised him and that he was frightened; now I had to let him make the next move. The seconds felt like hours. I decided that if he came towards me, I would rev the engine and charge straight at him. I held the gaze of his big yellow eyes and took in all the details of his shining yellow-and-black coat. His mouth was open and his top lip was drawn back, revealing his long white teeth. He twitched his long tail slightly, then rose and strolled almost casually away into the trees.

Strangely enough, I hadn't been frightened; I had been quite calm. I had been taught by experts about big cats in the wild, and I had a plan of what to do if the jaguar had attacked me. The old adage 'knowledge dispels fear' came to mind. In fact, I had actually enjoyed the experience.

WE EXPERIENCED TWO serious medical incidents while I was in Guyana. The first was a night-time road traffic accident, when a security guard crashed a four-wheel bike which rolled over on top of him. Our system worked admirably: by the time I arrived at the accident site, the first-aiders I had trained had treated the man correctly under Fred's supervision. The ambulance arrived ten minutes later and we took the unconscious man to the medical centre. Once there we treated him for head injuries and cleaned up his wounds. He had lacerations on his face that required nearly eighty stitches. An aircraft came within the hour and we flew him to the Georgetown hospital. The local doctor was on the flight, but he believed this was all a well-planned exercise and didn't even look at the patient.

The guard returned to the mine four weeks later and strolled into one of my classes, smiling. I kicked him out for coming in late – I hadn't recognised him, there was almost no scarring from the sutures I had put on his face and it was only when he told me who he was and that he had come to say thank you that I figured it out. I felt very proud of myself and my team – all the work had been worthwhile.

The second incident also happened late at night. Two Amerindians had visited the local whorehouse over the river and, after drinking far too much, they had argued with one of the girls about her price. She had refused them and they had tried to rape her. This resulted in the hot-blooded girl drawing a machete across one man's scalp and then burying the same blade in the other attacker's back. I was alone at two in the morning with two bleeding Indians. Both my nurses were away, so my technician assisted.

Luckily for the first man, the blade had hit bone and been deflected. I cleaned them both, stitched them up and filled them with antibiotics – the drugs would work better on the natives than they would on most Westerners because they had never been exposed to them before.

AT THE VERY end of my three-month contract I ran a major accident exercise, utilising the canteen as a casualty clearing station for forty accident victims. Omai were impressed, and asked me to work directly for them.

I had loved the job, and would happily have abandoned my security company if they'd made me a serious offer, but my friend in human resources sabotaged the situation. The plans to build a new medical centre were struck out of the mine budget, saving the company a million dollars. They decided that my centre was perfectly adequate for their needs. My contract was not renewed, but at least this time I went home with a shining reference.

I THINK TEACHING has always been my true vocation in life. I knew from the time I was sixteen that I had a true affinity with it, and other people noticed this too. I love standing up in front of a class and getting things across to people: it's like being a performer on stage. People appreciate what you do and this makes you feel good, boosts your self-esteem. While you're up there, you're the man.

I started teaching a little karate. By 1994 my security business had folded, incurring large losses, and I decided to make karate teaching my future. Although I was good at it I was too old to make a great name for myself as a competitor. I gradually expanded my one-hour-a-week class, turning it into my first karate club at the Riverside Racquet Centre in Chiswick, London. It wasn't so much the karate I loved as the teaching. Karate was the vehicle that allowed me to do what I felt I was destined to do.

Several companies called me and asked me to work for them in places like Colombia, Zaire and Algeria, but in spite of the high wages on offer I stayed put and persevered with building my karate business.

I had introduced my teacher, Tom, to the SAS a long time ago and he had become their unarmed combat instructor. As my own club grew, Tom began coming down to London to teach courses for me. By 1995, I had as many students as Tom himself, and numbers continued to expand. Things were going well, although Heather had to work hard to support the family during these years. Something then happened that nearly ruined everything we had worked so hard for.

IT HAD BEEN a long time since I had fought anyone: I was seven or eight pounds overweight and wore a short grey beard, looking considerably older than my thirty-eight years. One Saturday afternoon I was at a bar in a small south Wales village near Chepstow. The bar was filling up with a bunch of local men all in high spirits. They were coming to watch the rugby match between Wales and England being played at Cardiff Arms Park. The mood was typical of a group of rugby fans: cheerful banter being exchanged between the English and Welsh supporters.

I sat happily at the bar and cheered loudly as England beat Wales at Cardiff for the first time in many years. I turned to speak to a short Englishman sitting next to me. He'd had his back to me during the match so we hadn't spoken before. He was wearing a multi-coloured rugby shirt and I asked him what team the shirt was from. He looked over his left shoulder and with a sneer on his face said, 'You're nearly as fucking stupid as him,' glancing at the man he had been speaking to, 'can't you see it's a multi-nation shirt?' He turned back to his friend, a very tall, athletic-looking man with long blond hair.

'What are you so angry about?' I replied. 'We just won the rugby.'

'Listen you fat old cunt, why don't you just fuck off?'

I was taken aback. This was so out of context and I didn't know what I had done wrong.

'You're lucky my mate doesn't kill you,' he added.

I asked him what his problem was, saying that the afternoon had been cheerful enough and there was no need for his behaviour. I called him a 'little shit' and turned to walk away. As I turned, his left arm reached out and grabbed my right shoulder.

Years of preparation, training and violence had primed me for this moment.

Instinctively I spun towards him, raising my right elbow to ward off any blow that may have been coming, and simultaneously hitting him across the front of his face with the side of my right fist. I knew as soon as my hand struck that he was unconscious. He flew backwards over his bar stool, as rigid as a post, and landed on the back of his head. His tall friend moved into the fray from my left-hand side and I turned to face him. He paused, not knowing whether to attack or not. As he made his decision my mind raced. Was anyone behind me? Where was the escape route? Was there anyone else attacking? Was the man on the floor alive? Keeping my guard up and my eyes on the big man I nudged the unmoving figure with my left foot. 'Get up!' I ordered. He never moved, but the nudge was the spark that my new opponent needed.

'He's stamped on his head!' he shouted to the rest of the men in the bar.

Three men came at me. As they didn't throw any blows I raised my arms in surrender and offered no threat. They pushed me back against the wall, two of them holding an arm each, while a third pushed his forearm up against my chin. The big blond man stood to the rear as they held me, but seeing that I was now helpless, he lunged forward drawing back his right arm ready to throw a punch.

I bit the forearm that was now pushed into my face and as the arm drew back I ducked and struck the man holding my right arm with my right elbow. The man on the left released me as I spun away from the group. Seeing that I was now free the big man lost his courage and ran from the bar.

The remainder stood back warily waiting for my next move. 'I'm not going to do anything except leave.' I told them. They still seemed unsure what to do until the body on the floor moved and groaned. They turned to see how he was. I was relieved that the man was regaining consciousness, but felt that in the circumstances it would not be wise to hang around.

It didn't look good. I was unhurt, three men were injured – one seriously – and they were all friends. After interviewing the witnesses the police arrested me for malicious wounding with intent, grievous bodily harm and actual bodily harm.

MY WHOLE LIFE went on hold as the case went through the courts. I pleaded not guilty on the grounds of self defence. Seven months later I stood in the dock waiting for the jury's verdict.

As I stood there, I wondered whether I should have let them beat me up. I wouldn't then be facing four years inside: malicious wounding with intent carried a four year prison sentence. I wasn't frightened of prison, I was frightened of the effect that prison would have on my family. Perhaps I should have accepted the prosecution's offer of avoiding prison by pleading guilty to GBH. This would have meant walking with a fine and payment of costs, but still a conviction. However it was too late for such speculation. It was all down to the jury now.

Heather sat to my left in the public gallery. I stood to attention, prepared for the worst but praying that God would help me.

The jury had reached a verdict on two counts: the malicious wounding and the actual bodily harm, but not on the grievous bodily harm. The judge asked for their verdict on the first two counts.

The foreman stood and announced, 'not guilty'.

I was elated. I knew that I wouldn't go to prison, but it was too late. The press had discovered my background and the case was now national news. If I was found guilty of GBH, my growing karate business would crumble with my reputation.

The judge sent the jury out to come to a decision on the charge of grievous bodily harm. I sat in the dock waiting and chatting to the security guards. They were confident for me and I wanted to believe them. The clock ticked slowly by for twenty minutes before the jury returned.

The moment of truth had arrived. I looked at Heather. Her eyes were wet and her hands were shaking. I glanced at the jury and they were looking at me, not at the floor. I knew before the foreman said it, 'not guilty'.

I ran to Heather and we embraced and kissed, her tears running down my cheeks. I looked around and heard the final words of the Judge, 'An innocent man has been acquitted'.

Heather got pissed and I drove home. She deserved it, it was she who would have suffered most had I gone down. It had been a terrifying ordeal.

THE KARATE BUSINESS continued to grow, fortunately unaffected by the trial, and my Riverside Karate Club eventually had branches in Putney, Fulham, Northwood, Roehampton and Westonbirt. At last there was now some financial light at the end of the tunnel.

IN JANUARY 1998 my father, Geoff Horsfall, asked me to visit him. We had developed a friendly but distant relationship over the years. We had little in common, but he was always glad to see Heather and the children. Age had withered him; now sixty-nine, he was small and frail. He sat me down and told me that he was dying of cancer. Before I left the house he hugged me and told me that he loved me. I hugged him back and said the same, without thinking too hard about it.

On the way home my reactions surprised me. I asked myself why had it taken him forty years to tell me that he loved me. The tears welled up in my eyes several times before I got home.

The year passed quickly, and we made greater efforts to see more of one another. I discovered things about his childhood that I had never known. He made sure that I knew how proud of me he truly was, and never missed a chance to tell me that I was loved. In October I received a call telling me that Geoff – my dad – was at death's door and had only twenty-four hours to live. Heather and I rushed to be by his side, as did my brothers and sister. He had deteriorated rapidly; this once-big man, who'd served the Army with everything he had to give, was reduced to a shadow. He weighed only a hundred pounds, and although lucid, he was incontinent and weak – but he retained his dignity and refused to be nursed by the women of the family. We all respected his wish to remain at home and took on the task of looking after him twenty-four hours a day. He was still a tough old man, and he struggled on, pain-free, for the next four days.

During this time, my family grew closer than we had ever been, and there were many joyous and beautiful moments. My eight-year-old son Oliver said his prayers by my father's bedside and asked God's help for all the cancer sufferers of the world. Friends visited, and made him smile. He apologised for his condition endlessly and thanked us often. On the fourth day he suddenly started to feel the pain as his insides disintegrated, and the doctor gave him morphine.

Geoff Horsfall died peacefully on Friday, 30 October. His wife Theresa and all his children were present; I kissed his head and read Psalm 23. We all cried and grieved together.

Later, I returned alone to his bedside and sat beside him and released my grief in racking sobs. I asked him why he had been such a bastard to me as a child. As I sat there the answer came into my head. 'I was only doing the best I could, the only way I knew how'. At last I understood.

All my demons were exorcised at last: my fear of rejection and my resentment of authority figures; my anger with my father and the bullies at whose hands I had suffered. I had conquered the bullies years before, but at last, with my father's belated reassurance, I had conquered myself.

THE MOST IMPORTANT things in my life are my immediate family and my friends. With these few people to support me I am wealthy beyond my wildest dreams. I have faced isolation, low self-esteem, bullying, extreme violence, malice, fear of death and of damaging my family, and come through. I've learned that rank, strength, skill, money and fame cannot in themselves make one person superior to another. The only thing that can do that is integrity.

All my life there have been two conflicting sides to my personality: the man who wanted to help others and be kind, and the victim who was determined never to be bullied again. This conflict, together with my childhood experiences, made me a loner with a chip on his shoulder. Many people would consider me a 'tough guy' today. I would disagree with them. A man doesn't have to act tough to be tough. He can laugh, cry and be stupid sometimes, but it's what he knows about himself that is important. Truly tough men are usually the kindest and most gentle of creatures, who understand that real toughness demands tolerance, patience, and consideration towards and understanding of all people, no matter how badly they behave.

Once a little boy came up to me and said, 'Are you the toughest guy in the world?'

I said, 'No, I'm not the toughest guy in the world. I think the toughest guy who ever lived was Jesus Christ. Look what he went through, and he forgave everybody and he loved everybody.' (To be honest, this impressed his mum more than it impressed him.)

Someone once said, 'We all want to be loved, if not loved then liked, if not liked then respected, if not respected then feared, and if not feared, they will settle for being hated.'

In my early years I fell into this downward spiral of despair. The cure was love.

Index

Index